Contemporary Philosophical Proposals for the University

Aaron Stoller • Eli Kramer
Editors

Contemporary Philosophical Proposals for the University

Toward a Philosophy of Higher Education

Editors
Aaron Stoller
First Year Exerience
Colorado College First Year Exerience
Colorado Springs, CO, USA

Eli Kramer
Department of the Philosophy
of Culture, Institute of Philosophy
of the University of Warsaw
Warsaw, Poland

ISBN 978-3-319-89145-3 ISBN 978-3-319-72128-6 (eBook)
https://doi.org/10.1007/978-3-319-72128-6

Printed on acid-free paper

This Palgrave Macmillan imprint is published by Springer Nature
The registered company is Springer International Publishing AG
The registered company address is: Gewerbestrasse 11, 6330 Cham, Switzerland

For my parents, David and Nancy
—A.S.
For Joanna
—E.K.

Preface

In the USA and abroad, higher education is at a critical juncture. The guiding policies, structures, and concerns of universities and colleges are increasingly being framed and reconstructed by the logic of neoliberalism. While these reform efforts may be couched in the language of innovation, they are designed to do little more than reshape the institution in both the interest and image of industry. Throughout higher education, faculty and administrators are largely paralyzed in the face of these neoliberal reforms. Part of why neoliberalism has gained traction in the university is that scholars across all fields have given up the task of being directly reflective about higher learning. Faculty and administrators have developed neither the critical discourses necessary to resist corporate critiques nor the kind of theoretically informed, alternative imaginaries through which they might create their own meaningful institutional change.

In the face of these pressing realities, this collection serves two central purposes.

First, this volume begins to revive a long-standing discourse within the discipline of philosophy, which we believe is a powerful tool to combat and creatively reimagine many of the contemporary problems of the university. In many ways, the collection can be best understood as emerging from John Dewey's legacy who, as is often forgotten in disciplines outside philosophy, was not strictly an educational theorist but was a philosopher who considered education to be a central theoretical concern. Dewey's writings on education are nested within a wider, original philosophical system because he understood philosophy to be in its etymological sense a general theory of education.

Following Dewey, this collection includes essays by philosophers who believe the discipline must give serious consideration to issues in higher education (broadly understood). This volume revives a discussion within philosophy regarding the scope, direction, and organization of the institutional contexts that serve as the lifeblood of the field but which have been considered philosophically insignificant or altogether ignored. It also engages philosophy in a meta-critical discussion of the role of philosophy and philosophers in an institutional context that is arguably increasingly undermining the possibility of authentic higher learning. Lastly, it challenges the discipline to engage even further with practical engagement with public problems. Dewey famously argues that "philosophy recovers itself when it ceases to be a device for dealing with the problems of philosophers and becomes a method, cultivated by philosophers, for dealing with the problems of men."[1]

Second, we hope this collection will also contribute to and catalyze a growing critical discourse in higher education studies and practice. We believe it will support other critical literatures challenging economized higher education while also offering reconstructive pathways for resolving and transforming institutional structures and cultures. In doing so, this collection contributes to the scholarship of higher education studies by opening up lines of discourse within the discipline of philosophy that connect to broader issues of concern across the entire field. It also serves as a theoretical resource for critically minded administrators and faculty who wish to analyze and change policies and structures at their home institutions. It will introduce them to a wide range of possible educational imaginaries, as well as provide them with productive suggestions for pragmatic change on campuses.

In light of our aims and in the spirit of Dewey's philosophical approach, the essays are organized into one, broad reconstructive philosophy of higher education.

In the introductory essay, "Toward a Philosophy of Higher Education," the editors sketch several critical foundations for a reconstructive philosophy of higher education and advocate for it as a way of approaching future projects in philosophy of higher education.

The first full section, "The Problematic Situation: Challenges Facing Higher Education," provides a philosophical analysis of the situation in which higher education finds itself. Crispin Sartwell explores the problematic legacy of linguistic constructivism in campus political life, while Gabriel Keehn, Morgan Anderson, and Deron Boyles explore the detrimental nature of the hegemonic neoliberal technology craze in higher education. The section ends with Dwayne Tunstall's revealing reflection on the limited nature of "diversity policies" in colleges and universities.

The second section, "The Wellspring of Experience: Reflections on Robust Higher Education," provides alternative educational imaginaries from experiences over a lifetime in higher education. L. Jackson Newell offers an Emersonian personal narrative in order to articulate his vision of liberal learning and higher education. George Allan, through his years of experience in leadership at Dickinson College, illuminates the meaningful discussions that make up the heart of any college or university.

The third section, "Generalization: Reconstructive Proposals for the University," takes a broader, reflective view of the nature and purpose of higher education. Ronald Barnett explores the relationship between culture and the university, proposing an ecological systematic scheme for the modern university. In a classic summative piece, Martha Nussbaum articulates what a broad cosmopolitan liberal, higher education for citizenship looks like in our increasingly globally connected world. Thaddeus Metz provides an alternative vantage point on the purpose of higher education as it would be understood from the context of sub-Saharan Africa.

In the penultimate section, we return to the earth and grit of experience in, "Return to Experience: Reconstruction Put Into Practice." In their reconstructive essay, Danielle Lake, Amy McFarland, and Jessica Jennrich tell the story of how they put their feminist pragmatism inspired, the transdisciplinary vision of higher education into practice at Grand Valley State University, and what lessons that provided for future reconstructions of higher education.

Finally, we look to the future of philosophical reconstruction of higher education in "Future Inquiry: Higher Education in the Coming Century." In this section, Randall Auxier challenges us to think through the implications of the impending, epochal human-technological transformation, often dubbed the "singularity," and how process philosophy can aid the transformation of higher education and the disciplines for this coming world.

The chapters in the collection are truly diverse. They include philosophers from across the globe representing disparate philosophical schools, as well as various career stages, statuses, and standpoints within the university. This diversity is mirrored not only in the approaches and conclusions of the essays but even within their rhetorical styles, which vary from personal narratives and case studies to philosophical genealogies, to traditional philosophical essays, and to systematic theories. The collection, both in whole and in its many parts, also strikes a delicate balance between rigorous philosophical inquiry and practical application of ideas to contemporary problems in higher education.

What the authors share in common is a commitment to the importance of higher education as a concern within the discipline of philosophy, as well as a sense of urgency that something must be done. We believe this collection is the first step toward significant philosophical reconstruction of the university and higher education more broadly. More importantly, we hope the collection inspires others to take seriously the challenge of harnessing the energy of our intellectual institutions for our most pressing needs.

Colorado Springs, CO, USA Aaron Stoller
Warsaw, Poland Eli Kramer

Note

1. John Dewey, "The Need for the Recovery of Philosophy," in *The Collected Works of John Dewey: The Middle Works of John Dewey: 1899-1924: Journal Articles, Essays, and Miscellany Published in the 1916-1917 Period*, volume 10, edited by Jo Ann Boydston (Carbondale and Edwardsville, IL: Southern Illinois University Press, 2008), 46.

Acknowledgments

We are very grateful to Randall Auxier, who has continually provided feedback, guidance, and support for the edited collection. We would also like to thank Milana Vernikova and Mara Berkoff for their enthusiasm for the project and for shepherding the collection through the publishing process. Special thanks go to our supportive families, especially Eli's partner Joanna Smętek and Aaron's partner Catherine, and daughters Claiborne, Eliot, and Cate. Finally, we are incredibly grateful to our authors and to all those who continue to reflect on and reconstruct our institutions of higher learning.

Contents

Notes on Contributors

George Allan is a professor of philosophy emeritus at Dickinson College. His PhD is from Yale, 1963. He was on the Dickinson faculty from 1963 to 1996 and was its senior academic officer from 1974 to 1995. Allan has published three books exploring the metaphysical foundations for social value and three books in philosophy of education, most recently *Modes of Learning: Whitehead's Metaphysics and the Stages of Education*. He has published over 100 articles in metaphysics, social philosophy, philosophy of history, philosophy of education, and issues in higher education, usually from a process or pragmatic perspective.

Morgan Anderson is a doctoral student in education policy, with a concentration in social foundations at Georgia State University. Her research interests include corporate school reform and issues related to technology in education. Her work has appeared in *Studies in Philosophy and Education*, *Journal of Thought*, and *Philosophical Studies in Education*.

Randall Auxier is a professor of philosophy and communication studies at Southern Illinois University, Carbondale. He is the author of *Time, Will, and Purpose* (2013) and *Metaphysical Graffiti* (2017) and the co-author of *The Quantum of Explanation* (2017). He co-founded and edited *The Pluralist* and edited many books and is an author of numerous articles and book chapters. He specialized in the philosophy of culture, in particular, as it relates to issues of time and possibility, in science, myth, religion, art, and education.

Ronald Barnett is emeritus professor of higher education at University College London Institute of Education, where he also held senior leadership positions. He is a past-chair of the Society for Research into Higher Education (SRHE), was awarded the inaugural prize by the European Association for Educational Research for his 'outstanding contribution to Higher Education Research, Policy and Practice', and is a fellow of the Academy of Social Sciences, the SRHE, and the Higher Education Academy (HEA). He is a visiting professor at several universities and has been a guest speaker in 40 countries. For over 30 years, he has been advancing a social philosophy of the university, identifying creative concepts and practical principles that might enhance universities and higher education. His (26) books include—most recently—a trilogy, *Being a University* (2011), *Imagining the University* (2013), and *Understanding the University* (2016). In press (with Routledge) is *The Ecological University: A Feasible Utopia.*

Deron Boyles is a professor of philosophy of education in the Department of Educational Policy Studies at Georgia State University. His research interests include school commercialism, epistemology, critical pedagogy, and the philosophy of John Dewey. His work has been published in such journals as *Philosophy of Education*, *Social Epistemology*, *Journal of Thought*, *Education & Culture*, *Philosophical Studies in Education*, *Inter-American Journal of Philosophy*, *Educational Foundations*, *Journal of Curriculum Theory*, *History of Education Quarterly*, *Educational Studies*, and *Educational Theory*. His first book, *American Education and Corporations: The Free Market Goes to School*, won the Critics' Choice Award from AESA in 2000. He is the editor of two books, *Schools or Markets?: Commercialism, Privatization, and School-Business Partnerships* (2005) and *The Corporate Assault on Youth: Commercialism, Exploitation, and the End of Innocence* (2008). He is the co-author, with Benjamin Baez, of *The Politics of Inquiry: Education Research and the "Culture of Science,"* which was awarded the CHOICE Outstanding Academic Title for 2009 and the AESA Critics' Choice Award for 2010. He is also the co-author, with Kenneth J. Potts, of *From a Gadfly to a Hornet*, an intellectual biography of Joseph Kinmont Hart and the role of academic freedom in higher education. He is the recipient of the 2007 Outstanding Faculty Teaching Award, the 2012 Outstanding Service Award, and the 2017 Recognition of Faculty Excellence Award from the College of Education at Georgia State University. In 2010, he was presented with the James and Helen Merritt Award for Distinguished Service to Philosophy of Education. Boyles received his PhD from Vanderbilt

University in 1991 and is a fellow in the Philosophy of Education Society, past president of the American Educational Studies Association, and past president of the John Dewey Society.

Jessica Jennrich works at Grand Valley State University as the director of the Women's Center and as an adjunct faculty member in Education and Women and Gender Studies. She is currently involved in a number of higher education and feminist organizations and is a reviewer for *Diversity Journal* and *Higher Education Journal.* Jessica is a former grant partner and guest writer for the American Association for University Women policy magazine. Jessica earned her bachelor's degree at Bowling Green State University in English, her master's degree from Eastern Michigan University in Women's and Gender Studies, and her doctorate at the University of Missouri in Educational Leadership and Policy Analysis.

Gabriel Keehn is a PhD student at Georgia State University in the department of Educational Policy Studies. His research focuses on the intersection of anarchism, individualism, and democratic theory. His work has appeared in *Educational Theory*, *Philosophical Studies in Education*, and the Philosophy of *Education Society Yearbook*, among others.

Eli Kramer is an affiliated researcher at the Department of the Philosophy of Culture of the University of Warsaw Institute of Philosophy and a co-director of the John Dewey Society Democracy in Education Initiative. He is also a philosophy PhD candidate at Southern Illinois University, Carbondale. His work has appeared in journals such as the *Philosophy of Education Yearbook* and *The Journal of School and Society* and as an introduction to a new anthology on Richard Rorty entitled, *Rorty and Beyond* (Lexington Books, forthcoming). His areas of speciality are in American and European idealism, early American philosophy, philosophy of culture, process philosophy, and metaethics. His research focuses on the history and philosophy of higher learning and the nature of philosophical practice.

Danielle Lake is a 2017 winner of the John Saltmarsh Award for Emerging Leaders in Civic Engagement and is an assistant professor in the Liberal Studies Department at Grand Valley State University. As a public philosopher, her work seeks to engage with, in, and through the public in order to address collective problems. Her interests include wicked problems and the processes most conducive to meliorating large-scale, dynamic, and systemic messes, including systemic engagement, design thinking, democratic deliberation, and participatory action research. Recent publications can be found at http://works.bepress.com/danielle_lake/.

Amy McFarland is an assistant professor of food and agricultural studies in the Frederik Meijer Honors College and the academic coordinator for the Sustainable Agriculture Project at Grand Valley State University. Her research focuses on social and environmental impacts of food systems from production to consumption and urban greening. Amy is interested in pursuing transdisciplinary strategies for enhancing the collaboration among food system stakeholders to improve sustainability efforts. She obtained her PhD from Texas A&M University.

Thaddeus Metz is currently a distinguished professor (2015–2019) at the University of Johannesburg in South Africa. Author of more than 200 scholarly works in moral, political, and legal philosophy, his recent work on education includes *How the West Was One: The Western as Individualist, the African as Communitarian* in M. Peters and C. Mika (eds) *The Dilemma of Western Philosophy* (Routledge, 2017); *Managerialism as Anti-Social: Some Implications of Ubuntu for Knowledge Production* in M. Cross and A. Ndofirepi (eds) *Knowledge and Change in African Universities* (Sense Publishers, 2017); and *Africanising Institutional Culture* in P. Tabensky and S. Matthews (eds) *Being at Home* (University of KwaZulu-Natal Press, 2015).

L. Jackson Newell is a professor of higher education at the University of Utah from 1974 to 2000 and served for 16 years as dean of liberal education where he built a nationally celebrated arts and sciences core curriculum required of all undergraduates. He took leave to serve as president of Deep Springs College from 1995 to 2004 and then returned to teach in the University of Utah Honors College. Among Jack's teaching awards are the Hatch Prize for Teaching Excellence, designation as a Presidential Teaching Scholar, appointment to the special rank of university professor, and the Sweet Distinguished Honors Professorship. His recent books include *The Electric Edge of Academe: The Saga of Lucien L. Nunn and Deep Springs College* (2015), *Hope, Heart and the Humanities* (2016), and *Community and Conscience* (2018).

Martha Nussbaum is the Ernst Freund Distinguished Service Professor of Law and Ethics, appointed in the Law School and Philosophy Department at the University of Chicago. She is the author of many books, including *Cultivating Humanity, Not For Profit: Why Democracy Needs the Humanities,* and *Anger and Forgiveness: Resentment, Generosity, Justice.* She has also edited 21 books. Among her awards are the Grawemeyer Award in

Education (2002), the Centennial Medal of the Graduate School of Arts and Sciences at Harvard University (2010), the Prince of Asturias Prize in the Social Sciences (2012), the American Philosophical Association's Philip Quinn Prize (2015), and the Kyoto Prize in Arts and Philosophy (2016).

Crispin Sartwell is an associate professor of philosophy at Dickinson College in Carlisle, PA. His books include *Political Aesthetics* (Cornell, 2010) and *Entanglements: a System of Philosophy* (SUNY, 2017). His essays and reviews have appeared in *Harper's*, *The Atlantic*, *The New York Times*, *The Wall Street Journal*, and the *Times Literary Supplement*.

Aaron Stoller is a philosopher and educational theorist who specializes in the work of John Dewey. His research centers on the epistemological foundations of higher education with a particular focus on progressive pedagogies, curricular theory, and reimagining the nature and practices of the liberal arts. His work has been published in such journals as *Studies in Philosophy and Education*, *The Journal of Aesthetics and Phenomenology*, *Research in Education*, *Transactions of the C. S. Peirce Society*, *The Journal of Curriculum Studies*, and *The Journal of Aesthetic Education*. He is the author of *Knowing and Learning as Creative Action* (2014). He lives in Colorado Springs, CO, where he teaches at Colorado College and directs the First-Year Experience Program.

Dwayne A. Tunstall is an associate professor of philosophy at Grand Valley State University. He is the author of two monographs: *Yes, But Not Quite: Encountering Josiah Royce's Ethico-Religious Insight* (2009) and *Doing Philosophy Personally: Thinking About Metaphysics, Theism, and Antiblack Racism* (2013). He is also a co-editor for the Dictionary of Literary Biographies, Volume 366: Orientalist Writers (2012). He has written numerous articles, book chapters, and book reviews on a variety of topics, including Africana philosophy, classical American philosophy, diversity in education, religious ethics, and social philosophy.

Check for updates

CHAPTER 1

Introduction: Toward a Philosophy of Higher Education

Aaron Stoller and Eli Kramer

Since the late 1960s the political right and business leaders have called for a more utilitarian approach to higher education, rejecting what many see as the uselessness of academic knowledge particularly as it exists in the liberal arts.[1] In the last 20 years, the intensity of these calls has increased, manifesting into the accountability and assessment movement and throwing higher education into something of an identity crisis.

This crisis has troubled the academy's cultural, social, and economic role. It has also illuminated a difficult reality of most institutions of higher education, which is that they have few resources available to radically reimagine the purposes, scope, and structures of the tradition in the face of these kinds of external pressures. Ronald Barnett and Kelly Coate argue, for example, that there has been virtually no modern debate or meaningful scholarship developed around the idea of curriculum in higher education. Instead, any talk of curriculum is framed exclusively within the context of teaching methods for content delivery.[2]

In the face of mounting skepticism, most institutions have not responded through creative revision to organizational, departmental, and

A. Stoller (✉)
Colorado College, Colorado Springs, CO, USA

E. Kramer
Department of the Philosophy of Culture, Institute of Philosophy of the University of Warsaw, Warsaw, Poland

A. Stoller, E. Kramer (eds.), *Contemporary Philosophical Proposals for the University*, https://doi.org/10.1007/978-3-319-72128-6_1

pedagogical structures, but instead by trading some amount of encroaching bureaucratic oversight for their ability to maintain the curricular status quo in increasingly smaller spheres of autonomy.

The lack of robust institutional response could be explained, in part, by the history of higher education in the United States. Until very recently, American colleges and universities were largely protected institutions. In the twentieth century they received a tremendous amount of financial support from the state and a truly explosive increase in student population. Further, their very existence brought economic and cultural capital to towns and states around the country.[3] Their academic subjects were seen as an obvious democratic and economic necessity. With this protection they developed their own complex, heterogeneous, and, at times, antagonistic aims and purposes. As David Labaree argues, higher education in America "…was a system, but it had no overall structure of governance and it did not emerge from a plan. It just happened, through an evolutionary process that had direction but no purpose. We have a higher education system in the same sense that we have a solar system, each of which emerged over time according to its own rules. These rules shaped the behavior of the system but they were not the product of intelligent design."[4] Perhaps it would be more precise to say there was no rationalist autocratic architect. Modern American colleges and universities are a jungle of creatures with instincts, aims, and purposes that developed over generations, which still belong to a shared ecosystem. While higher education in the United States has a long and complex history, the institution has developed devoid of a single intentional conceptual orientation because it was largely unnecessary for its own flourishing. As a result, it has few resources available to describe and articulate a robust rationale describing its practices and impacts.

This situation is compounded by graduate schools responsible for training academic faculty. Most American graduate programs have maintained a sharp disciplinary orientation and view their role largely as training charismatic academic researchers who will flourish in terms of their grant attainment and publication record.[5] This training is codified by tenure and promotion processes that are built around the same set of narrow, disciplinary-specific values and achievements. The faculty have been trained, in other words, to see their research as the true value they bring to institutions. Their pedagogical and administrative labor—the aspect of their labor that is most actively involved into the reconstitution of the institution, itself—is seen either as unnecessary to their lives as scholars or as a direct distraction to it. Unlike in previous generations, many faculty today in the United States have neither the interest nor incentive to cultivate a robust theoretical understanding of the institutional and organizational ecosystems that support their work as scholars.

For those who wish to engage and resist these external pressures, the available literatures are largely anemic in the face of the complexity and immediacy of the problems we now face.

The majority of traditional educational research, for example, has given little sustained treatment to the university as an ontologically distinct unit. Instead, the largest and most well-established bodies of scholarship in educational research are directed at the K-12 system or focused on adult education. While there are strands of this research that are of significant use to scholars interested in systems of higher education, it rarely considers higher education a distinct field and therefore does not engage directly with issues unique to colleges and universities.

The smaller, though active, strands of educational research that focus on issues in higher education are often neither critical nor theoretical in their approach. The two main streams of this kind of contemporary higher education research are the scholarship of teaching and learning (SOTL) and higher educational leadership and policy studies. The former focuses exclusively on pedagogical issues in higher education, while the latter is concerned improving administrative and co-curricular practices. Both fields typically draw on a range of qualitative and quantitative approaches and are concerned supporting and reinforcing the status quo. As such, they do not offer robust, critical imaginaries capable of reconstructing institutions of higher learning.

A third body of scholarship is found within the discipline of philosophy. Philosophers as wide ranging as Kant, Humboldt (Wilhelm), Hutchins, Whitehead, and Derrida played a key role in some of the most significant and imaginative university reforms of the last several hundred years. Yet while philosophy has a historical involvement within higher education, the work failed to materialize into a discourse creating sustainable material change in the trajectory of present higher education. There are at least two reasons for this failure. The first is that while philosophical examinations and reconstructions of the university have existed nearly as long as the institution, itself, they have been produced ad hoc by scholars in response to particular, localized issues or events. The modern discipline has simply never understood education, much less higher education, as a core concern. The second reason is that the majority of current philosophers writing about higher education have concerned themselves with broad investigations into the idea of education. While many of these texts offer creative imaginaries for the future of the institution, they remain disconnected from the material and political conditions of institutions. As such, they offer no path forward to faculty and administrators who might operationalize their vision or reconstruct it for a local campus community.

A more recent discourse called Critical University Studies (CUS) has developed, filling a significant void in the landscape of higher education research and practice. Jeffrey Williams locates the history of the field in terms of the emergence, since the early 1990s, of "the rise of 'academic capitalism' and the corporatization of the university; ... the deteriorating conditions of academic labor; and ...the problems of students and their escalating debt."[6] This critical turn is a movement away from traditional streams within higher education, as it seeks to critique university practices and overturn unjust structures. It also stands in contrast to traditional philosophical literature in higher education. In a recent review of the field, Krystian Szadkowski ties CUS to currents in the disciplines of "education, history, cultural studies, sociology and sociology of work" while setting it against "philosophical investigations of the idea of education."[7] While CUS's work is explicitly involved in critiquing the material conditions, policies, and economies of university practice as they currently exist, it often fails to offer robust and ameliorative imaginaries that might be deployed by faculty and administrators to push their institutions in new directions.

Our intent through the rest of the essay is to create a path forward for philosophical work in higher education that is sensitive to the discursive, organizational, economic, epistemic, and political cultures of the institution. We believe the discipline is well positioned to support, engage, and extend the critical turn begun by CUS, if and only if the work of philosophy of higher education is undertaken in the right way. The purpose of this essay is therefore explicitly *not* to provide a grand theory of higher education that might be overlaid onto university practice. Instead, as we will argue, any viable philosophy of higher education must not only recognize but be prepared to account for and harness the heterogeneity of theoretical, organizational, economic, epistemic, and professional perspectives that are the ground of an institution of higher learning.

The Question of Method

We begin by considering the question of method in philosophy as it was taken up by John Dewey. Here we are interested in Dewey's work less for his specific conclusions about education and more for his approach to philosophy of education. Dewey was, himself, highly skeptical of the viability of a philosophy of higher education[8] and instead focused his work on primary and secondary schooling systems. Yet his approach to philosophy of education presents a particularly important conceptualization of the work of philosophy in higher education precisely because he links the work of theory to the social and political cultures of school and society.

In *Reconstruction in Philosophy*, Dewey argues that two major historical insights made space for a pragmatic approach to philosophy. The first insight is what he calls "psychology based on biology" by which he means evolutionary naturalism, which allowed us to conceptualize ourselves as biological organisms adapting to an unstable environment.[9] Pragmatic philosophy begins with the notion that life, by its very definition, is active. Life is not a static essence, but an event which is constantly adapting to and anticipating changes in the environment in order to not only survive but also thrive. This claim in itself dissolves the Cartesianism underlying most approaches to philosophy and education.

The second insight is that the process of experimental inquiry is the primary method of knowing. Dewey writes that "knowing is literally something which we do; that analysis is ultimately physical and active; that meanings in their logical quality are standpoints, attitudes, and methods of behaving toward facts, and that active experimentation is essential to verification."[10] For Dewey, the project of knowledge is not a decontextualized, universalized, thing-in-itself but instead is a tool crafted by and for particular situations and cultures through a systematic process of inquiry. Here Dewey dissolves the foundationalist epistemologies inherited from the Platonic tradition.

While this reconstruction of two of the most fundamental categories of philosophy is in itself enough to disrupt most contemporary approaches to education, Dewey argues that Darwin's influence on philosophy did something more radical, which is to shift the primary method of philosophical work.[11] Dewey describes this new approach to the philosophic method as the "denotative-empirical" method. While his method was most directly outlined in *Experience and Nature*, his concern for a more grounded approach to philosophy was present as early as *Psychology*.[12]

Dewey's aim was to more directly tie the work of philosophical theory to the needs and issues that emerge from the everyday. He writes that "in the natural sciences there is a union of experience and nature which is not greeted as a monstrosity; on the contrary, the inquirer must use empirical method if his findings are to be treated as genuinely scientific."[13] As a result "ventures of this theoretical sort start from and terminate in directly experienced subject-matter."[14] In making this claim, Dewey is not suggesting that philosophy give way to a reductively instrumentalist approach. Instead, he was developing a way of approaching philosophy that would be of deeper and more immediate value to human experience.[15]

Thomas M. Alexander argues that this approach is an attempt at building "a method of 'disclosing' experience without transforming into a mere theoretical object."[16] In this way "the scientific method is not identical with the denotative method, but is rather illuminated by it. The denotative method attempts to make us fully *aware* of the world *beyond* our 'ideas' of it. ....The denotative method is meant to contextualize the *cognitive* interests of philosophy with the *noncognitive* scope of life."[17] We might say, then, that the aim of the denotative method is not only to recover philosophy so that it is more directly linked with the problems of life but also to take experience on its own terms and, in so doing, realize that it cannot be strictly reduced to scientific causal properties.

This reconstruction of the aim and method of philosophy brings the relationship between education and philosophy into sharper view. Dewey argues that "if we are willing to conceive education as the process of forming fundamental dispositions, intellectual and emotional, toward nature and fellow-men, philosophy may even be defined *as the general theory of education*."[18] Education offers particularly fertile ground in experience, enabling us to view philosophical problems where they emerge and where our approach to answering them has deep social and personal impacts.[19]

For Dewey, education is the site where culture reproduces itself, and it is also an individual process of meaningful individual growth. As Walter Feinberg argues, "Dewey's educational subject is … the social order itself and the opportunities it might create for democratic social-self reproduction."[20] Education is therefore a process of reproduction rather than transmission. Education does not simply change what we know, it changes what we *want to know*: our beliefs about the world, our dispositions toward the world, and our habits for engaging the world.

As such, education is not an anemic subfield of philosophy, but stands at its very center because it is an explication, critique, and reconstruction of the social conditions from which new forms of practice and new beliefs might emerge.[21] Dewey makes this clear most explicitly in *Democracy and Education*, writing that "the most penetrating definition of philosophy which can be given is, then, that it is the theory of education in its most general phases. .... The reconstruction of philosophy, of education, and of social ideals and methods thus go hand in hand."[22] The new, methodological labor of philosophy becomes most apparent in education. It is not in building grand theories set apart from the experienced conditions in and through which education occurs, but in redirecting (i.e. educating) action toward more meaningful and productive ends.

For Dewey, the central question of philosophy of education is understanding how to organize the practices of schooling, which includes academic content, into a form that will best prepare students to become empathetic, creative, and active participants in a democratic order.

From Theory to Praxis in Higher Education

Yet Dewey's conclusions about education cannot be easily or directly grafted onto the work of philosophy in higher education precisely because the cultures of practice are vastly different than K-12. In the first instance, colleges and universities are not grounded in a culture of teachers and teaching, but instead are heterogeneous collectives of disciplinary inquirers, each with their own epistemic discourses, sets of material practices, patterns of thought and evaluation, and rhetorical strategies. In the second instance, virtually none of the faculty at colleges and universities have extensive training in pedagogical or curricular theory. Their primary identity and labor lies within the domain of their disciplinary research. The result is that most colleges and universities have little to no theoretical or philosophical perspective unpinning the dimension of their labor that falls outside the domain of their research. Virtually no college or university has a common discourse for pedagogy, a common language for curricular design, and/or theoretical agreement on the role of the institution in culture. Instead educational discourse, if it exists at all, occurs at the level of the discipline or department. The differences between the two cultures of education in fact highlight the necessity and centrality of Dewey's approach to a philosophy of education that maintains close ties to the experienced and material cultures of the institution.

Dewey's debate with Robert Maynard Hutchins over the aims and structure of the liberal arts curriculum presents an interesting case study regarding two ways the philosophic method might transact with the cultures of practice to produce a philosophy of higher education. Hutchins' approach is illustrative of a more traditional approach in which philosophical theory is constructed and overlaid onto experience, while Dewey understands philosophy as working from experience to theory and back to experience.

When Hutchins' *The Higher Learning in America* was published in 1936, it was instantly hailed as a significant contribution to theory and practice of higher education. In the tradition of John Henry Cardinal Newman, the text examined the foundations and practices of postsecondary education, concluding that a proper view of higher learning is the study and refinement of first principles (metaphysics), with its empirical branches applying and occasionally refining it.

Dewey was not impressed with Hutchins' proposal, as their lengthy and public debate illustrates. While Dewey shared Hutchins' concern for the maintenance of the college as a special cultural site which does not operate directly in the service of industry, he disagreed with a number Hutchins' central claims.

Perhaps the most significant point of disagreement is Hutchins' assertion that the college curriculum should remain a place of contemplation that cultivates the life of the mind through initiating students into a common heritage of great (if not universal) ideas.[23] In making this claim, Hutchins identifies himself as an apologist for a tradition which began with Aristotle's theory of knowledge as contemplation and developed through the medieval curriculum which grounded itself upon the seven liberal arts, "trivium" of communicative arts (logic, rhetoric, literary studies) and a "quadrivium" of mathematical studies (arithmetic, music, geometry, and astronomy)."[24] More significantly, Hutchins sublimates the cultures and histories of the diverse disciplines at the University of Chicago underneath a kind of theoretical monoculture that depends on the assumption that all disciplines hold the same metaphysical and epistemological beliefs about the world and the nature of their work.

Dewey's rejection of Hutchins' proposal has been frequently interpreted as a rejection of the rationalistic and hierarchical view of the project of knowledge embedded in Hutchins' view of the traditional liberal arts curriculum. This reading is not incorrect but is not broad enough to capture the full scope of Dewey's concern.

For Dewey, disciplines are cultures of practice that emerge in response to particular classes of problems both in the world and in response to lines of inquiry within the disciplines, themselves. Dewey's critique of Hutchins, therefore, is as much about epistemological and metaphysical differences in their particular philosophical systems, as it is about the role of disciplines and education in social, cultural, and political contexts, as well as the role of philosophy in mediating that relationship. For Dewey, the university cannot be simply about metaphysical contemplation because such a course of study is neither appropriate for a student in a modern world, nor does such a curricular position make space for the heterogeneous communities of inquiry that already exist at colleges and universities.

However problematic Hutchins' proposal might be considered, it was situated in a very real set of concerns which plagued the university then and now. Hutchins arrived at the University of Chicago in 1929 and found a professorate filled with what he understood to be "pragmatists." Dewey, as an important founding faculty member of university, had left his mark on it by the time he left in 1904. When Hutchins arrived Dewey's legacy had been sedimented. The faculty had little to no interest in his classicist policy initiatives to make a rigorous undergraduate program for the sake of cultivating the life of the mind. Hutchins saw pragmatists as part of the instrumentalized research orientation of the University of Chicago, and further, as foolish for not defending the life of the mind. He was worried that progressive theory of the university could all too easily slip into a vulgar anti-intellectual vocationalism. Although Hutchins had a limited understanding of Dewey's alternative, he had a tactical point about how, when a university is instrumentalized, its reflective and systematic aspects can be dragged down by all too simplistic understandings of what is useful to a culture. Hutchins understood all too well that philosophical discourse is part of a complex political context and needs thoughtful deployment to not feed anti-intellectual and anti-democratic movements.

In contrast to what he believed was brute instrumentalism of the pragmatists, Hutchins developed a foundationalist and largely normative vision for undergraduate education. This vision was robust, philosophically grounded, and charted a bold course for the University of Chicago. It was not, however, tied to the cultures of disciplinary practice that made up that institution.

The Dewey-Hutchins debate is largely representative of the problematic situation contemporary institutions of higher education find themselves in today. The narrowness of our current imaginary forces an unfortunate and unnecessary binary between two visions of higher education. On one hand, institutions follow an unreflective and utilitarian vision that follows the interests of culture, as illustrated in Hutchins' view of the Chicago pragmatists. On the other hand, they attempt to retreat entirely from the concerns of culture, finding justification in an Aristotelian conception of their work, as illustrated in Hutchins' proposal for undergraduate education.

What we are suggesting is a third way: a reconstructive philosophy of higher education that grounds itself in the real situation of colleges and universities, and then builds robust alternatives (imaginaries) that can harness their productive heterogeneities, and be reorganized and refined as new problems and needs emerge. In other words, we advocate for a philosophically supported higher education that can reflect and refine its present culture, without retreating from it or becoming reduced to a narrow utilitarian function within it.

Philosophy functions in higher education as a point of connection between disciplinary boundaries, steering the institution in a direction which offers the possibility of meaningful growth both for students and culture, as a whole. Yet, it must also be representative (in theory and practices) of the diverse practices and beliefs that are largely the ground of postsecondary institutions. A theory of higher education must not marginalize this fact but instead take root in its fertile soil.

Reconstruction in Philosophy of Higher Education: A Brief Review

Although philosophy of higher education in previous generations has sometimes been too far removed from disciplinary experience, practice, and material culture, to improve the very institutions it seeks to serve, there are notable exceptions. Many of the significant questions of philosophy of higher education have arisen from genuine problems in colleges and universities, and the significant responses were meant to advance novel solutions to address those problems. Below we provide historical examples of the philosophy of higher education as an entry point for thinking about the elements of a robust philosophy of higher education.

The University in Culture

One of the major historical streams in reconstructive philosophy of higher education has been politically and ethically positioning higher education as a whole. Kant's *The Conflict of the Faculties* is one of the earliest modern attempts to make normative theoretical claims about the structure of the university, beyond the dogmatic formula and curriculum of the medieval university. For Kant, the state should have little influence (for its own benefit) on the project of the advancement of knowledge, save as it impinges on the practical side of the higher faculties (faculty, law, and medicine). These conclusions were drawn from his experience at the University of Königsberg, his understanding of the production of knowledge as a philosopher and theoretical physicist, and the dangers he saw of the Prussian state sliding into dogmatic mythic and religious fervor. Kant left a generation of Neo-Kantians an open-ended question on the relationship between the aspiring nation-state and the university.[25] Humboldt, as a liberal politician and higher education leader/creator, although granting more interaction between the university and the nation-state than Kant, still retained many restrictions that might encumber the activity and growth of scholars and culture.[26]

By the time Bill Readings wrote *The University in Ruins* in the 1990s such an alliance was beginning to unravel, for in the new transnational corporate economy it is not nation-states but transnational capitalist corporations that the university must align with in order to survive. Although nation-states should certainly be blamed for much of the disastrous violence of the twentieth century, they at least understood the project of higher learning to be an invaluable human cultural project. Readings argued that we are now entering an era where those in power see human cultural projects as superfluous to what they deem most important: the efficiency of the current economic paradigm to perpetuate itself.[27] A sufficiently robust reconstructive philosophy of higher education that would harness the energies needed to address this political and ethical crisis has yet to be formed.

The Institutional Structure of the University

A second thread of philosophical reconstruction in higher education is a debate regarding whether the university is a rational, centrally ordered institution, or whether it is a heterogeneous, pluralistic institution. Since at least Giambattista Vico's famous oration *On the Study Methods of Our Times*,[28] reconstructive philosophy of higher education has struggled to balance the concrete particular activities of each discipline with the speculative whole that is presupposed within them (the university itself). Neo-Kantians, Thomists, phenomenologists, and even post-structuralists such as Derrida all suggest that there is a coherency (or at least desire for coherency) embedded within diverse disciplinary practices that have made universities what they are today. By the mid-twentieth century, this began to be questioned, and ideas such as the multiversity begin to take root. Those in the Burkean conservative tradition of philosophy such as Michael Oakeshott suggest that tradition has built heterogeneous but efficacious higher education institutions that need not be rationally ordered as some sort of well-oiled machine.[29] In recent years the heterogeneity and the plurality of knowledge have been explored by younger disciplines. For example, as P.J. Gumport has argued, Women and Gender studies provides an example of a discipline which recognizes the heterogeneity and plurality of knowledge as both necessary and positive for the mission of the university.[30] Along these lines, in recent years philosophers like Ronald Barnett have argued that the super complex plurality of the university is a holistic aim in itself.[31]

At the heart of this reconstructive work is a concern with how loosely coupled university practice can be without losing a positive effect on cultural life. Philosophers split on whether the university ought to simplify (the position of Newman or Hutchins) or if one should embrace and utilize super complexity (the position of Oakeshott and Barnett). Although very few suggest that university education should be for everyone, some like Dewey have a democratic egalitarian vision of the aims of who the university serves,[32] while others such as Nietzsche see the university as an elitist institution for a select few aimed to advance culture by their very activity.[33]

Some philosophers have operationalized such theories toward new models of the university. For example, when he was dean of the College of Education at University College London, Ronald Barnett created a transition culture into what he now calls an "ecological university". Derrida has also helped such a transitional culture toward a more holistic and public higher education by his work in creating the "Collège international de Philosophie," a unique free philosophical institution of higher education.

The Academic in Culture

A third historical stream in reconstructive philosophy of higher education concerns the role of academics as social and political agents. Richard Rorty argued that the traditional notion of academic freedom as the search for truth free of political bias is inherently flawed. For him, "[d]ebate at

English Department faculty meetings is no less, and no more, rational than at the conferences where justices of the Supreme Court discuss pending cases."[34] Instead, academic work is always already tied to political aims. For Rorty, the most significant criterion of a university's success is its social impacts: does it, in fact, contribute to social hope?

Hans-Georg Gadamer takes up the impact of this reconceptualization of academic freedom, arguing that the notion of the knowledge worker as an unbiased expert has led to detrimental unintended consequences for democracy. Specifically, he argues that "[t]he increasing importance of the role which the expert plays in our society is rather a serious symptom for the increasing ignorance of the decision makers."[35] The result has been no less than the anti-intellectualization of the body politic, who place the mantle of knowledge on the expert class.

Jim Garrison and Gert Biesta make these concerns more concrete and place them in relationship to specific political and economic influences in the contemporary university. Garrison argues that the American scholar has lost her way. While scholars across the disciplinary spectrum have the potential to combat the ideological forces bearing down on institutions of higher learning, "scholars are less likely to intervene in the flux of public events than at any other time in recent history."[36] Garrison finds this situation not simply morally objectionable and politically dangerous, but "one could find no greater rejection of Emerson's vision of the active and engaged public scholar."[37] Instead, he calls on scholars to turn their attention to the neoliberal forces bearing down on institutions of higher learning.

Like Garrison, Biesta questions the impact of the scholar in the face of the privatization of the university and of knowledge production, more generally. For him, the historic role of "the expert" in democratic culture has eroded as knowledge work has shifted from the public to the private sphere. Biesta suggests that while the university can no longer claim a monopoly on expert knowledge, it still serves a vital and central function in through what he calls the democratization of knowledge. For Biesta, "The key question…is whether the interpretation of the scientific worldview as an account of what reality is really like, is inevitable."[38] Following John Dewey and Bruno Latour, Biesta argues that it is not inevitable and, further, that knowledge workers in the university must play a central role in the processes of inquiry that will shape and ultimately direct knowledge toward a democratically productive end.

The Aims and Structures of the Curriculum

A fourth stream of reconstruction concerns the nature and impacts of the university curriculum. José Ortega y Gasset makes a case that curriculum has been and should continue to be the central contested space of educational reform efforts. This is because Ortega y Gasset believes that the heart of the institution is found in its curriculum which, in the case of the Spanish universities, must be not simply be critiqued but imaginatively reconstructed based on criteria authentic to the culture and people it serves. Ortega y Gasset argues instead that Spanish universities must reject their traditional emphasis on the training of academic researchers. Instead, he argues that "we must turn the present university upside down, so to speak, and stand it upon precisely the opposite principle. Instead of teaching what ought to be taught, according to some Utopian desire, we must teach only what can be taught; that is what can be learned."[39] For Ortega y Gasset, this reversal means a reconstruction of the central core of the curriculum around "culture." Here, the disciplines are not taught and research is not conducted for its own sake, but in meaningful relationship to the needs of localized peoples.

Jane Roland Martin's critique of the curriculum and the institutional structures of the academy bears a resemblance to Ortega y Gasset's in that she claims it most often does not serve the needs of the people. Martin offers a contemporary feminist critique of both the institution and its curriculum. While it is the case that the percentage of women as students in the academy finally mirrors the overall population, Martin points out that this has not come with a parallel change in the policies, practices, and curricula of the institution. She specifically takes issue with "the chilly coeducational classroom climate for women in institutions of higher education, the inadequate representation of women in the professoriate, and the relative silences about and misrepresentations of women in higher education's curriculum."[40] Martin proposes a novel way of conceptualizing the problem which is rooted in immigrant imagery and has the effect of pulling together of what have been seen as unrelated phenomena.[41] She leverages this imaginary to argue that while women have been assimilated into the university, they have not been acculturated into it. Such a move would require significant change with regard to the masculinist cultures, policies, and pedagogies which currently dominate systems of higher education. For Martin, this reconstruction involves a constellation of efforts that center on a reconceptualization of the curriculum and classroom pedagogies, which serve as the intellectual heart of the institution.

Ronald Barnett also raises the question of the relationship between the university curriculum (the known) and its students (the knowing subject).[42] The curriculum has traditionally been viewed as a landscape of disciplinary data to which faculty serve as guides. That landscape bore no direct relationship to the students who are considered recipients of disciplinary truths. Barnett mounts a significant challenge to this conceptualization, arguing that curricula and the pedagogy which support it are not only value-laden but also must account for the knowing subject and his or her process of coming to know. He puts forward a set of principles aimed at reconstructing the relationship between knowing and being as expressed in and through the curriculum.

Toward a Reconstructive Philosophy of Higher Education

Today, the problems of higher education call not only for new philosophical reconstructions but also the development of a sustained discourse around these issues. Instead of proposing a theory of higher education, we return to the question of method. Where ought we to begin our analysis of higher education and what are the kinds of things for which a successful theory must account? Here we draw forward and revise some of the historical concerns of philosophy of higher education while also adding new lines of thought in light of our contemporary context.

A philosophy must view higher education as an institutional type, accounting both for its distinctive elements and its organizational complexities.

If we accept the idea that higher learning is distinct from primary and secondary forms of schooling, then the work of philosophy of higher education must denote and reconstruct particular aspects of the institution in its work, seeking to build a discourse around higher education as a distinct structure. It must consider, for example, the project of teaching and learning in this particular context, as well as the relationship between pedagogy and disciplinary research. A viable theory must also be capable of accounting for the economic, organizational, and political cultures that situate and frame the work of faculty, administrators, and students. In doing so, it must have some kind of theory of the institution that seeks organizational justice and provides a platform for future innovation. It must not ignore, for example, the structural forces that shape the orientation and outputs of workers, such as tenure and promotion systems. It must denote the concerns of labor and the needs of all workers (from faculty to facilities staff) in the system. It must also be broad enough to seek forms of epistemic justice that account for the aims and knowledges of all members of the college or university community.

A philosophy of higher education must build on the complex network of actors and cultures in the system.

Tony Becher and Paul Trowler's work in anthropology of higher education suggests that if we want to understand, critique, and build policy and theory in higher education, we need to take disciplinary cultures as our primary unit of analysis, rather than the institution as a homogenous unit. This is because, as their research shows, faculty organize their professional lives (i.e. teaching, research, service) in ways that are related to and emerge out of their disciplinary paradigms, as well as the specific intellectual tasks on which they are engaged.[43] A theory of higher education, then, must denote, build upon, and work to reconstruct a set of heterogeneous disciplinary cultures, each with their own norms, assumptions, and behaviors.

We would add to Becher and Trowler's conclusion that a theory of higher education must not reduce the labor and value of the institution to the work of faculty. Instead, it must understand the institution as a much richer and complex set of persons and practices. It is clear that the kinds of expertise necessary to sustain and cultivate an institution have changed dramatically, even in the last 20 years. Disciplinary expertise is now a necessary but not sufficient form of knowledge to advance our institutions. A theory must embrace the fact that disciplinary experts exist alongside expert counselors, development officers, pedagogues, accountants, housing personnel, and architects, all of whom are vital to the functioning of the whole. It must also meaningfully connect expertise inside and outside the academy. The academy no longer begins and ends in disciplinary knowledge but is a complex ecosystem that must be reorganized to meet the complexities of the world.

A philosophy of higher education advances a cohesive and critical imaginary for higher education in relationship to various, social, political, economic, and ethical contexts and concerns.

Within philosophy there has been a longstanding interest in the proper aims of higher education. Today, that question takes on significantly more urgency and requires much more critical nuance than it ever has before.

The cultural role and, in fact, the very necessity of colleges and universities have been destabilized. The university finds itself in the midst of increased skepticism from the broader public in terms of its value within and applicability to cultural concerns.[44] Compounding this issue is that the demands of culture today are much more significant than preparing a "citizen" (in the narrow sense of that term associated with voting and state politics). We need to educate individuals and communities prepared to understand and face challenges presented by wicked problems such as global climate change, systemic poverty, and water access. We need to develop aims and forms of education that directly confront the fact that the carrying capacity of the earth may soon be exhausted. At the same time, we are also increasingly aware of the limitations of the disciplines and disciplinary forms of knowledge. Disciplines, as singular paradigms and methodologies, are insufficient to engage and solve the very wicked problems for which we are educating our students.

In spite of these pressing realities, the extent of our collective imaginary regarding higher education is limited to an outdated and insufficient binary between, on one hand, the institution in service to industry and, on the other, in service to a narrow conception of liberal representative democracy. Today, theory must situate the institution in meaningful, critical, and dialogical relationship with local and global cultures. It must also be broad enough to account for and reconstruct the institutional structures (e.g. disciplinary boundaries, curricula and pedagogies, grading practices) that reflect and reinforce the outdated values that that are no longer functional. In doing so, it must be capable of going deep enough to reimagine how faculty and administrators are trained to carry out their work. Most faculty have neither the training nor support to reconstruct their pedagogical practices outside of a simple content distribution model rooted in traditional disciplinary structures. In this regard, a theory must work to radically reimagine the content, practices, and structures of institutions in order to develop theory that is capable and equipped enough to engage the world in which we now find ourselves.

A philosophy of higher education must develop a robust account of teaching, learning, and knowing.

The anemic role of the institution in culture can be tied in many ways to an outmoded view of teaching, learning, and knowing that became encoded in the structures and practices of the institution.

Today we have significantly more complex understanding of the process and aims of learning. Rather than a view of growth as a strictly individual, mental, and academic process, we understand learning as an embodied, psychosocial process that takes place in and through the various communities we inhabit and problems we encounter. Yet our pedagogical practices and curricular structures still reflect a largely parochial view of teaching and learning inherited from the late nineteenth and early twentieth centuries. It is simply no longer appropriate to view a curriculum as a body of content and pedagogy as a simple distribution of content from the knowledgeable to the uneducated.

This institutional stagnation is somewhat ironic given the fact that the epistemological frameworks of most disciplines have shifted from positivistic foundationalism (that was made popular over the last 100 years) to some version of an understanding that knowledge is an intertwining, value-laden, and organic cultural project. Yet the organization of our disciplines and our practices of research has not yet begun to make anything like this shift.

A robust theory of higher education must also find ways to reconstruct the relationships between and among disciplines in both theory and practice. It must find robust ways to relate research programs to learning processes. It also must hold an expansive view of the teaching and learning mission of an institution, including how and why learning occurs in and across various contexts (e.g. disciplinary, formal and informal, cultural), and give students meaningful agency in curricular processes.

A philosophy of higher education must advance a theoretical discourse that appropriately denotes its practices and its aims.

One of the major failings of contemporary higher education is the lack of a theoretical discourse that describes its labor and its value *on its own terms.* This is perhaps one of the most important impacts of Dewey's denotative method in relationship to a robust theory of higher education, but also the most misunderstood or ignored.

Developing a rich, theoretical discourse for higher education is urgent and has immediate, practical consequences. Without a critical and theoretical language, we can neither conceptualize (and therefore meaningfully reconstruct) our practice, nor can we resist outside forces which seek to colonize our practice. It is a lack of theoretical language, particularly in the context of teaching, learning, and knowing, that has shackled many of our practices and structures to the status quo of the tradition. We are simply unable to imagine alternatives to practice because we see our pedagogical and institutional labor as a theoretical dead zone.

Without a rich discourse, we are also unable to justify our practice to a culture that has begun to question the goals, structures, and impacts of the university. As such, our institutions remain vulnerable to outside imaginaries co-opting our work. Most of our faculty colleagues, for example, can do little more than intuit their frustration with the contemporary assessment movement, but they have neither the conceptual resources to explain why it is problematic nor the discursive resources to offer counter narratives that contradict its assumptions and effects.

The contemporary accountability and assessment movement has shined a spotlight on the fact that the majority of institutions of higher education simply have no rich language of practice. As such, our institutions have been forced to adopt and internalize the language thrust upon us by culture. Our pedagogical practices are reduced to single-factor causal models and behavioral outputs. Our curricular architectures become efficient road maps caught within false and largely unhelpful binary between "skills" and "content." Our organizational and administrative models are co-opted by the language of Taylorism taking the form of the total quality management (TQM) movement of organizational theory.[45]

Ultimately, when we fail to develop critical and theoretically informed discourses that are authentic to our practice, we can do little more than assume the status quo.

Conclusion

Creating an engaged discourse around robust, reconstructive philosophies of higher education to drive institutional change can no longer be considered luxurious addition to academic work but is necessary and central in the face of cultural pressures that will eventually subsume the university if left unchecked.

We are aware that difficulties faced in attempting to do this work are many. Within the discipline, education is most often considered little more than a footnote to the "real" work of philosophy and jettisoned off to peripheral, if not separate, discourses. Within the political and intellectual economies of our local institutions, the same prejudices hold true: participating in reconstructive action within our organizational structures, turning our research to pedagogical and curricular concerns, or directly relating our work to the public (e.g. transdisciplinarity) are all still considered taboo activities that can spell career suicide for academics. Even our institutional structures, themselves, are arranged such that a rich, reflexive discourse that might engage the diversity of standpoints in the system is largely absent.

Yet, in the face of these difficulties, we believe that philosophy as a discipline and a practice is well suited to leading this kind of work, given the critical orientation of its work, its capacity for theory building, and its situatedness within cross-, meta-, and interdisciplinary conversations. The subfields within the discipline (e.g. philosophy of science, social science, literature, technology, etc.) have long concerned themselves with the practices, epistemic and metaphysical frameworks, and truth claims produced across a range of disciplinary tribes and levels of generality. This perspective yields the very real possibility for establishing common discourses across disciplinary domains and for locating points of divergence and convergence that can yield to fruitful directions for education practice.

This collection provides a propaedeutic to that work. A philosophy of higher education that harnesses the energies of the university will be in a strong position to address the most pressing questions of human life and culture. Despite the challenges they face, universities and colleges very heterogeneity and diversity of praxis are also their strength. Universities and colleges have a powerful range of stakeholders to advance our most pressing inquiries. It is for this reason that the time is now to reconstruct the philosophy of higher education.

Notes

1. Dan Berrett, "The Day the Purpose of College Changed," *The Chronicle of Higher Education*, January 26, 2015. Accessed October 11, 2017. http://www.chronicle.com/article/The-Day-the-Purpose-of-College/151359/
2. Ronald Barnett and Kelly Coate, *Engaging the curriculum*. (United Kingdom: McGraw-Hill Education, 2004), 13–17.
3. David Labaree, "2013 Dewey Lecture: College – What is it Good For?," *Education and Culture* 30, no. 1 (2014): 5.
4. David Labaree, "2013 Dewey Lecture: College – What is it Good For?," 4.
5. See William Clark, *Academic charisma and the origins of the research university*. (Chicago: University of Chicago Press, 2008).
6. Jeffrey J. Williams, "Deconstructing academe: the birth of critical university Studies," *The Chronicle of Higher Education*, February 19, 2012. Accessed October 11, 2017. http://chronicle.com/article/An-Emerging-Field-Deconstructs/130791/
7. Krystian Szadkowski, "University's Third Mission as a Challenge to Marxist Theory," *CPP Research Papers Series* 36 (2013): 10; 11.
8. John Dewey, "From Absolutism to Experimentalism," in *The Later Works of John Dewey, Volume 5*, ed. J.A. Boydston (Carbondale: Southern Illinois University Press, 1930/1984), 156.

9. John Dewey, "Reconstruction in Philosophy," in *The Middle Works of John Dewey, Volume 12,* ed. J.A. Boydston (Carbondale: Southern Illinois University Press, 1920/1982), 127–128.
10. John Dewey, "An Added Note as the 'Practical' in *Essays in Experimental Logic," in The Middle Works of John Dewey, Volume 10,* ed. J.A. Boydston (Carbondale: Southern Illinois University Press, 1917/1980), 367.
11. John Dewey, "The Need for a Recovery of Philosophy," *in The Middle Works of John Dewey, Volume 10,* ed. J.A. Boydston (Carbondale: Southern Illinois University Press, 1917/1946), 46.
12. Thomas M. Alexander, "Dewey's Denotative-Empirical Method: A Thread Through the Labyrinth," *The Journal of Speculative Philosophy* 18, no. 3 (2004): 249.
13. John Dewey, *Experience and Nature* in *The Later Works of John Dewey, Volume 1,* ed. J.A. Boydston (Carbondale: Southern Illinois University Press, 1925/1981), 11.
14. John Dewey, *Experience and Nature* in *The Later Works of John Dewey,* 11.
15. Ibid., 18.
16. Thomas M. Alexander, "Dewey's Denotative-Empirical Method: A Thread Through the Labyrinth," *The Journal of Speculative Philosophy* 18, no. 3 (2004): 249.
17. Thomas M. Alexander, "Dewey's Denotative-Empirical Method: A Thread Through the Labyrinth," 252.
18. John Dewey, *Democracy and Education* in *The Middle Works of John Dewey, Volume 9,* ed. J.A. Boydston (Carbondale: Southern Illinois University Press, 1916/1980), 338.
19. John Dewey, *Democracy and Education* in *The Middle Works of John Dewey,* 338.
20. Walter Feinberg, *What is a Public Education and Why We Need It* (Maryland: Lexington Books, 2016), 7.
21. Jim Garrison, "Dewey's philosophy as education" In *Reading Dewey: Interpretations for a Postmodern Generation,* ed. Larry Hickman (Indianapolis: Indiana University Press, 1998), 75.
22. John Dewey, *Democracy and Education* in *The Middle Works of John Dewey,* 341.
23. Donald N. Levine, *Powers of the Mind: The Reinvention of Liberal Learning in America* (Chicago: University of Chicago Press, 2008), 181–182.
24. Leonard Waks, "Experimentalism and the Higher Learning: John Dewey's Theory of the University," forthcoming. Accessed October 11, 2017. https://www.academia.edu/11688441/EXPERIMENTALISM_AND_THE_HIGHER_LEARNING_JOHN_DEWEY_S_THEORY_OF_THE_UNIVERSITY

25. Immanuel Kant, "The Conflict of the Philosophy Faculty with the Theology Faculty," in *The Conflict of the Faculties = Der Streit Der FakultaÌten*, trans. Mary J. Gregor (Lincoln, NE: University of Nebraska Press, 1798/2011).
26. Wilhelm Von Humboldt, "On the Spirit and the Organizational Framework of Intellectual Institutions in Berlin [in University Reform in Germany]," *Minerva* 8 (1900/1970).
27. Bill Readings, "The Idea of Excellence," in *The University in Ruins* (Cambridge, MA: Harvard University Press, 1999).
28. Giambattista Vico, *On the Study Methods of Our Times*, trans. Elio Gianturco and Donald Phillip Verene (Ithaca: Cornell University Press, 1990).
29. Michael Oakeshott, "The Idea of a University," in *The Voice of Liberal Learning: Michael Oakeshott on Education* (New Haven: Yale University Press, 1950/1989).
30. Patricia J. Gumport, "Chapter 7: Changing Conditions for Knowledge Creation," in *Academic Pathfinders: Knowledge Creation and Feminist Scholarship* (Westport, CT: Greenwood Press, 2002).
31. Ronald Barnett, "Supercomplexity: The New Universal," in *Realizing the University in an Age of Supercomplexity* (Philadelphia, PA: Open University Press, 1999).
32. Leonard Waks, "Experimentalism and the Higher Learning: John Dewey's Theory of the University." https://www.academia.edu/11688441/EXPERIMENTALISM_AND_THE_HIGHER_LEARNING_JOHN_DEWEY_S_THEORY_OF_THE_UNIVERSITY
33. Friedrich Wilhelm Nietzsche, "Fifth Lecture," in *On the Future of Our Educational Institutions*, trans. Michael Grenke (South Bend, IN: Augustine's Press, 1872/2004).
34. Richard Rorty, "Does Academic Freedom Have Philosophical Presuppositions?," *Academe* 80, no. 6 (1994): 55–56.
35. Hans-Georg Gadamer, "The Limitations of the Expert," in *Hans-Georg Gadamer on Education, Poetry, and History: Applied Hermeneutics*, ed. Dieter Misgeld and Graeme Nicholson (Albany: State University of New York Press, 1992), 182.
36. Jim Garrison, "Emerson's 'The American Scholar' and the Current Status of Philosophy of Education," *Taboo* 4, no. 1 (2000).
37. Jim Garrison, "Emerson's 'The American Scholar' and the Current Status of Philosophy of Education," 102.
38. Gert Biesta, "Towards the Knowledge Democracy? Knowledge Production and the Civic Role of the University," *Studies in Philosophy and Education* 26, no. 5 (2007): 473.
39. José Ortega Y Gasset, "The Fundamental Question," in *Mission of the University* (New York: Routledge, 1946/1991), 50.

40. Jane Roland Martin, "Bound for the Promised Land: The Gendered Character of Higher Education," *Duke Journal of Gender Law & Policy* 4 (1997): 3.
41. Jane Roland Martin, "Bound for the Promised Land: The Gendered Character of Higher Education," 3.
42. Ronald Barnett, R. Knowing and becoming in the higher education curriculum. *Studies in Higher Education*, *34*(4) (2009).
43. Tony Becher and Paul Trowler. *Academic tribes and territories: Intellectual enquiry and the culture of disciplines.* (UK: McGraw-Hill Education, 2001) 23.
44. Dan Berrett, "The Day the Purpose of College Changed,"
45. See Lawrence and Sharma (2002).

PART I

The Problematic Situation: Challenges Facing Higher Education

CHAPTER 2

Postmodern Worldmaking and the Unanimous Academy

Crispin Sartwell

It seems to me that today's academic leftism is historically discontinuous with its progressive ancestors in its focus on the control of the language, on limiting the expression of rival or incompatible views and attitudes. This agenda is pursued by techniques ranging from speech codes to riots to informal social sanctions. The American left, through much of the century, defended free speech and did not centralize the repression of expression as a central liberatory strategy: control of the language was not an emphasis of Martin Luther King, for example, to say nothing of Mario Savio. I may as well make my position plain. I do not regard myself as being on the political right, but I think the ideological uniformity of universities—particularly in the humanities and social sciences—is unfortunate on numerous grounds. I believe that in the long run it is compromising academic research and pedagogy and blurring the line between education and indoctrination (and I think there is such a line). A consensus is by definition unexamined from an external point of view, and the means by which this one is enforced—amounting above all to what was once called "peer pressure"—is a formula for irrationality.[1]

The present approach—pursuing social justice through the repression of retrograde opinions and attitudes—first loomed in its present form during the "culture wars" of the late 1980s and early 1990s. Here I explore

C. Sartwell (✉)
Dickinson College, Carlisle, PA, USA

A. Stoller, E. Kramer (eds.), *Contemporary Philosophical Proposals for the University*, https://doi.org/10.1007/978-3-319-72128-6_2

one intellectual or theoretical element connecting that period to this. It is a position about the relation of language and the world that, though developed at the high water mark of "postmodern theory," has percolated into many disciplines and moments. It is stated explicitly in many campus free speech controversies and has become common cultural coin. The view might be formulated simplistically in the words of a Nike ad from the late 1990s: "We are the stories we tell." Or, as I have often heard it put around campus, "Words have power."

Linguistic Constructivism and "Political Correctness"

Many strands have led leftism into its various situations today, on campus and off. Larger social forces obviously shape it, from the condition of the economy to shifting gender roles. The strand I focus on here is intra-intellectual, a development that unfolded on the level of theory, and in the academy. One thing characteristic of the academic left, connecting 2017 to 1990, is the attribution of great power to language as an instrument of oppression and potentially, hence, as an instrument of liberation. In its strongest forms, the position characterizes language as the source and environment of human experience, or even as the source and nature of reality as a whole. Sometimes, in other words, the position seems tantamount to a fundamental ontology. Again, it is often expressed informally by the sentence "words have power" and variants. That in turn often introduces a line of argument meant to break down the distinctions between speech and conduct, including violence, to motivate various speech restrictions.

In the 1980s, my teacher Richard Rorty narrated the history of philosophy as culminating in "the linguistic turn," as focusing ever-more tightly on language. He saw both continental philosophy and analytic philosophy as moving in that direction, and in his story of intellectual history, he centralized figures such as Heidegger, Gadamer, Derrida, Wittgenstein, Quine, and Davidson. With great insouciance he directly drew from their work seemingly flat conclusions of the sort that they would certainly reject, and in some cases did reject, that our reality is made linguistically, hence socially, hence cooperatively or even by consensus. There is no sense in or indeed possibility of speaking of a reality external to language, according to this line of thought. Rorty's narrative of intellectual history had an element of descriptive truth: the twentieth century really was obsessed with language in myriad ways; almost all the great thinkers centralized it. Many argued that philosophy was concerned with nothing but language or practiced forms of philosophy occupied exclusively with linguistic analysis or play. Rorty-style linguistic constructivism was taken up with great enthusiasm, for example, in departments of literature and communication, which are of course directly concerned with language; it potentially exalted these subjects into fundamental sources of truth. Rorty said that philosophy is a way of writing or a genre of literature and that philosophers should withdraw in favor of poets and novelists.

I do not mean, in what follows, to hold Rorty responsible for what came, around 1990, to be called "political correctness," supposing there is such a thing and that, if there is, it's a bad thing, both of which are controversial. But Rorty was an emblematic and influential figure. He explicitly endorsed PC and lent the whole approach intellectual heft. Above all, he was one of a number of figures who helped articulate the position I am calling "linguistic constructivism" (he often called it "textualism") which has trickled down to become a sort of common wisdom.

Achieving Our Country, published in 1997, was Rorty's late-breaking contribution to the culture wars circa 1990 and his prescient contribution to the culture wars circa 2017. He flatly argued that universities, all of them, should be "progressive" institutions, meaning by the term a particular position on or zone of the left-right political spectrum.

> Encouraging students to be what mocking neoconservatives call "politically correct" has made our country a far better place. American leftist academics have a lot to be proud of. Their conservative critics, who have no remedies to propose either for American sadism or for American selfishness, have a great deal to be ashamed of.
>
> What these critics condemn as the politicizing of the universities is an expression of the same outrage against cruelty which moved the students and faculty at Charles University in Prague to resist the Communists in 1948, and the students and faculty at South African universities to resist apartheid laws. All universities worthy of the name have always been centers of social protest. If American universities ever cease to be such centers, they will lose both their self-respect and the respect of the learned world. It is doubtful whether the current critics who are called 'conservative intellectuals' deserve this description. For intellectuals are supposed to be aware of, and speak to, issues of social justice.[2]

The connection of student protests in Prague to speech codes being enforced by institutions in the 1990s is strained, but it is perhaps more plausible now, as student protesters at places like Berkeley, NYU, and Middlebury silence or "no-platform" speakers they regard as right wing. But at any rate, Rorty's view encourages, or indeed tolerates, only a narrow range of progressive political positions in the university; with a good conscience it imagines the university as politically homogeneous, or even purges non-progressives preemptively from the realm of the intellectual. I'm not sure we should be telling intellectuals, before they even get going, what they are "supposed to be aware of" or how they ought to address those matters with which they are concerned. It is an argument, for example, for screening young faculty on the basis of their political positions, which I believe is precisely what has happened over the last 20 years.

After the election of Donald Trump, *Achieving Our Country* underwent something of a revival, as Rorty had talked about white conservative resentment and the possibility of an American "strongman." Here, I am more interested in the sort of views about truth that could lead figures like Rorty to tie the very ideas of truth and reality so closely with a set of political positions or to confound truth itself with, let us say, democratic socialism. This would be of limited interest, but I do think that Rorty captured a moment in the way people think about truth and that the sort of view he was expressing about truth in the 1980s is now something like common wisdom in the academy. I can't imagine that we still live in the "postmodern" era. But postmodern views about truth—often in their least sophisticated and least plausible forms—have saturated academia and emanated outward from there. Perhaps that's in part because the upper ends of the media and politics are dominated by people trained in the institutions that Rorty was calling for, and trained by Rorty's generation of scholars.

"The Postmodern View of Truth"

Any way you look at it, work on truth by figures thought of as postmodern is remarkably various. There is no view about truth shared by Foucault, Derrida, Lyotard, Rorty, Baudrillard, Deleuze, Latour, and Charles Taylor. Folding these people all up together and then condemning them as relativists was common when they were at their height, an attack far too generalized and far too mechanical. Rorty himself, who was as relativist as any, had deft ways of deflecting the charge or rendering it nonsensical: he said that even the formulation of the charge of relativism depended on a particular view of truth and hence was question-begging or merely anachronistic; the charge, he asserted, could not even arise. Rorty's postmodern pragmatism is not at all the same as deconstruction. He repudiated virtually everything about Foucault, particularly the way Foucault conceived truth as and in relation to power. Calling Deleuze a relativist is the most ham-handed misconstrual. And so on. I want to narrow the figures and positions down to versions of linguistic constructivism which centralize language as the site of worldmaking, or as the only scene of truth, among which I would include Rorty's and Hans-Georg Gadamer's. These positions are characterized by the idea that we have no access to a reality beyond or outside language: at a minimum that there is no sense in or possibility of talking about such a thing, and at a maximum that there isn't any such thing. Gadamer's version is as clear as anyone's:

> Language is not a delimited realm of the speakable, over against which other realms that are not speakable might stand. Rather, language is all-encompassing. There is nothing that is fundamentally excluded from being said... Language is the fundamental mode of operation of our being-in-the-world and the all-embracing form of the composition of the world.[3]

Figures such as Alasdair MacIntyre emphasized the construction of the human subject: it is a social construction; it is a linguistic construction; and it is a narrative construction. Each of us is centrally articulated or made what we are by inhabiting our various social roles; these are largely understood through narratives which set out the goals we pursue within such roles and the ways we ought to pursue them. "In what does the unity of an individual life consist? The answer is that its unity is the unity of a narrative...The unity of human life is the unity of narrative quest."[4] A remarkable range of thinkers, otherwise to be found on various sides of various debates, converged on something along these lines in the 1980s, but the view had many intellectual sources, both remote and proximate: Hegelian historicism, post-Heideggerian philosophy of language including certain versions or readings of deconstructionism ("there is nothing outside the text"), later Wittgenstein. Rorty's version was distinctive, among other things, for annexing analytic resources: Sellars on science; Quine on the indeterminacy of translation; Davidson on truth. Feminist and critical race theorists were in a period of defining and problematizing gender and racial categories, among others, as social constructions, analyzable in part as, or identical in part to, linguistic taxonomies or representational systems. At a certain moment it seemed that all intellectual history was funneling into this sort of position; Rorty certainly thought so.

Ricoeur put forward an influential version according to which narrative is the very form of temporal experience: a version of transcendental idealism with a decisively linguistic inflection:

> Between the activity of narrating a story and the temporal character of human experience there exists a correlation that is not merely accidental but that presents a transcultural form of necessity. To put it another way, time becomes human to the extent that it is articulated through a narrative mode, and narrative attains its full meaning when it becomes a condition of temporal experience.[5]

Personal identity consists in narrative, according to Ricoeur, as to MacIntyre. "Without the recourse to narration, the problem of personal identity would in fact be condemned to an antinomy with no solution. Either we must posit a subject identical with itself through the diversity of its different states, or, following Hume and Nietzsche, we must hold that this identical subject is nothing more than a substantialist illusion."[6] Less sophisticated versions came from literature and communications professors, and even from advertising.

Rorty, Gadamer, Ricoeur, and MacIntyre do not have the same view; but they have what we might think of as the same spirit, or in all their diversity they share one important premise; they centralize the linguistic construction of reality and of the self. I would connect this family of positions to the history of modern philosophy, which treated human experience as representational. Linguistic constructionism is an extension, elaboration, and qualification of, or a cure for, the sort of views that treat human sense experience and intellection basically in terms of picturing: the "ideas" of the classical rationalists and empiricists, phenomena or sense data, mental images, seemings, appearances, and Carnap's "autopsychological objects." The world, if any, ticks on in one way or another, while we immediately experience the deliverances of our senses, which are construed as representational systems. Rationalists, empiricists, and idealists shared the representational theory of mind: the view that we experience external reality, if at all, through the mediation of representations or that the mind is a representational system.

One thing that is conspicuously lacking in such accounts, whether it's Descartes's or Kant's or Schopenhauer's, the phenomenalists', phenomenologists', or positivists', is the social element in the articulation of human experience and hence reality. Schopenhauer's version threatens a collapse into solipsism:

> [Man]does not know a sun and an earth, but only an eye that sees a sun, a hand that feels an earth; the world around him is there only as a representation, in other words, only in reference to another thing, namely that which represents, and this is himself. If any truth can be expressed a priori, it is this; for it is a statement of that form of all possible and conceivable experience... Therefore no truth is more certain, more independent of all others, and less in need of proof than this, namely that everything that exists for knowledge, and hence the whole of this world, is only an object in relation to the subject, perception of a perceiver, in a word, representation.[7]

Among the other sorts of skepticism that loomed from this history was the "problem of other minds."

By the twentieth century, however, many had come to appreciate that each of us is social from birth or before, that culture helps create our experience. A number of intellectual and political strands converged to make the twentieth the century of the social: Marxism, the pragmatism of Mead and Dewey, the rise of cultural anthropology, later Wittgenstein. The last, in an exemplary way, shows that language is one way to make the social turn while retaining much of the representational theory of mind. We might consider the *Tractatus* as a pivot point; in it, though language becomes pictorial, pictures also become linguistic, a theme taken up in different ways by Nelson Goodman (an exemplary linguistic constructivist), W.J.T. Mitchell, and E.H. Gombrich, for example. To say that pictorial systems are languages or are like languages is also to say that they are social systems, conventional systems. A private language is impossible.

This need not yield the sort of linguistic constructivism I am describing. We might think of postmodern philosophy as in some ways a compressed modern philosophy, and once we identify the screen or framework that stands between us and the world "as it really is," we face a number of options. We could go for some kind of "representational realism," according to which we have good reasons to think that our representations or vocabularies inform us truly, that pictures or descriptions may be more or less realistic or accurate, and hence that we can have (mediated) access to and knowledge about a material or spatiotemporal environment in which we are embedded. For Descartes, God guarantees that our representations or ideas correspond to the world, more or less. Or we could just bite the bullet with Berkeley and Rorty: "material reality," "the world," and "truth" mean something only about or within the representational system itself; material reality is itself a set of representations in consciousness, or "material reality" itself is a form of words, a way of speaking. And then we could go "constructionist" a la Kant and Ricoeur: the experience we inhabit, built from the form of our sensibility, or from our cultural practices and narratives, is reality itself. Linguistically constructed time and a constructed self are objective *for us*, hard and fast enough to satisfy our residual yearning after the real. But on this view the supposed opposition between reality and representation breaks down.

On the constructivist position, truth is internal to the procession of ideas in a sensorium (in idealist modern philosophy) or to the structures of a language in a culture (in this version of postmodernism). The apparent question about truth outside of any language cannot even be put, as Rorty so often said, for it can only be formulated in a language. It makes sense to say, given our practices, our imagery, our vocabulary, our raising, that "the sky is blue" is true. But outside of such a context, the question of truth cannot arise, and to raise it is merely delusory or nonsensical. There is no outside. This is where the charge of relativism has bite, and this is also where it is deflected or short-circuited; relativism itself presupposes a reality underlying the descriptions, the practices, and so on, which those descriptions and narratives represent or construe or articulate in different ways. But the move to the external view is impossible; it presupposes that your own vocabulary is not a vocabulary.

On this view, words have power indeed. They are in some sense, for us, the source of reality. They are not a map of a pre-existing terrain, but what makes our experience possible.

Rorty's Pragmatism

Rorty explicitly ties his approach to the academy to a theory about the nature of truth. I believe he is also describing the status of his own discourse, enacting in his text the theory of truth he describes. His views about truth characterize his authorial stance and his sense of what writing, including his own, is for.

> Dewey abandoned the idea that one can say how things really are, as opposed to how they might best be described in order to meet some particular human need. In this respect he is in agreement with Nietzsche, and with such critics of 'the metaphysics of presence' as Derrida and Heidegger. For all these philosophers, objectivity is a matter of intersubjective consensus among human beings, not of accurate representation of something nonhuman.

> Insofar as human beings do not share the same needs, they may disagree about what is objectively the case. But the resolution of such disagreement cannot be an appeal to the way reality, apart from any human need, really is. The resolution can only be political: one must use democratic institutions and procedures to conciliate these various needs, and thereby widen the range of consensus about how things are. (*Achieving Our* Country, 34–35)

This is in many ways a characteristic passage; it is a particularly clear, and disarmingly offhand, summary of Rorty's whole philosophy. As so often in Rorty, you'd do well to suspect that this is not a fully accurate presentation of Dewey on truth, much less Nietzsche, Derrida, or Heidegger. But it is a clear statement of Rorty's.

The pragmatists held, at a first rough stab, that truth is what works. And then the work in what works comes in the details: works in what respects, how, for whom? But Rorty has a particular way of reading "works," related to the classical pragmatists' but certainly not identical to it. For a claim to work, it must have good political effects, which can be described as good effects in building a consensus; to speak the truth is to be persuasive, effective, and also progressive. Reality, we might say, is consensual, and consensus is built through language or through persuasive storytelling, poetry, and even science as linguistically articulated. "True" comes to mean "persuasive," though persuasive in a particular context (democratic institutions) for particular reasons (reducing cruelty).

More broadly, to say of some claim that it is "true" or "objective" is to say that it is of help moving toward the realization of human purposes. For example, to tell the truth about history is to relate a narrative of progress; in particular, what is true about American history is what helps us construct a narrative of the overcoming of suffering and oppression based on factors such as race and gender; we narrate our history as an overcoming of divisions and the story of the realization of equality and freedom, and telling that story will itself help it to be realized insofar as it commands a consensus. Education is a key for making that come to pass: not a way of coming into contact with a harsh or ambiguous reality, but a way of constructing a better reality to come. Rorty asks us to "substitute hope for knowledge" (106).

> We can still be old-fashioned liberals even if, like Dewey, we give up the correspondence theory of truth and start treating moral and scientific beliefs as tools for achieving greater human happiness, rather than as representations of the intrinsic nature of reality. We can be this kind of liberal even after we turn our backs on Descartes, linguistify subjectivity, and see everything

> around us and within us as one more replaceable social construction... You have to describe the country in terms of what you passionately hope it will become, as well as in terms of what you know it to be now. You have to be loyal to a dream country rather than the one to which you wake up every morning. Unless such loyalty exists, the ideal has no chance of becoming actual. (*Achieving Our Country*, 96, 101)

What is particularly striking about a position like this is that it permits no distinction between truth-telling or factual research and political persuasion. To say that a particular narrative would, if believed, have good or progressive or useful effects *is to say that it is true.* Then, for example, responsible and objective scholarship would be incompatible with telling a retrograde story, or purporting to uncover or emphasize "facts," which, if believed, would have reactionary political effects. The test of scholarship and pedagogy remains truth. But truth is precisely a progressive consensus. One amazing feature of this position is that to object to it is to speak falsely, by its own criteria of truth.

Spread of an Era

Rorty regarded himself as crystallizing a period, and indeed people were coming to similar conclusions across disciplines, in literature, education, and communications, for example. In academic communications programs, the insight was, as we might say, weaponized. People developed systematic theories for shaping public opinion, by reshaping the narrative or reframing the picture:

> The essential tool of the manager of meaning is the ability to frame... To hold the frame of a subject is to choose one particular meaning (or set of meanings) over another... Frames exert their power not only through what they bring to light but also through what they leave out. In framing, when we create a bias towards one interpretation of our subject, we exclude other aspects, including those that may produce opposite or alternative interpretations... Two different frames of the situation, two different socially constructed realities.[8]

This has none of Rorty's sophistication, much less Gadamer or Ricoeur's. It hints that there is an underlying reality that is being interpreted or distorted or reconstructed in framing. From that, a host of objections emerge to the whole activity. To begin with, it appears to consist of mere propaganda, manipulation, or (not to put too fine a point on it) lies. But if there is no reality external to the frame, there is no truth that is being distorted, only truth in what is being constructed. An underlying linguistic transcendentalism would allow you to reframe with a good conscience. This and related material in "strategic communications," which had a golden age in the 1990s, came on the scene as something of a science, with empirical data. It coincided also with a new set of technologies for assessing as well as reshaping public opinion: the focus group, for instance, ever-more sophisticated survey materials, and then big data and clicks, Karl Rove and Joe Trippi, pharmaceutical advertising, and new forms of PC.

In the 1990s and 2000s, academic communications programs underwent explosive growth by all measures (majors and professorships, including "schools" of communication).[9] In some respects, communications studies superseded the traditional humanities or took over the function of a "humanistic" or "liberal arts" education. Text and argument were understood in terms of their "effects" in manufacturing public opinion or persuading many people to buy something or vote in a certain way or endorse certain positions. The science of media effects to some extent superseded the art of literary interpretation, or the quest for rational underpinnings. Of course, that there are any distinctions between those things is just what people like Rorty were throwing into doubt.

The study of persuasion is among the most ancient subjects in the West, an obsession of the Athenians and the Romans alike. And the connection of rhetoric to truth is a most traditional question. Socrates opposed his own dialectic to the persuasive tactics of the Sophists precisely on the grounds that it had a different relation to the truth, which he tried to establish as eternal and unchanging, a truth about as non-pragmatist and non-constructivist as could be imagined. Protagoras did not threaten the Socratic position when he offered to make the worse argument seem better, but he started to develop an alternative when he argued that "Man is the measure," that truth is internal to human practices and perhaps specifically to human discourse, denying the transcendence or alienation of truth from human experience.

Aristotle, in his characteristic way, tries to ameliorate this opposition, saying that "rhetoric is useful because things that are true and things that are just have a natural tendency to prevail," so that speakers should be armed to resist plausible arguments for false conclusions, and are blameworthy if they fail. "Things that are true and things that are better are by their nature practically always easier to prove and more persuasive."[10]

The purpose of rhetoric, for Aristotle, is not to persuade simpliciter, but to persuade in service of the truth. Obviously on such an account, the truth is not necessarily whatever turns out to be persuasive in a particular case. I might just remark that this is close to the sort of position Dewey develops in his *Logic* and that Rorty's reading of Dewey as identifying truth with persuasiveness and consensus is at best misleading.

It's not that pragmatist or narrativist accounts of truth drove developments in strategic communications, but they did suggest that the activity was one not merely of sales or consensus-building, but of "worldmaking," to use Nelson Goodman's phrase:

> If I ask about the world, you can offer to tell me how it is under one or more frames of reference; but if I insist that you tell me how it is apart from all frames, what can you say? We are confined to ways of describing whatever is described. Our universe, so to speak, consists of these ways rather than of a world.[11]

This move takes one sort of question out of play: namely, whether one is being "true to the world" or somehow representing reality correctly. Admittedly, those are extremely difficult ideas to formulate plausibly.

Linguistic Constructivism and the Academy

There are many possible philosophical objections to this sort of linguistic constructivism. But here I just want to make a series of what I take to be quasi-practical points that bear on higher education in particular. I think that many of the moments and moves by which Goodman, Rorty, or Ricoeur got us here were optional, and that the whole procedure could have been interrupted at many points; I do not think it is philosophically convincing, but I do not intend to argue that here. Whatever the case, I would like briefly to explore some of the practical and theoretical difficulties that emerge if we entirely lose the distinction between reality and language, or between the world and its description, ourselves and our stories, time and narrative. Or, in what sort of situation, as scholars and educators, has this line of thought landed us?

One thing that happens is that we lose the distinction between action and expression; indeed, in some ways linguistic expression appears to be the most efficacious action of all: the creation of reality. Then, for example, linguistic expressions are "violent" insofar as the reality that has arisen on their foundation inflicts suffering; if words are at the heart of the construction of race, for example, then words are in some sense a crystallized history of centuries of exploitation, brutalization, genocide, and exclusion. It would still need something of an argument to get from a position like that to the position that racial oppression might be ameliorated through a regime of speech control. And yet that seems a rather obvious extension; if we could control the discourse about race, that would itself be a substantial contribution to remediating racism, which is a way of describing the world and not just a practice of discrimination. Racism is a form of consciousness embodied in symbols, stories, taxonomies, images circulating around us and through each of us: a frame, as it were. It matters very much, for example, how trans people or women of color or for that matter white men are depicted in films, television shows, novels, billboards, textbooks, and so on; for those are the very heart of the construction of racist culture. Hence controlling such things, or turning them toward conveying progressive characters and narratives of inclusion, could be a substantial contribution to social justice and hence a means of telling the truth rather than a mere regime of censorship.

In this circumstance, higher education is seen as having a particularly potent role to play, both as an arena in which dominant symbol systems, narratives, codes, and so on can be challenged and as a way to inculcate new ones in the elites of tomorrow, or potentially in everyone, to the extent that higher education has become a necessity for participating in the economy. Higher education, we might say, is a key place to do the work of reframing. Challenging the narratives is changing reality itself, a grand project indeed, and one which connects high theory with practical achievement. What seems a profound insight of this view—sometimes more or less conscious, sometimes not—is that truth simply is what points toward or invents or articulates a positive future condition; Rorty, as we have seen, made this move flatly. Then the redescription that he demands faces no external test; there is no framework external to it from which it could be probed, much less discredited. The progressive narrative, put forward in media, arts, and education in particular, is a statement of the truth, a factual statement, because it is an instrument for achieving a future we want, or one that we should want. At that point, repressing certain points of view, or even more or less intellectually cleansing the academy of non-leftists, becomes defensible all the way down to the fundamental ontological level. It is a service to the truth as well as to justice. It's at this point that the vision transcends or diverges from the ideal of democracy as a source of knowledge, or what Dewey calls "science," for example, and I think it has already had disastrous implications for American higher education.

I don't think such a view can be refuted without constructing an alternative metaphysical picture and an alternative theory of truth, one that is more compelling for one reason or another, or many. I have tried to do that elsewhere. But here I might try a few pointed questions. For example, is there any evidence that telling a positive story, or constructing a positive history, does actually have good practical results? For example, if we believed that America was an inspiring story of freedom in which members of various groups would eventually take up a free and equal place, would that make it more likely that these groups will take up a free and equal place? I would like to see some evidence of that, and it strikes me offhand that the best strategy for improvement, and in general the best or most adaptive approach no matter the circumstances, would be to face up to the real history and the real situation. That might well be a precondition of ameliorating it, and the extent of my hope might not correspond very well to the strength of my action. Of course, that there is any such thing as the real history and real situation, in contrast to the inspiring narrative, is the point at issue, so I am begging the question. But I seem to myself to be talking in a way that could be understood: isn't it the most promising strategy to become more aware of the actual situation rather than to sweep it up into a good narrative?

Here is an example: by and large, American white people speak differently now than we did in 1960. The civil rights movement, among its many achievements, conveyed to us that certain terms and the expression of certain attitudes of hostility, fear, or condescension were highly inappropriate. Add a bit of textualism or linguistic constructivism and we perhaps came to believe that these items—as they appeared in consciousness as well as conversation—were at the heart of racism, constituted racism. To a very great extent, we edited these words out of our vocabulary and enforced that on one another. After we had, we took ourselves to have transformed ourselves, or never to have been polluted, and we took American racism to be over. The very remarkable thing is that the structural racism of the society continued and in some ways even intensified. It got to the point in the 1990s at which people could support policies of mass incarceration without even appearing to be aware of the racial implications, because they did not appear to be aware of race at all; race was not represented in their vocabularies or imagery, and yet race as an historical phenomenon just went right on or even grew more intense as the vocabulary dissipated.

This is quite a typical set of developments, I think; one place to see it is in the "march of euphemism," as the non-offensive term we introduce today to replace the offensive term ("retarded" for "cretinous," perhaps) becomes the epithet of tomorrow. I am not denying that language plays a role in the construction of such things as race, but race is also a vast range of hard material conditions: ships and shackles, cotton and cannonballs, ghettoes and buses, prison cells and pistols, bodies and beatings. The vocabulary is part of the material conditions, and the material conditions find their way into the vocabulary, but they are not exactly the same thing. The words are often the easiest things to change and control—words may be powerful, but talk is cheap—and often they are the least effective way to start. It is easier to make people talk as you think they ought to talk than to make them become who you think they ought to be.

I am asserting, in other words, that even for the sake of the progressive program itself, we had better come off the linguistic constructivism, which really is making a hash of social sciences and history, for example. But whether you agree with that or not, I suppose I would ask, with Dewey: What if you're wrong? Dewey was, to his core, a fallibilist; he saw that anything we believed today could be revised tomorrow, and he had rather old-fashioned-seeming ideas about how these revisions could happen, under conditions of free debate that he associated with both democracy and science. The idea of cutting off many or even most possible factual or normative positions because they are held to be false on *a priori* grounds—grounds arising from the nature of truth and language—would have struck him as a formula for coming to impose a fantasy or an ideology. I advise you not be so confident in your vision of the future or your theory of reality: both are quite fallible and quite revisable. The thing becomes dangerous when it arrogates to itself the right to repress or silence discourse, precisely because of the supposed power of language.

What if, after all, we are not stories and are not collectively making our world by language but collectively remaking and coping with it as a physical system? First, I would ask what the results would be for the way we are constituting the professoriate and how we are teaching. But then I would also want to know whether the grounds on which such claims have been dismissed as false are really adequate. Or: are you silencing people by rioting against them, or by disciplining them for speech, or simply by ostracizing them in the academy, in service of a vision which is really immune to revision? From where can the challenge come, if the institution is purged of dissent? And from where can it come, if the orthodox positions are identified at the outset with the nature of truth itself? According to themselves, they cannot be challenged. That makes the future look monological indeed.

Possible Developments

The intellectual structure I have described makes positive prescriptions difficult: the whole thing is designed to provide no exit: it disqualifies everyone who is not taking the consensus position from the outset. It silences dissenting voices in the service of its theory of truth, and literally tries to insulate people in the academy from speakers, ideas, and debate. It removes itself from criticism by demonstrating on *a priori* grounds that all dissent is false and evil. Once you wander into this line of thinking, there is no escape, except into falsehood and reaction. You have two options: accept the truth or leave the academy, and the purge has, obviously, been successful. It seems a particularly hopeless situation, and perhaps I ought simply to capitulate or leave.

On the other hand, this too shall pass. There have been many instances in which the academy has been swept up into bad pedagogical procedures and theories, yet there is always some new one on the horizon. Consensus is a beautiful thing, no doubt, and it makes many people comfortable and happy and lends them an apparently complete certainty. However, it makes other people want to jump out of their skins, and the progressive academy through its whole history has turned some of its students and professors into rejectionists, reactionary rebels. I really do understand how going to Wesleyan might turn someone into a neo-fascist. No doubt this is a very unfortunate reaction, and yet enforcing a consensus is impossible where there are no enemies, and the consensus position depends on its exclusions conceptually, and even explicitly: it is "anti-racist," "anti-fascist," "anti-capitalist," "anti-transphobic," and so on. It produces and depends on its own other, one reason the future it envisions will not come to pass. That, I guarantee.

If postmodern philosophy trickled down and became common wisdom, perhaps something of the same process will occur with post-postmodern philosophy, which I think has already taken a decisive term against linguistic constructivism. Various renewed flavors of "realism" have emerged in recent years, such as the "speculative realism" of Graham Harman, Paul Levi-Bryant, and others. This has even migrated from the academy, and I have had discussions of Harman's "object-oriented ontology" with artists and curators at gallery openings, for example. Harman's and Levi-Bryant's work has also involved re-narrating the history of twentieth-century philosophy, and Harman's Heidegger is entirely incompatible with Rorty's, for example. Many other developments show that this isn't 1990. Analytic philosophy has turned back toward basic questions in ontology, for example, and when it does, these days it usually presupposes or explicitly argues from some sort of realism about the world.

Meanwhile, I'd pursue any practical measures possible, as limited as they appear in the context of the consensus reality and the concept of reality as consensus. I'd support organizations that call for free speech on campus or that defend the PC exiles. I'd keep trying to find platforms for controversial speakers. I'd keep up a constant stream of slight transgressions of the informal speech codes: play with the prohibitions, say stuff that leaves people a little puzzled as to exactly why what you're saying is offensive. Now, for any junior professor to take such approaches would be to end her career, while most of her senior colleagues have no doubt already been thoroughly processed. So perhaps the thing has to come from students, or from the occasional tenured dissenter. Still, any of us should do what we think we can, including developing alternatives to the university.

I don't know how to accomplish this, exactly, but we could do with a lot more of Dewey's pragmatism and a lot less of Rorty's. Dewey's progressive politics and educational program, his vision of science and democracy, are quite incompatible with linguistic constructivism. Whatever Dewey might have said about postmodern philosophy if he had been around in 1990, his own notion of progress toward truth or toward democracy or toward a decent and useful academy countenanced or celebrated the most free-wheeling debate and a free development of individuals as well as groups: science and democracy, in short. And the people who are working in a pragmatist mode right now are by and large not sheer linguistic idealists.

So this might not help dissenters at the moment, who are reviled within or extruded from the academy, but looking at the thing in an historical frame, one can reasonably expect that there will be a next phase eventually, as indeed there has to be, given how implausible positions like linguistic constructivism actually are. In addition, PC in its draconian forms would be incomprehensible outside of the left-right political spectrum. It has both depended on and intensified the extreme polarization we now face. But the left-right political spectrum is a tissue of incoherence far more suitable for 1850 than 2020, and it is liable to disintegrate at the slightest touch from the outside. We should be working on that. In short, one factor in bringing the next possibility, and the proper task of a philosopher, is just a demonstration of the weakness of the assertions and arguments. We can all find hope in how confused, how vulnerable, and how dishonest these positions are, which is one reason their advocates are so keen on suppressing dissent. But I do think they have already collapsed intellectually, like the various forms of positivism and representational realism they attacked, and perhaps that presages their collapse institutionally.

As I write this (May 2017), there does seem to be a shift to the right in the politics of both the USA and the UK. One thing that is very likely to revivify the value of free expression on campus is an atmosphere of right-wing intolerance, or a wave of right-wing speech repression. Let left-wing speakers be no-platformed by, for example, withholding federal funding, or by protests by right-wing students, and the notion of academic freedom—a notion that today's academics must regard as some sort of fascist or capitalist ideology—might suddenly seem to them an inspiring ideal, or at any rate to be necessary in order for them to have careers. Let speech restrictions threaten the health insurance of progressives, in other words, and free speech and free inquiry will very suddenly regain their allure on the left. Admittedly, it is a rather dark moment if the hope for freedom depends on a right-wing crackdown, but there it is.

Unlike Rorty, I don't think things are likely to get better overall, and I don't think telling a story is a good way to make them get better; making things better starts by facing up. But things do change.

Notes

1. See Crispin Sartwell, "Anti-Social Epistemology," *Social Epistemology Review and Reply Collective* 4, no. 6 (2015), 62–75.
2. Richard Rorty, *Achieving Our Country: Leftist Thought in Twentieth-Century America* (Cambridge, Massachusetts: Harvard University Press), 83.
3. Hans-Georg Gadamer, *Philosophical Hermeneutics* (Berkeley: University of California Press, 1976), 3, 63.
4. Alasdair MacIntyre, *After Virtue* (Notre Dame: Notre Dame University Press, 1984), 218–19.
5. Paul Ricoeur, *Time and Narrative*, vol 1, trans. Kathleen McLaughlin and David Pellauer (Chicago: University of Chicago Press, 1984), 52.

6. Paul Ricoeur, *Time and Narrative*, vol 3, trans. Kathleen McLaughlin and David Pellauer (Chicago: University of Chicago Press, 1984), 256.
7. Arthur Schopenhauer, *The World as Will and Representation* (New York: Dover, 1966 [1844]), 3.
8. Gail Fairhurst and Robert Sarr, *The Art of Framing: Managing the Language of Leadership* (New York: Jossey-Bass, 1996), 5–6.
9. Some indications of this are given in survey data from the American Academy of Arts and Sciences, which says there were over 13,000 professors of communications in American universities in 2014. (http://www.humanitiesindicators.org/content/indicatordoc.aspx?i=575).
10. Aristotle, *Rhetoric* 13555b, trans. W. Rhys Roberts in *The Complete Works of Aristotle* (Princeton: Princeton University Press, 1984), 2154.
11. Nelson Goodman, *Ways of Worldmaking* (Indianapolis: Hackett, 1978), 3.

CHAPTER 3

Neoliberalism, Technology, and the University: Max Weber's Concept of Rationalization as a Critique of Online Classes in Higher Education

Gabriel Keehn, Morgan Anderson, and Deron Boyles

Introduction

Market-based solutions to complex human problems are a hallmark of the neoliberal era. While the assault on all things public has heightened, particularly since the "Great Recession" that further destabilized faith in public institutions, education has felt this attack most acutely. As Kenneth Saltman notes, "[e]ducation has been transformed more through privatization than any other aspect of neoliberal economic doctrine."[1] Corporate school reform has not been restricted to the K-12 sector; the battle between public and private interests is playing out in universities as well.[2]

Conceptualizing the teaching and learning process as a consumer transaction has been a feature of educational policy for the past several decades.[3] In K-12 schooling, this has manifested in a myopic focus on standardization, measurement, and accountability where knowledge is viewed as something to be transferred, and teachers are understood as unimaginative content deliverers.[4] As Sanford Schram notes, however, "[h]igher education

G. Keehn (✉) • M. Anderson • D. Boyles
Georgia State University, Atlanta, GA, USA

A. Stoller, E. Kramer (eds.), *Contemporary Philosophical Proposals for the University*, https://doi.org/10.1007/978-3-319-72128-6_3

has not been immune to the pressures to introduce neoliberal reforms."[5] Indeed, the neoliberal occupation of the university has been well documented. Universities are not only mimicking the policies of primary and secondary education, they are often left to mitigate the destruction left behind by market-based reforms. Such reforms starve public schools of funding thus leading to a decline in the number of college eligible students and an increase in students entering college in need of remedial support.[6] These reforms have also ushered in the commercial logic of convenience that suggests offering more and more online classes is primarily a way to increase enrollment.

Neoliberal policies over the past several decades have contributed to the ongoing dismantling of the university as a site of both authentic inquiry and humane, scholarly interaction. The increasing reliance on precarious labor such as adjuncts and graduate students as cost-cutting measures, and the ongoing assault on the humanities, are just a few examples that scholars have pointed to as evidence of neoliberal encroachment.[7] Andrew Nadolny and Suzanne Ryan note, for example, that "[i]n recent decades, the dominance of neoliberal economic rationalization in universities has resulted in institutions becoming reliant on an adjunct teaching workforce as flexible labor pool to buffer against uncertain revenues."[8] When faculty are made contingent in this way, teaching online classes is rarely optional; it is often required. Adjuncts, part-time instructors, and graduate students are not in a position to resist the top-down pressure to offer online classes.

Furthermore, when the humanities are defended, they are frequently justified in terms of careerism. Philosophy gets reduced to "critical thinking skills" for law school preparation, and English gets abridged to "communication skills" for workplace advancement. Megan Laverty argues that universities "imply that the humanities derive their value exclusively from their ability to provide extrinsic benefits, such as cultural literacy or critical thinking."[9] Such attempts to transform the university into, as Steven Ward argues, "servants of the economy" have resulted in the reduction of the messy tasks of teaching and learning to a system of efficiency, accountability, and control.[10] The school, and subsequently the university, as Alasdair MacIntyre has noted, is now hegemonically conceived of as "an input-output machine."[11] Accordingly, universities are hypervigilant about graduating students in four years and tracking how much money graduates make in their post-university jobs. The value of a university education is not understood as knowledge for the sake of knowledge, but efficient information transfer to quickly enter the world of work. Nowhere in these conversations do we appear to wonder about ethics, understanding, compassion, or self-worth outside of the pecuniary interests of global corporations and transnational capitalism. As Schram notes, we are observing a period where "US institutions of higher learning are now prioritizing cost-efficiency in the provision of education as a commodity at the expense of promoting the liberal learning essential to fostering a democratic citizenry."[12]

We argue that this particular neoliberal turn of the university has largely been made possible by technology, generally, and that online classes, specifically, are a hindrance to democratic citizenship and real learning. While critiques of technology have been made for many, many years, the late 1980s and 1990s saw a particular glut of works by those critical of the coming of "advanced technology" in education.[13] Formal academics and general scholars had growing suspicions of the role of technology in advancing the neoliberal agenda in the university. In 1998, for example, David Noble warned that technology such as CD ROMS and websites would result in the commodification of classroom teaching, as lessons could be transformed into marketable goods.[14] He noted, "[w]ith the commodization of instruction, this transformation of academia is now reaching the breaking point."[15] Nearly 20 years after Noble's assertion, technology is no longer merely encroaching into university life—*technology itself defines university life*. Online platforms such as "Blackboard" and "iCollege" are now the portals through which nearly every university student manages almost all aspects of student life. The introduction of such technology allows for greater convenience in tasks such as registering for classes or obtaining financial aid, and this technological infrastructure at face value seems relatively benign. Our concern is that such technology no longer just *assists* university life but *subsumes* it. Here, we are specifically concerned with the trend away from "Harkness-type" classrooms toward fully online instruction and the degree to which this shift represents the fulfillment of Weber's concept of rationalization.[16] It is to this concept that we now turn.

Weber's Ascetic Vocationalism and Rationalization

In order to understand the process of rationalization and its applicability to the contemporary landscape of higher education, and particularly to the recent movement toward online learning broadly outlined above, it is critical to situate the concept within the overall structure of Weber's thought. For Weber, the process of rationalization entails a movement toward an increased routinization of calculability, efficiency, mechanization, and the proliferation of administrative bureaucracy in all spheres of human interaction. Broadly speaking, Weber associated increased rationalization with the increased dominance of capitalistic economic practices, and often spoke of "economic rationality" or "capitalist rationality."

There is a complex array of ways in which the ideas of rationality, rationalism, and rationalization are utilized in Weber's work, some methodological and some theoretical. Weber himself notes at least three different modalities of the term "rationalism:" "(1) 'theoretical mastery of the world by means of increasingly precise and abstract concepts,' (2) 'methodological attainment of a definitely given and practical end by means of an increasingly precise calculation of adequate means,' and (3) 'systematic arrangement.'"[17] As Lars Udehn points out, it is number (2) which is most central to Weber's understanding of rationalism and rationalization, as it isolates the type of means-ends reasoning that Weber argues characterizes modern capitalism more than any other feature. This understanding of rationalism is also critically important because it is the defining feature of the consuming subject, the supposed *homo economicus*, that drives modern capitalist development. The other two understandings of rationalism act as either theoretical presuppositions (as in the case of [1]) or as preconditions for the possibility of (2) (as in the case of [3]). That is, the systematic arrangement of the social world, for example, through laws or ethical systems, is "a material precondition for instrumentally rational action, because it gives rise to regular behavior, and regular behavior is a precondition for an adequate calculation of means and ends."[18] This last point is crucial to the process of rationalization, as one of the basic necessities of rational social action under capitalism is, as Weber puts it, "its meaningful orientation to the expectations that others will act in a certain way, and to the presumable chances of success for one's own action resulting therefrom."[19]

Rationalism in this socioeconomic sense, however, is not something that Weber simply posits as a pre-existing given in the modern capitalist order, and it would be a mistake to simply equate Weber's understanding of rationalization with capitalism *simpliciter*. Rather, Weber sees rationalization as a fundamentally historical process, advancing slowly from the earliest forms of human civilization through early Christianity and ultimately Puritanism, terminating in what he dubs "modern capitalism," as opposed to pre-rationalistic capitalist activity. Incorporating this historico-economic dimension and the attendant complications that dimension introduces is important to understanding the concept. As he puts the point, "One can very well 'rationalize' life according to very different ultimate points of view and in different directions; 'rationalism' is a historical concept that encompasses a world of differences."[20]

Given his overriding concern with elucidating the historical developments which have contributed to the development of rationalization, Weber isolates as a necessary precondition to the current state of rationalized capitalism the doctrine of what he calls "worldly asceticism" or "ascetic vocationalism." This doctrine, which Weber traces back to the Reformation and the rise of Calvinist Protestantism, is one that Rogers Brubaker suggests is not simply a new ethical attitude but also represents a shift in the very personality structure of human subjects.[21]

Without detailing the complex nuances of Calvinist theory, Weber isolates four aspects of ascetic vocationalism that have led to the modern vision of *homo economicus.* First, there is the Calvinist vision of what it means to be called by the Christian idea of God. In previous incarnations of Christian morality, as in monasticism, the highest expression of religious faith was to detach from all earthly pleasures and tasks to focus on the mystical attainment of spiritual enlightenment. In Protestantism, however, the most important vocation for the human person was to demonstrate faith through worldly activity, or "works."[22] Turning the focus of human activity away from the spiritual or transcendental realm to the worldly, for Weber, set the stage for the rationalization of the personality of the individual. Secondly, Calvinism's understanding of the nature of God, and specifically God's relationship to humanity, leads to a view of humans not as vessels of God (due to God's unavoidably transcendental nature) but only ever as *tools* of God.[23] This, in turn, contributes to the type of means-ends reasoning that is a fundamental aspect of capitalist calculability. Third, Weber tied the suspicion toward "all the sensuous and emotional elements in culture and religion" that Calvinism advocated to the pre-capitalist values of impersonalism, individualism, and anti-hedonism. [24] Finally, and most crucially for Weber, is the Calvinist doctrine of predestination, that is, the idea that individuals are fundamentally powerless to either know or change their fate. However, as Brubaker points out, while fatalism seems to be the only logical consequence of the doctrine of predestination, the historical data suggests that the psychological consequence of Calvinist predestination was precisely the opposite.[25] Rather than submitting to a fatalistic view of the world which suggested that the actions one took were immaterial to the nature of one's fate, the Puritanical and Calvinist Protestants rather took the view that one should work doubly hard at "intense, methodically controlled activity in a worldly calling [vocation] as a means of attaining certainty of their own election."[26] Significantly, as Weber emphasizes, one of the key indicators that the Puritans looked to in determining the likelihood of salvation for individuals was economic success in one's vocation. Once the secularization of capital took place and the religious flavor of this ethic had fallen away, what was left was the type of "nose-to-the-grindstone" work ethic that places financial success at the pinnacle of human achievement. As Weber notes, "The essential elements of the spirit of capitalism are the same as the content of the Puritan worldly asceticism…"[27]

This type of ethic is also clearly visible in current corporatized higher education, which emphasizes further and further degrees of parochialism and the division of vocations, as well as a high-stakes atmosphere of surveillance, standards, and accountability. While, as in capitalist rationalism generally, the religious dimension to this type of work ethic has largely fallen away, the general commitments which drove it originally—individualism, control of the inner self, discipline, and rationalization of all worldly activity—exist in various forms in higher education. Think, for example, of the sort of ascetic rationalism of the online classroom culture in universities today. It seems to us that the lone figures of a professor and individual students stuck to their individual computers and perpetually engaged in individual "postings" and mindless "chats" bears a striking resemblance to the toiling figure of the shoemaker, blacksmith, or any number of traditional vocational figures which served for Weber as the exemplars of the ascetic vocationalist spirit.[28]

Weber's most sustained inquiry into the historical origins of the current era of capitalist rationalization is *The Protestant Ethic and The Spirit of Capitalism*, in which he explores and chronicles the development of religious rationalization, secularism, and ultimately capitalist economic hegemony as a product of these other trends. The large-scale picture Weber paints is broadly one of gradual progression from the more traditional and mythological forms of social organization exhibited in early Occidental history up through the rise of more explicitly scientifically oriented rationalism, secularism, demystification, and ultimately the arrival of modern capitalism and bureaucracy, the two forces that Weber believed were most significant to the development of the modern condition. Jürgen Habermas characterizes the general arc of Weber's argument this way:

> What Weber depicted was not only the secularization of Western culture, but also and especially the development of modern societies from the viewpoint of rationalization. The new structures of society were marked by the differentiation of the two functionally intermeshing systems that had taken shape around the organizational cores of the capitalist enterprise and the bureaucratic state apparatus. Weber understood this process as the institutionalization of purposive-rational economic and administrative action. To the degree that everyday life was affected by this cultural and societal rationalization, traditional forms of life – which in the early modern period were differentiated primarily according to one's trade – were dissolved.[29]

Key to Habermas' description is the way in which bureaucratization and rationalization come to infect daily life. Of specific concern is how activities, relationships, and ways of living that had previously been seen as inherently human, organic, and face-to-face were gradually turned into rote, mechanistic interactions governed by rationalistic market forces and bureaucratically imposed rules and norms. As we will show, it is this aspect of the rationalization process which we can see clearly enacted in higher education today and, for our purposes, especially in online classes.

Importantly, this historical shift was quite a long time in coming. As William Clark painstakingly details, the shift from Medieval universities to Enlightenment universities to what we now call research universities was a slow drift away from more familial, authentic human relationships toward entrepreneurialism and celebrity.[30] In the context of European universities, Clark explains the differences between and among French, English, German, and Jesuit institutions of higher education and shows how the German university hegemonically prevailed as "the" model for modern research universities. Briefly, the medieval universities of England, Oxford and Cambridge, were characterized by a focus on colleges. German Protestant universities, on the other hand, were focused on faculties (four, actually: theology, law, medicine, and philosophy and the arts).[31] Jesuit universities were in a category almost to themselves insofar as faculty members were structurally precluded (in most instances) from staying at one university for more than five years. This required Jesuit professors to learn different topics and fields along with their students. They were assigned by administrators to teach x and y topics at z university. Differently, English universities at this time concentrated power in the heads of colleges. German universities vested control in faculties via faculty senates.

This issue of control and power is important to understand because the shift over time has been from, as Clark puts it, "ministries to markets."

> After 1763, two systems arose. There was an aristocratic, courtly system, based on connections, gifts, and favors, and mostly for higher subjects and offices, versus a bourgeois, bureaucratic system, based on examination, work, and merit, and mostly for mid- to lower subjects and officers. This second system fit the rationalizing winds blowing over academia. In Prussia and elsewhere in the German lands, the rationalization of academic life took place within the framework of bureaucratization and good policing, as it was called.[32]

Current universities can trace their link to the market to the 1830s when various disciplines benefited from "being in fashion." After the 1860s, the link between "laboratory-based university research to medicine and technology clearly drove the expansion" of market logic tied to academia.[33] Today we see this logic in action when pre-college students are "sold" on the idea that if they would major in a STEM field, they will have increased scholarships, lower or no debt, and more academic support. In all, the shifts in bureaucratic power and the rationalization of market logic are traceable to Medieval universities and forward through German Protestant universities to what US research universities now do and represent.

While it is tempting to see Weber's discussion of the progression of rationalization as a type of linear, causal process, it is vital to note that Weber himself did not see it this way. Rather, as he writes at one point in *The Protestant Ethic*, "If this essay makes any contribution at all, may it be to bring out the complexity of the only superficially simple concept of the rational."[34] That said, Weber also identified what he saw as some of the common driving themes of the rationalization process, particularly in the modern social order, apart from the various types of religious rationalization which Western society had undergone in the lead-up to scientific, capitalist rationalism.[35] Weber remarks in his introduction to *The Protestant Ethic* that Western society differs from all other social forms, both historical and contemporary, in its "specific and peculiar rationalism."[36] It is a schematic understanding of the peculiarities of Western rationalism that Weber identified and to which we now turn.

Following Brubaker, we find it helpful to group the various examples of rationalization in modern society into four major groups, which each share a set of unifying themes. The groups isolated by Brubaker are: capitalism and calculability, legal formalism, bureaucratic administration, and asceticism and the ethic of vocation. For our purposes, we have already detailed the final group, ascetic vocationalism. In what follows, we explain Weber's arguments about capitalism and calculability. We then collapse the second and third groupings, as their fundamental structures and logics are deeply related. For Brubaker, each of these categories also exhibits one or more of the unifying themes of Weber's understanding of modern rationalization, that is, knowledge, impersonality, and control. In the next section, we will explain each of Brubaker's groupings in turn and provide illustrative examples from the current state of higher education to justify our claim that online classes are one (but not the only) manifestation of Weber's concerns about rationalization.

Calculability and the Capitalist Spirit

It is in his discussions of capitalist rationality that Weber uses the term in perhaps its most straightforward sense, or at least the sense that will likely be most familiar to his readers. That is, Weber is generally comfortable, particularly in *The Protestant Ethic*, in adopting the non-evaluative usage of "rational" to mean what the term normally means in capitalist discourse, that is, instrumentally oriented toward exchanges for commodities with the ultimate end goal of value maximization and satisfaction of desires. The freely choosing *homo economicus* posited by capitalism is rational in her pursuit of her own self-interests within the confines of her market transactions. This is not to say that Weber's analytical usage of the term "rational" in this context implies that Weber himself had no critiques of the presuppositions embedded in the term. He writes at one point in *Economy and Society* that the pure rationalism of market interactions are "an abomination to every system of fraternal ethics."[37] For Weber, the rise of capitalist market calculability as a prescriptive ideal was less important from an economic perspective than it was from a psychological one, and his theory of capitalism can, from this point of view, be understood primarily as an ontology and genealogy of the modern self.[38] Weber underscores the importance not of capitalism itself but of the spirit it engenders in those who must live under it, writing in a rejoinder to a prominent critic of *The Protestant Ethic*: "The advancement of an expanding capitalism was not my *central* interest; rather it was the development of *humankind* as it was produced to the confluence of religiously and economically determined factors."[39] The attitudes of *homo economicus* both toward herself and toward her fellow humans, that is, feelings of dispassionate calculation, competition, exchange value, and the free exercise of rationality in market choices, are what Weber sees as the particular, and especially ethically dubious, core of modern Western capitalism.

Here the resonances with contemporary higher education are difficult to avoid, as many of the various neoliberal reform efforts explicitly mobilize the discourse of *homo economicus* as one of their guiding presuppositions. Take, for example, the increasingly common notion that universities are first and foremost businesses that must compete for students, who are oftentimes addressed explicitly as "customers." Relatedly, the student-consumers of university education are viewed as freely choosing social agents who rationally and impartially balance their market options and choose on the basis of their considered self-interest. It is with this assumption in mind that universities market themselves and attempt to "incentivize" consumption of their product, through demonstration of student success, higher quality facilities and amenities, or convenience of access, as in the context of online learning programs. Under capitalism, all relationships must become inherently quantitative, calculable, and measurable in terms of exchange value. As Brubaker puts the point, "Every good and service, every asset and liability, every factor that is (literally) taken into account is assigned a numerical money value."[40] This attitude is a clear illustration of Weber's vision of how capitalist calculation infiltrates relationships, in this case the educative endeavor, that had previously escaped quantification.

Bureaucratic Formalism

The second major aspect of modern rationalization in the West, for Weber, is the advancement of bureaucratic administrative control. Indeed, the historical advance of rationalism seems to necessitate more and more complex and hierarchical forms of bureaucracy. The form of bureaucratic control exhibits most distinctly the theme of the impersonality of modern rationalization. Weber argues that the impersonal, dispassionate form of *homo economicus* which dominates capitalist economic relations leads directly to the development of similarly dispassionate forms of administrative oversight. There is, in other words, a "distinctive ethos"[41] to the rational bureaucratic form which necessitates a commitment to "impersonal and functional purposes and…a spirit of formalistic impersonality…without hatred or passion, and hence without affection or enthusiasm."[42] Aside from the cold indifference of bureaucratic administration, Weber also singled out the precise and mechanistic nature of bureaucracy. Weber explicitly drew comparisons between bureaucracy versus previous forms of organizational hierarchy and machines versus pre-industrial forms of production. He is worth quoting at length:

> The fully developed bureaucratic apparatus compares with other organizations exactly as does the machine with the non-mechanical modes of production. Precision, speed, unambiguity…continuity…unity, strict subordination, reduction of friction and of material and personal costs—these are raised to the optimum point in the strictly bureaucratic administration.[43]

Brubaker ties the advance of bureaucratic control to not only rationalism but also the precise type of parochial technical knowledge that is required of bureaucrats to make the system run efficiently.[44] In this sense, bureaucracy becomes even more like the machine in Weber's metaphor. Not only is it more efficient, cold, and precise than its predecessors (e.g. online classes), it also ushers in a new class of laborers (e.g. young professors, clinical faculty, and part-time instructors) who are trained specifically in the technical details of its operation, details that the general public are generally ignorant of and must remain subordinate to.

In higher education, the various learning management systems (LMS) are clear examples of the way Weber envisioned the development of bureaucratic administration.[45] Some of the most popular LMS adopted by universities are Blackboard, Moodle, Sakai, Lore, and iCollege.[46] This "e-learning" or "web-based learning" is "defined as the delivery of education in a flexible and easy way through the use of the internet to support individual learning or organizational performance goals."[47] It is said by supporters of e-learning that "by eliminating the barriers of time and distance, individuals can now take charge of their own lifelong learning."[48] Furthermore, "Learning Management Systems represent an evolution from the processes and systems developed by certain institutions to register students on specific courses and keep records of students' activities."[49] We could not disagree more.

Relationships that used to be fundamentally messy, human, and unquantifiable are suddenly regimented, sanitized, and surveilled. The myriad ways in which both professors and students are "held accountable" first and foremost *not* to each other as human beings engaged in authentic relationships but rather to their bureaucratic overlords, who they may well never actually meet, are illustrative of the power of bureaucracy in contemporary higher education.[50] The systems of surveillance, from counting the number of "posts," to online tracking of student work activity, to the "customer satisfaction surveys" students are asked to fill out at the conclusion of a semester, are all processed, data-mined, and archived by bureaucratic officials who have no relationship whatsoever with the people represented in their data, but only ever execute mechanistic, rote operations in exerting their distanced and impersonal control over the rest of the university system.[51] Of course, this is not a personal indictment of bureaucrats, but rather illustrates the ways in which the current systems of bureaucratic administration and formal authority structurally isolate individuals from one another, sanitize human relationships, and make deviations from the established lines of power and change nearly impossible. It is this formal power structure inherent in bureaucracy that Weber found so problematic.

Markets, Universities, and Online Learning: Rationalization Run Amok

While much has been written on the many and varied aspects of technology in education, we have used online learning as a specific site for Weberian critique. Our goal was illustrative in the sense that Weber's theory has direct and practical implications for both teaching and learning and what it means to be a university. The bureaucratic and economic reality is that online classes are convenient and appeal to students as customers' understanding of the purpose of university life: get in, get out, and get a (high-paying) job. By focusing on online platforms and their utility, we highlight the limits of technology that seemingly go unnoticed or are largely unremarked upon in the scholarly literature.[52] Indeed, the utilization of online instruction is only one of the many features of the neoliberal university that rarely faces critique, but it supports the "growing interest in the mass processing of students."[53] By the year 2011, 32 percent of college students were enrolled in at least one online class, and by 2012, more than 6.7 million college students nationwide were enrolled in "traditional, credit-bearing online courses."[54] These numbers have since increased, as universities continue to "incentivize" the creation of fully online and hybrid courses among faculty. While some have argued that online instruction democratizes higher learning by offering increased access to degree granting institutions, we believe that the proliferation of online learning is an instrument of the rationalization of the university. In other words, the trend toward online instruction cannot support the democratization of education, as argued by Jorge Larreamendy-Joerns and Gaea Leinhardt, as it supports the mechanization, technocratization, and rationalization of teaching and learning.[55] Put differently, Noble argues that "this new commercial ethos has irreversibly corrupted the university as a site of reliably independent thought and...inquiry, placing in jeopardy a precious and irreplaceable public resource."[56] Arguably worse, as Hubert Dreyfus explains, is the degree to which online classes evidence student withdrawal and lack of engagement:

> Experiments in computer-supported cooperation have shown that people are more inclined to defect in on-line communications than in face-to-face interactions, and that a preliminary direct acquaintance between people reduces this effect. So, computer technology can even weaken trust relationships already holding in human organizations and relations, and aggravate problems of deception and trust.[57]

In summing up the general point we are making, Kenneth Benne is worth quoting at length. Writing in 1975, Benne is prescient regarding online classes:

> Whatever the media, however, the big selling point is often the extent to which these instructional devices are teacher proof. They are advertised as enabling the student to proceed with his [sic] own learning at his own individual pace and they are designed to relegate teachers to the role of technicians implementing a *prescribed* learning program.... Students can proceed to learn through interaction with their materials without any necessity of messy, subjective, and unpredictable dialogue with either their teachers or their fellow students. Such materials are urged as a technological solution to problems of large numbers of students and a paucity of well-prepared teachers. They are urged also as an efficient way of individualizing instruction, usually without awareness of the irony involved—that "individualization" in this usage seems to be equivalent to further "depersonalization" of the instructional process.[58]

Benne's ultimate point is to make sense of what happens to community when technology becomes the overriding superstructure of our lives. He refers to this as a form of absurdity and offers the following:

> A limerick which went the rounds recently shows, in exaggerated fashion to be sure, the absurdity that has been reached in the reliance upon educational technology as a substitute for the freely chosen action and suffering of human experience.
>
> The news is now out, clear and clean,
> That by aid of a teaching machine,
> King Oedipus Rex
> Has learned all about sex
> Without ever touching the queen.[59]

Our point is that, following Dreyfus and Benne, actual conversations and real experiences are not only more educative than virtual or technologically mediated ones but that the rationalization that has gone on around technology and education perverts authentic inquiry and the potential of what it means to be a student. Weber's notion of calculability recurs: students as *homo economicus* are expected to achieve dispassionate calculation, competition, and the free exercise of market choice *even when such choices are hegemonic*. Students literally buy into the idea that choosing an online course is better because it is more convenient (and easier) than it is to take the time and effort to physically attend class and face others and others' ideas. It is a form of narcissism characteristic of Americans for a long time, but heightened in the age of cell phones, tablets, e-readers, and online classes.[60] The problem, as we see it, is that the ubiquity of online classes reifies them as legitimate spaces for authentic learning. We maintain that online classes are merely a more efficient means of collecting credits for program completion and increasing enrollments. As such, online learning represents a culminating instance of Weber's concept of rationalization and should be challenged accordingly.

In the face of such hegemonic ubiquity, we can only call upon others to realize the limits of online classes and refuse to teach them. This requires wresting power back from bloated university administrations and culling the mindset that such courses are necessary. It means, in short, overthrowing economic rationality itself. Our point is both political and ethical. In the general arena of state politics, the clear majority of representatives and senators are not only business people, they also advocate reduced state funding to higher education. This establishes the vicious cycle that makes grant-getting increasingly central to faculty life. Ethically, we wonder about the degree to which underfunding universities is actually part of a master-plan attack on public education itself. As Noble points out, this is a battle over labor and the kind and quality of that labor. He is worth quoting at length:

> Once faculty and courses go online, administrators gain much greater direct control over faculty performance and course content than ever before and the potential for administrative scrutiny, supervision, regimentation, discipline, and even censorship increase dramatically. At the same time, the use of technology entails an inevitable extension of working time and an intensification of work as faculty struggle at all hours of the day and night to stay on top of the technology and respond, via chat rooms, virtual office hours, and e-mail, to both students and administrators to whom they have now become instantly and continuously accessible....Once faculty put their course material online, moreover, the knowledge and course design skill embodied in the material is taken out of their possession, transferred to the machinery and placed in the hands of administration....In short, the new technology of education, like the automation of other industries, robs faculty of their knowledge and skills, their control over their working lives, the product of their labor, and, ultimately, their means of livelihood.[61]

Two unrelated suggestions might follow: (1) recapture what were once known as Centers for Teaching and Learning but have become Centers of Instructional Innovation (or some other ghastly terminology) and (2) repeatedly pose three questions to anyone under the mistaken notion that online classes are virtuous.

For (1), this is both a practical and symbolic suggestion. That centers once (not unproblematically, of course) focused on quality teaching have been taken over by technophiles who think they already know what quality teaching is (think "best practices") should be laughable. Under the rationalization we have explored, however, it is not laughable, it is "the real world." We call for sit-ins by faculty and students who are committed to the art and craft of teaching over technological reification. Short of smashing computer screens, we urge faculty and students to develop clearly stated reasons why such centers have drifted too far into the (very expensive) virtual world of technorationality and to take over such centers, disrupting the taken-for-granted falsehoods that online classes are a good thing.

For (2), finally, we urge faculty, students, and administrators to consider three questions Neil Postman offered at a technology in education conference at Penn State University in the late 1990s. Paraphrased to fit our specific topic, Postman's questions are as follows:

- What problems do online classes solve?
- What problems do online classes cause?
- Who benefits most from online classes?

Interrogating these questions will reveal, we assert, that online classes solve fewer authentic problems than currently believed, cause more actual problems than currently understood, and that technology industries and their subsidiaries benefit the most from expensive but economically rationalized online offerings.

Notes

1. Kenneth Saltman, *The Politics of Education: A Critical Introduction* (Boulder, CO: Paradigm Publishing, 2014), 65.
2. See, for example, Frank Donoghue, *The Last Professors: The Corporate University and the Fate of the Humanities* (New York: Fordham University Press, 2007); Sheila Slaughter and Gary Rhoades, *Academic Capitalism and the New Economy: Markets, State, and Higher Education* (Baltimore: The Johns Hopkins University Press, 2004); and Sheila Slaughter and Larry L. Leslie, *Academic Capitalism: Politics, Policies, and the Entrepreneurial University* (Baltimore: The Johns Hopkins University Press, 1999).
3. Some argue that this trend can be traced to at least the early 1900s and the rise of Taylorism in education. See Raymond Callahan, *Education and the Cult of Efficiency: A Study of the Social Forces That Have Shaped the Administration of Public Schools* (Chicago, IL: University of Chicago Press, 1962). For diametrically opposed styles of research and writing, but nearly identical conclusions on the corrupting influences of business thinking in colleges and universities, see Thorstein Veblen, *The Higher Learning in America: A Memorandum on the Conduct of Universities by Business Men*, ed., Richard F. Teichgraeber III (Baltimore: The Johns Hopkins University Press, 1918/2015); and Upton Sinclair, *The Goose-Step: A Study of American Education* (Pasadena, CA: By the author, 1922). Ironically, while Veblen derided corporate intrusion into higher education, he held out hope that technology would provide "real" measures of social progress. See Thorstein Veblen, *The Instinct of Workmanship* (New York: Macmillan Co., 1914). See, also, Kenneth D. Benne, "Technology and Community: Conflicting Bases of Educational Authority," in Walter Feinberg and Henry Rosemont, Jr., eds., *Work, Technology, and Education: Dissenting Essays in the Intellectual Foundations of American Education* (Urbana, IL: University of Illinois Press, 1975): 142–165.
4. See Alfred North Whitehead, *The Aims of Education* (New York: New American Library, 1954).
5. Sanford F. Schram, "The Future of Higher Education and American Democracy: Introduction," *New Political Science* 36 (2014): 425–437, 427.
6. Ibid., 427–428.

7. See, for example, Martha Nussbaum, *Not for Profit: Why Democracy Needs the Humanities* (Princeton: Princeton University Press, 2010); Andrew Nadolny and Suzanne Ryan, "McUniversities Revisited: A Comparison of University and McDonald's Casual Employee Experiences in Australia," *Studies in Higher Education* 40, no. 1 (2015): 142–157; and Donna Adair Breault and David M. Callejo Pérez, *The Red Light in the Ivory Tower: Contexts and Implications of Entrepreneurial Education* (New York: Peter Lang, 2012).
8. Nadolny and Ryan, 143.
9. Megan Laverty, "'There Is No Substitute for a Sense of Reality:' Humanizing the Humanities," *Educational Theory* 65, no. 1 (2015): 611–754, 637.
10. Steven C. Ward, "From *E Pluribus Unum* to *Caveat Emptor:* How Neoliberal Policies are Capturing and Dismantling the Liberal University," *New Political Science* 36, no. 4 (2014): 459–473, 461.
11. Alasdair MacIntyre and Joseph Dunne, "Alasdair Macintyre on Education: In Dialogue with Joseph Dunne," in *Education and Practice: Upholding the Integrity of Teaching and Learning*, ed. Joseph Dunne and Pádraig Hogan (Malden, MA: Blackwell, 2004), 3.
12. Ibid.
13. See Langdon Winner, *The Whale and the Reactor: A Search for Limits in an Age of High Technology* (Chicago: University of Chicago Press, 1986); David F. Noble, *The Religion of Technology: The Divinity of Man and the Spirit of Invention* (New York: Penguin Books, 1997); Neil Postman, *Technopoly: The Surrender of Culture to Technology* (New York: Vintage, 1992); Alison Armstrong and Charles Casement, *The Child and the Machine: Why Computers May Put Our Children's Education at Risk* (Toronto: Key Porter Books, 1998); and Stanley Aronowitz, Barbara Martinsons, and Michael Menser, eds., *Technoscience and Cyber Culture* (New York: Routledge, 1996), among others.
14. David Noble, *Digital Diploma Mills* (Monthly Review Press, 2001), 8–11.
15. Ibid., 10. Noble, and others, presaged the controversy over faculty rights to their own syllabi and course materials. See Ann Springer, "Intellectual Property Legal Issues for Faculty and Faculty Unions," American Association of University Professors, https://www.aaup.org/issues/copyright-distance-education-intellectual-property/faculty-and-faculty-unions-2005. There are, of course, leading theorists who are generally supportive of technology, including online learning. For three of the more balanced and philosophically sound defenses of technology in education, see Leonard J. Waks, *Education 2.0: The Learning Web Revolution and the Transformation of the School* (New York: Routledge, 2013); Nicholas C. Burbules and Thomas A. Callister, Jr., *Watch IT: The Promises and Risks*

of Information Technologies for Education (Boulder, Colorado: Westview Press, 2000); and David Blacker, "Allowing Educational Technologies to Reveal: A Deweyan Perspective," *Educational Theory* 43, no. 2 (1993): 181–194.

16. See David I. Backer, "The Mass Psychology of Classroom Discourse," *Educational Theory* 67, no. 1 (2017): 67–82, 70.
17. Max Weber, *From Max Weber: Essays in Sociology,* eds. H.H. Gerth & C. Wright Mills (London: Routledge & Kegan Paul, 1970), 293.
18. Lars Udehn, "The Conflict Between Methodology and Rationalization in the Work of Max Weber," *Acta Sociologica* 24, no. 3 (1981): 131–147, 139.
19. Max Weber, *Economy and Society,* eds. Guenther Roth and Claus Wittich (Berkeley: University of California Press, 1978), 1375–1376.
20. Max Weber, *The Protestant Ethic and the Spirit of Capitalism*, trans. Talcott Parsons (London: Routledge Classics, 2001), 35.
21. Rogers Brubaker, *The Limits of Rationality: An Essay on the Social and Moral Thought of Max Weber* (London: Routledge, 1991), 24.
22. Weber, *The Protestant Ethic and the Spirit of Capitalism*, 121.
23. Ibid., 113–114.
24. Ibid., 105–106. See also 224, n. 30.
25. Brubaker, 24.
26. Ibid., 25.
27. Weber, *The Protestant Ethic and the Spirit of Capitalism*, 180.
28. See, also, Keith Hampton, Lauren Sessions Goulet, Eun Ja Her, and Lee Rainie, "Social Isolation and New Technology," Pew Research Center (2009): http://www.pewinternet.org/2009/11/04/social-isolation-and-new-technology/.
29. Jürgen Habermas, *The Philosophical Discourse of Modernity* (Cambridge: The MIT Press, 1990), 2.
30. William Clark, *Academic Charisma and the Origins of the Research University* (Chicago: University of Chicago Press, 2006).
31. Ibid., 28*ff.*
32. Ibid., 11.
33. Ibid., 464*ff.*
34. Weber, *The Protestant Ethic and the Spirit of Capitalism*, 194, n. 9.
35. While it is a topic we do not have the space to explore here, there is much excellent work on the topic of Weber's theories of religious rationalization and its development, as well as the various modalities of pre-capitalist rationality. See for some examples John R. Love, *Antiquity and Capitalism: Max Weber and the Sociological Foundations of Roman Civilization* (London: Routledge, 1991); Warren S. Goldstein, "Patterns of Secularization and Religious Rationalization in Emile Durkheim and Max

Weber," *Implicit Religion* 12, no. 2 (2009): 135–163; and Lutz Kaelber, "Weber's Lacuna: Medieval Religion and the Roots of Rationalization," *Journal of the History of Ideas* 57, no. 3 (1996): 465–485. For a different, deeply disturbing, extension of religion and technology, see Yuval Harari, *Homo Deus: A Brief History of Tomorrow* (New York: Harper, 2017).

36. Weber, *The Protestant Ethic and the Spirit of Capitalism*, 26.
37. Weber, *Economy and Society*, 637.
38. Sung Ho Kim, *Max Weber's Politics of Civil Society* (Cambridge: Cambridge University Press, 2004), 28.
39. Quoted in ibid.
40. Brubaker, 11.
41. Ibid., 21.
42. Weber, *Economy and Society*, 225. Online classes are only one illustration of this, but they are indicative of the rationality that merges commerce, convenience, and calculability together.
43. Ibid., 973.
44. Brubaker, 21.
45. Drawing on the work of George Ritzer, some scholars have argued that such trends represent the "McDonaldization" of the university. See George Ritzer, *The McDonaldization of Society* (New York: SAGE, 2007); Nadolny and Ryan, op. cit.; and Dennis Hayes and Robin Wynyard, *The McDonaldization of Higher Education* (New York: Praeger, 2002).
46. Shehryar Nabi, "7 Blackboard Competitors With Online Learning Solutions," *Education Dive* (January 2012) http://www.educationdive.com/news/7-blackboard-competitors-with-online-learning-solutions/35847/.
47. Tagreed Kattoua, Musa Al-Lozi, and Ala'adin Alrowwad, "A Review of Literature on E-Learning Systems in Higher Education," *International Journal of Business Management and Economic Research* 7, no. 5 (2016): 754–762, 754.
48. Ibid., 755.
49. N.N.M. Kasim and F. Khalid, "Choosing the Right Learning Management System (LMS) for the Higher Education Institution Context: A Systematic Review," *International Journal of Emerging Technologies in Learning* 11, no. 6 (Fall 2016): 55–61, 55.
50. We include quotation marks around "held accountable" and "incentivize" because the language is indicative of the most recent corporate turn in the university. We endorse discourse that focuses on being responsible, but not "accountable." Accountability is language of a market logic that positions power outside of faculties and is indicative of the degree to which Weber's notion of rationality has become deeply embedded in the discourses and practices that govern faculty and student lives. Said differently,

such rationalization represents a business approach to education that furthers a technological agenda whereby online classes are but one illustration of external control and surveillance.

51. See, for example, Jamie Costley and Christopher Lange, "The Effects of Instructor Control of Online Learning Environments on Satisfaction and Perceived Learning," *Electronic Journal of e-Learning* 16, no. 3 (2016): 169–180; and Retha Price, Tammy Arthur, and Kevin Pauli, "A Comparison of Factors Affecting Student Performance and Satisfaction in Online, Hybrid, and Traditional Courses," *Business Education Innovation Journal* 8, no. 2 (December 2016): 32–40.
52. There are exceptions, of course. See Nicholas Carr, *The Glass Cage: How Our Computers are Changing Us* (New York: W.W. Norton and Company, 2014); Hubert L. Dreyfus, *On the Internet* (New York: Routledge, 2001); Larry Cuban, *Oversold and Underused: Computers in the Classroom* (Cambridge: Harvard University Press, 2001); Jaron Lanier, *You are Not a Gadget: A Manifesto* (New York: Alfred, A. Knopf, 2010); Todd Oppenheimer, *The Flickering Mind: The False Promise of Technology in the Classroom and How Learning Can be Saved* (New York: Random House, 2003); and Sherry Turkle, *Reclaiming Conversation: The Power of Talk in the Digital Age* (New York: Penguin Press, 2015). Other than Dreyfus and Cuban, however, these works are written for a popular audience and are more journalistic than scholarly.
53. Schram, 427.
54. Peter Shea, "A National Study of Differences Between Online and Classroom-Only Community College Students in Time to First Associate Degree Attainment, Transfer, and Dropout," *Online Learning* 20, no. 3 (September 2016): 14–15, 15.
55. See, for example, Jorge Larreamendy-Joerns and Gaea Leinhardt, "Going the Distance with Online Education," *Review of Educational Research* 76, no. 4 (December 2006): 567–605.
56. Noble, *Digital Diploma Mills*, 10.
57. Dreyfus, 118, n. 25. Clearly, we are not suggesting that *any and all* face-to-face interactions are superior to online interactions, but for education to take place, as Dreyfus points out, risks and confrontations of the educative sorts are best evidenced in actual classes where people are talking with one another.
58. Benne, 154.
59. Ibid., 154–155.
60. See Christopher Lasch, *The Culture of Narcissism: American Life in an Age of Diminishing Expectations* (New York: W.W. Norton and Company, 1979/1991).
61. Noble, 32–33.

CHAPTER 4

Promoting More than Just "Diversity" at Colleges and Universities

Dwayne A. Tunstall

What do many of us imagine when we talk and think about *diversity* on a college campus? We imagine a multiethnic and multiracial group of students, smiling at the camera, standing side by side, some of them with one arm around someone else's shoulders, standing in front of a wall.[1] Or we imagine a multiethnic group of students sitting on coaches and chairs in a cozy, well-lit lounge, with textbooks open, smiling at one another while they converse. These images are the stuff of institutional marketing in the early twenty-first century with respect to college and universities.[2] We image a blog post written by the president of the University of Dayton welcoming students, with an image of a student's hands holding a sign that states: "We may have different religions, languages, colored skin, but we all belong to one human race."[3] The background of that sign is white, with most of the letters in black. However, the commas indicating differences are colored blue, and the conjunction "but" and the words indicating our commonality (the second "we" and "one" in the second clause of that sign) are colored red.

I would not question the sincerity of University of Dayton's president when he affirms the value of diversity at his institution. Nor would I question the sincerity of the University of Dayton student who held the sign featured in the president's blog post. Yet, these messages and images

D. A. Tunstall (✉)
Grand Valley State University, Allendale, MI, USA

A. Stoller, E. Kramer (eds.), *Contemporary Philosophical Proposals for the University*, https://doi.org/10.1007/978-3-319-72128-6_4

reinforce a problematic view of diversity, in which *diversity* functions as a veneer to cover over the messy realities on their campuses, especially on the campuses of predominately white colleges and universities. These messy realities include the persisting racial and ethnic disparities in higher education enrollment and attainment, as well as racial and ethnic disparities in earnings, employment, and other social and economic outcomes between white communities and communities of color. This is especially true for Hispanic and black residents of the United States.[4] For example, "[w]hen looking at the cohort of all students entering college [in 2003–2004 and completed at least an associate degree by 2008–2009], degree completion is lower among black and Hispanic students than white and Asian students. Nearly half of Asian students who enroll in postsecondary institutions complete a bachelor's degree within six years, compared with 36 percent of white students and only 17 percent of black and Hispanic students."[5] Another one of these messy realities is that as recently as 2009 "approximately one-third of white and Asian high school students were from the top socioeconomic status quintile, compared to 10 percent or less of Hispanic and black students."[6] On the other hand, "Hispanic and black students were more than twice as likely to belong to families in the bottom socioeconomic status quintile as white and Asian students."[7] These disparities in socioeconomic status between white and Asian high school students and Hispanic and black high school students partially account for the gaps in degree attainment between these racial and ethnic groups.[8] We will revisit this topic later. A third messy reality that the college promotional materials on diversity obscure is the racial and ethnic disparities in the dropout rate for college students. Take the cohort of US college students who began their postsecondary studies in 2003–2004 and completed by 2008–2009, for example. The dropout rate for that cohort "was 44 percent among Hispanic students, 44 percent among black students, 34 percent among white students, and only 20 percent among Asian students."[9] Hispanic and black students who are fortunate enough to graduate with a postsecondary degree earn, on average, less than white and Asian college graduates.[10]

Rather than address these racial and ethnic disparities in college attainment and postgraduation earnings, *diversity* on college campuses often works like diversity does in the corporate world. It can seem more like a PR stunt than a genuine effort of all stakeholders to welcome people who differ from the groups with the most cultural, social, and economic capital. Accordingly, diversity efforts on many postsecondary educational institutions can be caricatured in a manner similar to how the sarcastic website *Rent-A-Minority* caricatures *diversity* in corporate America. Diversity efforts can recruit students from many underrepresented racial and ethnic demographics. We can recruit the "ethnically ambiguous" woman: "Mexican? Arab? Mixed? What even are they? It doesn't matter... the exotic Ethnically Ambiguous minority can be whoever or whatever you want her/him to be."[11] We can recruit the "Cheerful Woman of Color who won't embarrass anyone in the organization by being 'an angry black woman.'"[12] In addition, we can recruit smiling Muslim women who are guaranteed not to be associated with any terrorist group, allowing colleges and universities to affirm their commitment to diversity, but without any hint of Islamophobia. Of course, we can recruit the "intellectual black guy" who is "available to stand next to [white students, staff, or faculty] while [they] say racist things at parties. Because you can't be racist if one of your best friends is black, obvs."[13] These diverse images can then be used to make well-meaning people feel good about their efforts to make their campuses more diverse without having to do anything substantive to change their campuses' environments and cultures.

Perhaps there is a less problematic conception of diversity that is available to us in the context of US colleges and universities. I propose that the Association of American Colleges & Universities (AAC&U) has a conception of diversity that would better serve colleges and universities in the United States. What is the AAC&U's definition of diversity? For them, diversity consists of "[i]ndividual differences (e.g., personality, learning styles, and life experiences) and group/social differences (e.g., race/ethnicity, class, gender, sexual orientation, country of origin, and ability as well as cultural, political, religious, or other affiliations)."[14] *Diversity* is one of the core principles of the Making Excellence Inclusive initiative, which is the AAC&U's guiding principle for promoting student access and success, especially students from underrepresented groups, in the context of a liberal education in the early twenty-first century. *Diversity* cannot be promoted unless people act on two other core values—namely, inclusion and equity. Diversity without inclusion and equity could lead to this phenomenon: "A black person [like HUD Secretary, Dr. Ben Carson] can bumble into racially hurtful comments. A female executive can turn a blind eye to sexism in the ranks below her. A gay person can ignore or indulge homophobia. Diversity increases the odds that an organization sees the world more acutely, accurately and empathetically. But it's not the end of the effort, and it's no guarantee."[15]

For the AAC&U, inclusion is "[t]he active, intentional, and ongoing engagement with diversity—in the curriculum, in the co-curriculum, and in communities (intellectual, social, cultural, geographical) with which individuals might connect—in ways that increase awareness, content knowledge, cognitive sophistication, and empathic understanding of the complex ways individuals interact within systems and institutions."[16] Equity is "[t]he creation of opportunities for historically underrepresented populations to have equal access to and participate in educational programs that are capable of closing the achievement gaps in student success and completion."[17]

My home institution, Grand Valley State University (GVSU), has accepted this AAC&U Making Excellence Inclusive initiative as its own. At GVSU "diversity refers to the presence of difference and variety of personal experiences, values, and worldviews that arise from difference of culture and circumstance."[18] Celebrating diversity is part of GVSU responsibility "through a coordinated equity and inclusion strategy."[19] Such a strategy includes supporting "the success and engagement of all students, faculty, staff and campus visitors in creating a healthy and affirming climate."[20] In this context, "inclusion is 'the active, intentional, and ongoing engagement with diversity—in people, in the curriculum, in the co-curriculum, and in communities, and in communities (intellectual, social, cultural, geographical) with which individuals might connect—in ways that increase one's awareness, content knowledge, cognitive sophistication, and empathic understanding of the complex ways individuals interact within value systems and institution.'"[21] Promoting inclusion at GVSU involves "creating environments where individuals feel welcomed, respected, supported, and valued,"[22] whereas equity promotes genuine community of underserved and underrepresented populations. Promoting equity involves "identify[ing] and eliminat[ing] barriers preventing their full participation"[23] in the resources and life of the university and in their career development.

GVSU's Division of Inclusion and Equity does not simply promote diversity, inclusion, and equality. Administrators and staff at the Division of Inclusion and Equality actively use a social justice framework to promote these core values. The GVSU Division of Inclusive and Equity articulates its social justice framework for cultivating inclusive and equitable communities at GVSU in this manner: "The institution recognizes its responsibility to examine traditional power structures and to address unfair treatment of any university constituent within these structures. Moreover, Grand Valley intends to educate and empower all members of the community to think critically about systems of marginalization and oppression. This includes a deeper understanding of privilege and the need for all in the community to work toward equity and fairness in the pursuit of transformation of lives, professions, and societies."[24]

This social justice framework becomes more imperative given the shifting demographics, persistent social inequalities, and workforce imperatives facing US colleges and universities, particularly at regional state universities.[25] In their article, "Toward a Model of Inclusive Excellence and Change in Postsecondary Institutions," Damon A. Williams, Joseph B. Berger, and Shederick A. McClendon explain why shifting demographics make adopting a social justice framework imperative this way: "The overall U.S. population is becoming more ethnically and racially diverse as a result of lower birth rates among white compared to other groups and expanding immigration rates among Asian, Latino/a and Caribbean populations."[26] They also identify the implications of colleges and universities adopting this framework as they implement the AAC&U Making Excellence Inclusive initiative: "College and universities have unprecedented opportunities to diversity their student populations and draw on this diversity as a vehicle for learning for all students."[27]

Williams, Berger, and McClendon also explain why persistent societal inequalities make adopting a social justice framework imperative for US colleges and universities this way: "Persistent residential inequalities continue to reproduce educational inequalities at all levels of K-16 education."[28] These societal inequalities are caused by residential segregation, economic stratification, and disparities in educational outcomes.[29] They then identify the implications of colleges and universities adopting this framework as they implement the AAC&U Making Excellence Inclusive initiative: Leaders at postsecondary institutions will be required "to think deeply and more systematically about reducing disparities and meaningfully including diverse groups in higher education."[30]

In addition, Williams, Berger, and McClendon explain why workforce needs make adopting a social justice framework imperative for US colleges and universities as follows: "Employers require a diverse workforce in which individuals are technically savvy and capable of complex thinking, problem solving, and communicating and working with people different from themselves."[31] They note that "[c]olleges and universities must expand opportunities to diverse groups and develop academic and co-curricular experiences to prepare all students to interact productively in diverse work settings and to serve diverse clientele."[32]

Are there social justice frameworks that we can use to better understand the effects that persistent social and economic inequalities have on our institutions and more importantly on our students and local societies? Of course! One of the theories proponents of a social justice framework can use to identify and understand some of the historical and social causes of the persistent social and economic inequalities in the United States is Charles W. Mills's Racial Contract Theory. For Mills, the *Racial Contract* is both a concept and a theory that we can use to describe, explain, and understand how white supremacy operates in actual communities. By *white supremacy*, Mills means the actual institutions and social practices that perpetuate global racial hierarchies in which nonwhite peoples, especially people of sub-Saharan African descent, are regarded as being inferior to white people, especially people of western European descent, and in which white people are regarded as being superior to every other racial group. Mills's Racial Contract Theory is based on a methodological claim—namely, the claim that "as a political system, white supremacy can illuminatingly be theorized as based on a 'contract' between whites, a Racial Contract."[33]

According to proponents of the Racial Contract Theory, the Racial Contract shapes how white people interpret the world. One of the frames people learn to interpret the world in an anti-black racist society like ours is what Cheryl I. Harris and Devon W. Carbado call the *black criminality frame*.[34] In fact, the black criminality frame is one of the modes by which many white people in the United States interpret the lives and actions of African Americans. Many racially white people in the United States view the disparities between the rates of incarceration for African Americans and that of white Americans to be the result of black criminality, and not as the result of white supremacist structures. This frame obscures how a mix of federal housing policy in the first several decades of the twentieth century;[35] white flight from many major urban areas in the 1950s and 1960s; increased police surveillance of poor, hyper-segregated African American neighborhoods for the last 50 years; and changes in the economy over the last 50 years have created the conditions for many contemporary African Americans in urban and suburban areas to behave in ways that lead to them becoming incarcerated by the state.[36] Mills's Racial Contract Theory makes sense of how the mass incarceration of African Americans in the United States is the result of the institutions and practices constituting the criminal justice system working to disproportionately target and then punish African Americans living in racially segregated, poor urban and suburban neighborhoods. It also helps us make sense of how mass incarceration of African American and Latin Americans is a continuation of the Racial Contract at the heart of modern white supremacist system in the United States, with earlier historical and sociopolitical expressions of this system being the institution of slavery and Jim and Jane Crow laws.[37] This system in turn can be interpreted as the way by which white Americans—especially higher socioeconomic status, cisgender, ablest, heterosexual, racist, white American men—have maintained their privileged status since the founding of the United States.

Mills's Racial Contract Theory can also help us identify other inequalities in the United States based on racial and ethnic disparities, particularly the race-based disparities between Americans of African descent and other groups with respect to infant mortality rates, educational attainment, access to quality health care, wealth, and so on. Nevertheless, discussions of "Racial Contract" and "white supremacy" ring hollow for many, if not most, poor and working-class white Americans, living in economically devastated small towns that have been abandoned by their economically sustaining industries.

Proponents of the social justice framework should at least sometimes shift their discussions of social justice from racial disparities and inequalities to other forms of social and economic inequalities. That way, they can discuss realities facing poor and working-class white Americans. One of those realities is that roughly 50 percent of 30-year-olds in the United States earn less than their parents did when they were the same age in 2016.[38] Once one compares that fact with the fact that 90 percent of 30-year-olds in the United States earned more than their parents in 1940,[39] it becomes obvious that there has been a downward trend in social mobility for the last eight decades. In fact, US social mobility measured in this manner has fallen by more than 70 percent since from 1940 to 2016.[40] Along with deindustrialization of the Rust Belt during the mid-twentieth century and the replacement of well-paying manufacturing jobs for workers with only a high school degree with lower-paying service jobs and more specialized work that requires at least some college education, many poor and working-class Americans are no longer doing as well as their parents did at their age. Many of them have effectively been locked out of the American Dream. These economic and social realities can foster resentment against proponents of social justice who concentrate specifically on race-based inequalities and disparities. By acknowledging these realities for poor and working-class white Americans, and by recruiting more poor and working-class white students to elite universities, non-elite research universities, liberal arts colleges, and regional state universities, administrators, faculty, and staff at those institutions can have a better chance of improving access to a quality postsecondary education for this population of students.

Proponents of social justice frameworks to think about issues of inclusion and equity believe that everyone involved in the management and maintenance of US colleges and universities need to be sensitive to how many working-class people of all races and ethnicities are concerned about income and wealth inequalities. A proponent of this framework can take into consideration the data from the Current Population Survey (1963–2014) in which the difference between the income of families in the tenth percentile and the 90th percentile increased tremendously between 1963 and 2013. Families in the 90th percentile went from earning seven times more in income than families in the tenth percentile in 1963 ($93,390 vs. $13,024 in 2013 dollars) to earning 12 times more in income than them in 2013 ($159,002 vs. $12,951 in 2013 dollars). The difference between those families in the 50th percentile and those in the 90th percentile is less pronounced, but is still noticeable. The differences between these two percentiles went from families in the 90th percentile earning two times more than those in the 50th percentile in 1963 ($93,390 vs. $46,098 in 2013 dollars) to earning three times more than them in 2013 ($159,002 vs. $56,971 in 2013 dollars).

This is not to say that proponents of social justice frameworks are required to downplay racial disparities. After all, concerns about income and wealth inequalities in general can coexist with, say, concerns about disparities in earnings among different demographics. For example, as of 2015 the median hourly earnings for Asian men are 117 percent as much as for white men, whereas the median hourly earnings for Hispanic women are 58 percent of white men's earnings. White men out-earn black men, Hispanic men, and all groups of women. As noted by the Pew Research Center, "[e]stimates are for all civilian, non-institutionalized, full- or part-time workers ages 16 and older with positive earnings. Self-employed workers are excluded. Hispanics are of any race. Whites, blacks and Asians include only non-Hispanics. Asians include Native Hawaiians and Pacific Islanders." Of course, these statistics would be different if one disaggregated Asian men and Asian women, as well as immigrant African groups and descendants of sub-Saharan African slaves. The same is likely true when one disaggregates white men and white women's wealth by geographical region and educational level. Yet, these disparities can be explained in terms of class or socioeconomic differences.[41]

This is especially the case with respect to the disparities between African Americans (blacks) and white Americans on measures of wealth and income. Among blacks, the median household income was $44,100 in 2015, compared with $75,100 for whites. And among full- and part-time workers, the median hourly earnings of blacks were 75 percent of whites in 2015. In terms of wealth, the median net worth of white households was roughly 13 times that of black households in 2013 ($144,200 for white households, $11,200 for black households). The poverty rate among blacks is the highest among major racial and ethnic groups, but it has declined over time, from 31.1 percent in 1976 to 24.1 percent in 2015, according to Census Bureau data. By comparison, the overall US poverty rate has increased from 11.8 percent in 1976 to 13.5 percent in 2015.[42]

As college and university administrators, faculty, and staff think about how to make their campuses more inclusive and equitable communities, some of the issues mentioned above need to be not only acknowledged but taken as cues for more programs that aim to recruit and retain underrepresented students from various racial, ethnic, and socioeconomic backgrounds, along with other group/social differences (e.g., gender, sexual orientation, country of origin, and ability as well as cultural, political, or religious affiliations). The conception of diversity in the AAC&U Making Excellence Inclusive initiative is a step in this direction because it asks those of us working at US colleges and universities to not simply pay lip service to the importance of cultivating inclusive, equitable, and socially just communities at US colleges and universities, but also acknowledge the various inequalities and disparities that need to be addressed before we can create such communities at our institutions.

Notes

1. Jacob Lund, "Group of stylish young university students on campus. Multiracial young people standing together against wall in college." Stock photo ID: 184659830. Shutterstock.com. JPEG.
2. See Jeff Chang, "Is Diversity for White People?" in *We Gon' Be Alright: Notes on Race and Resegregation* (New York: Picador, 2016), 29–32, especially p. 31.
3. Eric F. Spina, "A Community of Welcome," President's Blog: From the Heart, University of Dayton, February 25, 2017, https://www.udayton.edu/blogs/president/2017/01/02/a_community_of_welcome.php.

4. U.S. Department of Education, Office of Planning, Evaluation and Policy Development and Office of the Under Secretary, *Advancing Diversity and Inclusion in Higher Education* (Washington, D.C., November 2016), 24–28, https://www2.ed.gov/rschstat/research/pubs/advancing-diversity-inclusion.pdf.
5. U.S. Department of Education, Office of Planning, Evaluation and Policy Development and Office of the Under Secretary, *Advancing Diversity and Inclusion in Higher Education*, 24.
6. Ibid., 18.
7. Ibid.
8. Ibid.
9. Ibid., 27.
10. Ibid., 24.
11. Arwa Mahdawi, *Rent-A-Minority,* http://rentaminority.com, accessed October 1, 2017.
12. Ibid.
13. Ibid.
14. "Making Excellence Inclusive," *Association of American Colleges and Universities,* https://www.aacu.org/making-excellence-inclusive, accessed August 31, 2017.
15. Frank Bruni, "Carson's Gray Matter," *The New York Times*, Opinion section (March 8, 2017), p. A23; available online at https://www.nytimes.com/2017/03/08/opinion/ben-carsons-gray-matter.html.
16. "Making Excellence Inclusive."
17. Ibid.
18. Grand Valley State University Division of Inclusion and Equity, *Framework for Inclusion and Equity at GVSU*, Allendale, MI, 2016. https://www.gvsu.edu/cms4/asset/8764E037-BDEC-7DDD-33FCF0A5048125AB/gv-inclusionbooklet-v3_for_website_3-18-2016.pdf.
19. Ibid.
20. Ibid.
21. Ibid.
22. Ibid.
23. Ibid.
24. Ibid.
25. Damon A. Williams, Joseph B. Berger, and Shederick A. McClendon, "Toward a Model of Inclusive Excellence and Change in Postsecondary Institutions" (Washington, D.C.: Association of American Colleges and Universities, 2005), p. 5.
26. Ibid.
27. Ibid.
28. Ibid.
29. Ibid.
30. Ibid.

31. Ibid.
32. Ibid.
33. Charles W. Mills, *Racial Contract* (Ithaca, NY: Cornell University Press, 1997, 7); see also Charles W. Mills, "The Racial Contract as Methodology (Not Hypothesis)," *Philosophia Africana* 5, no. 2 (March 2002): 77.
34. See Cheryl I. Harris and Devon W. Carbado, "Loot of Find: Fact or Frame?", in *Rereading America: Cultural Contexts for Critical Thinking and Writing*, 9th ed., edited by Gary Colombo, Robert Cullen, and Bonnie Lisle (Boston, MA: Bedford of St. Martin's, 2013), 533–536.
35. See Richard Rothstein, *The Color of Law: A Forgotten History of How Our Government Segregated America* (New York, NY: Liveright, 2017).
36. See Glenn C. Loury's Tanner Lectures on Human Values, which is part 1 of *Race, Incarceration, and American Values* (Cambridge, MA: MIT Press, 2008); also see Glenn C. Loury, "Racial Inequality in 21st Century America: Where do we go from Here?", *CASBS Symposium Series*, Stanford University, Stanford, CA., Feb 1, 2016. https://casbs.stanford.edu/second-2015-16-casbs-symposium-series-features-glenn-loury-video and "When Black Lives Matter: The Ethics of Race, Crime and Punishment in America," Lee Lecture, University of Oxford. May 25, 2017. https://www.brown.edu/Departments/Economics/Faculty/Glenn_Loury/louryhomepage/Lee%20Lecture.pdf.
37. See Michelle Alexander's *New Jim Crow: Mass Incarceration in the Age of Colorblindness*, rev. ed. (New York, NY: The New Press, 2012) for an account of how the mass incarceration of black and brown people, particularly men, is the most recent US race-based caste system, or a system under which unjust discrimination and marginalization of certain racial and ethnic groups is justified and enforced through law and custom.
38. See Raj Chetty, David Grusky, Maximilian Hell, Nathaniel Hendren, Robert Manduca, and Jimmy Narang's article, "The Fading American Dream: Trends in Absolute Income Mobility Since 1940," *Science* 356, no. 6336 (April 28, 2017): 398–406. This article is available online on the *Science* website. It is also available in the "Papers, Slides, and Summaries" section of *The Equality of Opportunity Project* website, accessed October 23, 2017.
39. Ibid.
40. Ibid.
41. Statistics stated in the above paragraph are from Eileen Patten, "Racial, gender wage gaps persist in U.S. despite some progress," Pew Research Center Fact Tank, July 1, 2016, http://www.pewresearch.org/fact-tank/2016/07/01/racial-gender-wage-gaps-persist-in-u-s-despite-some-progress/.
42. Statistics stated in this paragraph are from Kristen Bialik and Anthony Cilluffo, "6 facts about black Americans for Black History Month," *Pew Research Center Fact Tank*, February 22, 2017, http://www.pewresearch.org/fact-tank/2017/02/22/6-facts-about-black-americans-for-black-history-month/.

PART II

The Wellspring of Experience: Reflections on Robust Higher Education

CHAPTER 5

En Route: Toward a Philosophy and Practice of Liberal Education

L. Jackson Newell

A Prefatory Note

Brazilian educational philosopher, Paulo Freire, defined praxis as "reflection and action directed at the structures to be transformed."[1] The structures to which I have directed my reformist energy throughout my career have been the aims and methods of ***liberal education*** as the core teaching mission of American universities. Thomas Jefferson strove to possess a "liberal mind," one that was free to pursue truth and serve the public interest without being blinded by ideological, political, or religious predispositions.[2] This ideal, over which Jefferson himself sometimes faltered, has nonetheless guided my teaching.

L. Jackson Newell is professor emeritus of the history and philosophy of higher education at the University of Utah, former dean of Liberal Education at that institution, and president emeritus of Deep Springs College in California. He currently teaches in the Honors College at the University of Utah and was awarded the Distinguished Honors Professorship in 2016, at the age of 78. He has drawn from several previously published writings to present this, the most comprehensive statement of his philosophy of liberal education.

L. J. Newell (✉)
University of Utah, Salt Lake City, UT, USA

A. Stoller, E. Kramer (eds.), *Contemporary Philosophical Proposals for the University*, https://doi.org/10.1007/978-3-319-72128-6_5

Reflecting Freire's belief that the educator must be transformed in becoming a liberator, my pedagogy has grown across a lifetime of wide-ranging experience, inquiry, experimentation, and reflection. My passion is to lead students through their own encounters with concrete experience, intellectual and ethical exploration, and even spiritual discovery, to become free and responsible moral agents in their own right. This is the most direct way in which a college education becomes a public good. Liberal education is needed now as never before.

This essay is a tapestry of personal narrative, theoretical insights, intimate meditations, and practical conclusions in pursuit of liberal education. I invite you to join me on my educational journey. More importantly, I urge you to ponder your personal journey and define your own authentic philosophy and practice of college teaching.

An Unanticipated Prompt[3]

Martin Cantor arched his forearms and hands in a graceful dome, then explained that a caldera is formed when a volcano blows its insides out and collapses from its own weight. With this, his hands crumpled together and the arch of his forearms shuttered and surrendered to gravity. A little band of University of Utah students and professors led by evolutionary biologist Robert Vickery looked across the barren landscape at the gaping crater on Santiago Island and envisioned a cataclysmic event a million years removed. Having studied Charles Darwin's life and work, including his 1835 sojourn in the Galapagos Islands, we had come see for ourselves the creatures and habitat that crystallized the great scientist's ideas on the evolution of species.

For the next eight days, we followed Martin from island to island and from rugged Iguana-littered shorelines to the highland ranges of the giant tortoises. "I'll try to answer any question you ask me," he said, "but I refuse to lecture. You tell me what you want to know." By journey's end, we respected him not only as a fine naturalist but also as an uncommonly gifted teacher. Self-educated for this work, Martin was a guide certified by the Ecuadorian government. I knew immediately that I had much to learn from him.

When he finished high school in Guayaquil on the Ecuadorian mainland, Martin's love of nature and adventure propelled him to the remote Galapagos Islands where he was hired on as a dockhand. The archipelago had just been designated an Ecuadorian National Park at that time, and

UNESCO had only recently placed the Galapagos Islands on its World Heritage list for the preservation of natural and cultural treasures. The task of shepherding visitors and protecting endangered fauna and flora was just getting underway.

Curious about the natural and human history of the islands, and about the scientists, writers, and photographers who came to study them, Martin began by quizzing the visitors whose baggage he handled and to read the field manuals and scientific papers they left behind (increasingly at his urging). He became a keen observer of natural phenomena in his own right. Martin moved gradually from baggage handler to local expert and eventually to consummate guide for the succession of foreign scientists who came to the islands. When we met Martin, he spoke five languages; conversed comfortably with zoologists, botanists, and geologists from all over the world; and remained as inquisitive about everything in the Galapagos as the most recent traveler.

For me, who had studied the history and philosophy of higher education for decades, Martin was as interesting as the sea turtles and vermilion flycatchers to which he directed our attention. How had he come to know so much about the natural world, human nature, and foreign languages without availing himself of the elaborate curricula modern universities erect to do this job?

No doubt, Martin was a man of uncommon ability. But our universities are full of similarly gifted people. I asked myself, therefore, what elements came together to produce the knowledge and skill I admired in Martin. What were his habits? How had he learned?

Martin's motivation sprang from strong intrinsic interests, often complemented by urgent demands of his job. No teacher specified what he should learn, set his pace, or judged his progress. Self-discipline was the only discipline he knew, and his drive had not flagged with time. In the evenings as our little wooden boat, the San Antonio II, bobbed off shore, Martin spread his books and papers under the low light of the galley and poured over them—a scientific paper here, a literary essay there, and a few dog-eared field manuals that showed the effects of hard use. Learning, working, and living were all one for Martin; neither his life nor his education has ever been divided up, labeled, and thrust into compartments. Nor have graduation ceremonies ever suggested that his knowledge was complete.

I noted that Martin's education began with the immediate and the specific and proceeded outward in time and space. Personal observations preceded abstract concepts and theoretical explanations. Springing from a natural inquisitiveness about the unique animals, plants, and geology of the Galapagos Islands, Martin's interests gradually spread as he compared his growing knowledge of local animals and plants with what he learned to be the case elsewhere. His methods were concrete; he began with what he saw and then tested conclusions found in the scholarly literature against his own observations. Responding to a question about whether Galapagos land iguanas crossbreed with marine iguanas, Martin explained that some scientists believe they do. "But I'm a doubter," he said, "because I've never seen anything that looks like a cross. And I have never seen them together."

Martin acquired foreign languages when the need arose. He learned English and French in the process of showing North American, British, and French scientists around the islands. The party that followed us on the San Antonio II was coming from Frankfurt. This would be Martin's first solo guidance of a German-speaking group, and he was boning up the best he could. This meant, of course, tapping the resources at hand; he found out which of us spoke German and then good-humoredly practiced his colloquialisms on us. He had already mastered the grammar and scientific terminology. Learning German was a practical matter for him, not an end in itself. He approached the task with energy, imagination, and playfulness.

I became aware that Martin's highly developed interpersonal skills were an indispensable element of his self-education. His scientific and linguistic learning had been stimulated and nourished by the ways he interacted with other people. He learned in the same fashion he taught—by asking questions of people who knew more about something than he, and then engaging them in lively conversation.

In Martin's experience, there is no artificial or self-conscious partitioning of fact and value. As a university professor, I couldn't help but notice the absence of feigned value neutrality or the paucity of methodological rigidity. The penchant to make one's own observations and conclusions first, and then test them against expert judgments, was a special plea of Ralph Waldo Emerson in his 1837 essay, "The American Scholar,"[4] and a characteristic that pioneering humanistic psychologist Abraham Maslow found especially among the "self-actualized" people he identified.[5]

I am not suggesting that we close our universities or disband the public schools—and just let students learn what they can pick up on their own. But Martin's education does speak volumes about how we learn *naturally*.

A few colleges and universities—and some academic programs and professors everywhere—aim deliberately to bring out the "Martin" in their students. The College of the Atlantic, Berea, Deep Springs, Prescott, and Evergreen State are among the colleges that anchor their education in place and on lived experience. Nor is any college campus without professors who see teaching and learning in this way.

I returned to my campus determined to make more room in my undergraduate and graduate courses for the spontaneous joy of discovery—for my students and for myself. I was more determined than ever to spark students' own curiosity, to turn them loose individually and in small groups to solve problems, and to place increasing responsibility on them to participate in the evaluation of the quality of their own work. How better could I move them from dependence on me and my university to independence as self-motivated and self-directing scholars and human beings?

A Serendipitous Opportunity

When I got home from the Galapagos, I could not get Martin out of my mind. Being taught by him had awakened memories of my own most powerful learning experiences. Most of them had not taken place in classrooms either. Then, just a few weeks after my return from the Galapagos expedition, the university's Honors dean invited me to deliver the keynote address at the convocation for incoming students that fall. I went happily to work. It seemed entirely fitting that I could elucidate my newly emboldened teaching philosophy to a *student* audience rather than a gathering of scholarly colleagues. When the bright morning arrived, I offered this charge to the entering class.[6]

Welcome to the University of Utah Honors College. My purpose is to explore with you what effects (and the word "effects" is emphatically plural here) a good college education should have on students. What are the responsibilities you as students and we as professors bear along the path that we will tread together over the next four years? One of these is to explore, understand, and practice an ideal that is the mutual responsibility of all professors regardless of our disciplines: *liberal education.*

The open mind and broad understanding that emanates from liberal studies, learning that can help you become a free and responsible moral force, will underpin and provide context for every academic major offered on this campus. From music theory to social work and from bioengineering to psychology, a liberal education is yours for the taking, although it is often packaged as a set of seemingly unrelated courses called "general education" or labeled "distribution requirements." Chosen wisely and taken seriously, however, these courses can become the source of your human understanding—and thus the anchor of your professional and personal ethics….

Let's take a closer look at the map of this territory you enter today. While you won't be the first scholar to explore the region of ideas that will open up to you here, there are real frontiers out there and you may be the first to set eye or foot upon one of them. Think of your college adventure as distinctly twofold, because you will not only be expanding your knowledge and skills through your *outward* venture into the physical world and into the tangible realms of art history, geology, philosophy, or anthropology (to pick just four disciplines as examples), but, like any traveler or explorer, you can expect to learn as much about yourself as you do about the terrain. This dimension of your journey is an *inward* one, and the landscape is made up of the feelings, thoughts, and values that are inspired by your experiences. I am talking about your responses to what you discover and the meaning you choose to attach to your growing knowledge.

Your responses to what you learn may be subjective, and they will certainly be personal, but they are no less important than the mathematical formulas, scientific theories, or enduring works of art or literature that you study. Why? Because your values will ultimately guide your perceptions of truth, your use of knowledge, your application of hard-won skills. "Education," Socrates reputedly said, "must focus its main efforts on thinking about and examining our beliefs, studying them not as if they were alien objects, but rather from within, the beliefs as well as their study being seen as an integral part of the serious drama in which we are involved."

Essayist and theologian Thomas Merton asserted that education consists of "learning who one is, and what one has to offer the contemporary world, and how to make that offering valid."[7] When we think of education in these terms, it becomes quite clear why looking over your shoulder is bad business, and why predicting the outcomes of education is impossible.

Your professors are here as guides to lead you into the finest literature, scientific theories, and ideas, music, and art that we ourselves have come to know. And we will also go beyond the university's gates with you to observe and, where possible, take part in the social, cultural, and natural environments around us. Beyond the camaraderie engendered by these common experiences, however, your journey will also have an important solitary dimension. You must decide how earnestly you will strive to understand each new idea, and, if you accept it, you alone can decide what claim it will have on your actions. Will justice, equality, or mercy remain abstract terms to you, or will you plumb their depths and give life to these noble concepts in your dealings with others? You decide how you will live. Despite Socrates's and Merton's admonitions, and the best efforts of many able faculty, universities seldom give your inward excursion—your quest to forge a philosophy of life—its due. There are reasons for this imbalance, and some of them are good reasons. Let me explain.

While we can and should acknowledge and support each other's inward quest, we can't share it as fully as we share the texts, theories, and matter that are typically the objects of our study. Universities are sometimes called "households of reason." Reason, based on sensory observations, is the chief method of the external search—it is our means of making sense of things together—of the objects and processes we encounter around us. We like to think of observation and reason as being objective, because we yearn for clarity and, by nature, we want to be sure about things. Ambiguity gives us the willies.

In academic discourse, we generally confine our attention to matters that we can observe (directly or with technical instruments) and to claims that we can verify with evidence that reasonable people might consider seriously. The external quest, then, usually seeks to identify and understand what is in our universe—including ourselves—and how it all works. It is concerned primarily with *what is* rather than with *what ought to be*; it deals more with physical than with metaphysical questions. This quest is "external" in the sense that we depend upon verifiable evidence and accepted standards of reasoning to support our conjectures and reach our conclusions about the world around us.

But can our scientific hypotheses and aesthetic judgments really be objective? Try as we may, our creative work and scholarship seldom meet that lofty standard. On the one hand, we may not always focus on the most important elements in a situation, and, when we do, the instruments we employ to aid our senses are sometimes flawed, as is our ability to organize and make sense of the torrent of information we (with our omnipresent electronic devices, scientific instruments, questionnaires, and the like) may gather. More importantly, what we "see" and, therefore, what we report to one another are influenced substantially by what we assume to be true or hope to find. Sooner or later we must each reckon with the wisdom of this ironic twist of a common phrase: "If I hadn't believed it, I wouldn't have seen it!"

We have now come full circle. As we set out together to explore and further map the terrain of the physical universe we inhabit and the social and artistic worlds we have constructed, it is clear that we must proceed with humility sufficient to recognize the inherent subjectivity of our observations and knowledge—as well as the subjectivity of our own experience and interpretations. It is vitally important, therefore, that you examine your beliefs and values consciously and candidly, because they will exert a powerful influence not only on how you will live and what you will become but also on how you will learn and what you will believe.

I began by urging you to take your internal journey as seriously as the external one. Now I argue that the two are inseparably linked. Your task is to see and understand the ties between these two expeditions and to forge strong connections between what you learn and how you will live. How might we more fully link our needs for knowing and valuing and keep these two objectives equally vital? Our best hope is to create and maintain within the university a climate of intellectual and moral freedom that affords each student and professor the opportunity to fully develop and express her or his own thoughts and beliefs. The quality of our individual thoughts and the integrity of our personal beliefs depend not on their conformity with prevailing opinions but on their ability to weather encounters with new information, competing ideas, and contrasting values....

Without academic freedom, we cannot properly pursue our creative and scholarly objectives or be about the important work of defining and refining our personal and social values. We must welcome in this academy alternate interpretations of present realities and encourage the expression of a rich variety of personal beliefs about what is desirable for us and for our local, national, and global communities. By looking candidly at "what is," and considering contrasting views of "what might be," we open the door to the most distinctively human of all activities: thinking and acting to improve the human condition, including our own.

The aim of liberal education, Abraham Maslow believed, is to create a "fully functioning human being."[8] Such a person is alive in all the dimensions that make us human, being intellectually active and curious, emotionally aware and sensitive, spiritually resonate in the highest sense, and physically robust within our natural or imposed limits. Fully functioning people—healthy people—bring a matter-of-fact approach to the world, while living with uncommon delight. They simply accept human nature for what it is and seek to understand it. But they also strive, instinctively it seems, to bring some mercy and justice into their communities—harboring neither unrealistic hopes nor feelings of futility about their prospects for success. They know what they value and they do what they feel they must do.

Knowing. Valuing. Doing. Linking these ideals is the essence of liberal education. Set your own goals, establish lofty standards for yourself, and offer what you have to give to the contemporary world. And may you study and live with uncommon delight.

Seminal Influences

If Martin had animated my philosophy of college teaching, it was because he awakened my awareness of how I had learned best since childhood. First came reflections on the most powerful experiences in my own youth and early adulthood. They included annual family road trips from my native Ohio to my grandparents' ranch near Rocky Mountain National Park in Colorado. There I observed the natural world in all its glory, together with threats that were emerging even then to the integrity of the ecosystem that had seemed unassailable to my father in his youth on that land.

Running parallel to these summer experiences were sojourns every July to a remote island in Georgian Bay, Ontario, where my family and a few neighbors lived "off the grid" miles from Killbear Marina where we left our car and launched our small boat and motor. There I observed local guides, mechanics, and artisans whose skills baffled me and enriched our lives. My father was a physician who removed fishhooks and sutured lacerations in exchange for outboard motor repairs and nods toward favorite fishing holes. All of this made my schooling seem dull. I felt restless in the classroom. I was a lackluster academic achiever with an adventurous heart.

With the timorous agreement of my parents, and his, my friend Bill and I spent the summer of our 16th year driving a 1949 Chevrolet coupe over 9000 miles across the country and around the American West. Camping and cooking under the stars, we spent only $300 total—which we earned the previous spring as evening janitors at a local bank. We climbed Oregon peaks, camped under California redwoods, and descended to the bottom of the Grand Canyon, doing whatever moved us next. When we returned for our senior year in high school, my interest in school waxed strong. Why? Because biology, geography, geology, physics, and American history and literature had all come alive through the intense events of my summer travels. I wanted to understand what I had seen and done.

With that well-timed boost, my transcript began to glisten, and I applied as a long shot to uniquely democratic and participatory Deep Springs College. Located along the California-Nevada border, its students face a demanding liberal arts and sciences curriculum while bearing responsibility for managing just about everything in their community, including the working cattle ranch on which it is situated. Gigantic campus, diminutive student body—numbering just 26 each year. Like all the other students there, I was granted a full, expenses-paid scholarship, but it was not a gift. Rather, through the founder's deed of trust, I became a "beneficial owner," sharing responsibility for the health and future of this educational experiment—already a half-century old at that time. Deep Springs offers only the liberal education half of an undergraduate degree, so three years later my classmates and I sallied forth to other universities to complete our baccalaureate degrees. By now I was hooked on formal education in addition to learning anchored on real experience. The balance of my undergraduate studies heightened my desire to become a college professor. I chose history as my field.

Summer jobs continued to magnify my education. I was employed as a forest firefighter by the National Park Service each summer, benefitting from a series of assignments that culminated at Crater Lake where I served as foreman of the eight-member fire crew—all of us college students.

On the verge of retirement, the Chief Ranger, Jack Broadbent, was the last of his kind to serve without having earned a college degree. By the end of June, he had challenged me with some tough assignments and satisfied himself that I had adequately trained the other crew members. He called me into his office, noted the unusually cold and wet summer that virtually assured the absence of forest fires, and gave me a unique assignment: build a boathouse on Wizard Island to protect the rescue boat and a research vessel. With my crew, I was to design and construct the building to withstand the heavy snow load of severe winters and complete the task by Labor Day. He would supply all materials, tools, and equipment at my request, but he did not intend to check our work until we finished the assignment. Broadbent said he would hike down the trail with us and motor across the lake to inspect our work the day before Labor Day.

Neither I nor any crew member had ever worked so hard before. But we had been entrusted with an important job and we were not going to let Jack Broadbent down. He was an educator in disguise who possessed the vision to use a slack summer to see what he could get a band of college students to do and learn that season. Over 50 years later, our stone and log boathouse still graces the shore of Wizard Island. More importantly, eight initiates into adulthood learned what it means to be challenged, trusted, and supported by someone we admired.

The Launch

Prepared by a wide range of life experiences, as well as a bachelor's degree in history from Ohio State University and a master's degree in American history from Duke University, I launched my college teaching career at the age of 25 by a sad coincidence. A professor at Clemson University had died just days before fall semester opened and a cabal involving my major professor at Duke and the department chair at Clemson resulted in my emergency appointment to a one-year contract. My assignment was to teach five large sections of western civilization, two of which met on Saturday mornings. I learned the lecture method of teaching.

My plan to resume doctoral study was interrupted, however, by an offer to teach at Deep Springs College for two years—which I accepted. With classes averaging six students there, lecturing had no place. I had to master the Socratic method, fast. These back-to-back experiences with college teaching, even before my formal training as a professor was complete, proved invaluable over the decades to come.

After a stint as assistant dean of the College of Liberal Arts at the University of New Hampshire, I proceeded to Ohio State to complete my doctoral studies in the history and philosophy of higher education. Following two years as a postdoctoral fellow on that campus, I resumed my career path as assistant professor and (a most unlikely appointment) dean of Liberal Education, at the University of Utah. Throughout my 16 years as dean, I taught undergraduate courses and graduate seminars every year and maintained a respectable stream of publications. My commitment and identity as a professor first, and academic administrator second, served me well. I progressed quickly up the professorial ladder to the rank of professor.

While I loved what one of my graduate students described as "the cut and thrust of leadership," and became the primary architect of a nationally recognized liberal education program, I resigned the deanship at age 50. I set out to spend the rest of my career as a teacher-scholar. Emerson, I knew, had chided his friend Thoreau for leaving Walden Pond shortly after publishing his book about living there. Thoreau's response: "I left the woods for as good a reason as I went there.... I had several more lives to live, and could not spare any more time for that one. It is remarkable how easily we fall into a particular route, and make a beaten track for ourselves."[9] I had not forgotten this exchange.

Growing Consciousness of My Own Learning

When I slipped out of the whitewater rush of leadership, I luxuriated for a season in academe's calming backwaters—the university library and my faculty office. It was then that I immersed myself deeply in studying experiential learning theory—and realized how completely my own lived experiences illustrated David A. Kolb's experiential learning model (ELM).[10] Building on Aristotle's observation that we can learn some things only by doing them (riding a bicycle is an apt modern example), and then think about them and improve our technique afterward,[11] and on participatory educational concepts developed earlier by John Dewey and Jean Piaget, Kolb postulated a four-phased process to explain how individuals acquire vital knowledge and skill.

First, he argued, a person must become immersed in real rather than contrived experience. Then, following (or even during) one's involvement, it is important to reflect on what did and didn't work. Next should come analyzing what one learned, seeking concepts and comparisons with other's experiences to provide insight. Finally, reengage with higher and higher levels of responsibility for decision-making and results. Ideally, the cycle repeats, spiraling upward toward mastery.

The more I poured over Kolb's work, and renewed my appreciation of John Dewey's, the better I understood my own pathways to learning. Why not make my classrooms—my formal teaching—as real, as authentically human, and as reflective of the issues and ideas outside academe as my journey had seemed to me? Thus began a new phase of my education.

Saluting Forerunners[12]

As I reconsidered the conceptual bulwarks for my craft, I revisited theories that shaped my teaching, while also studying new ones. Howard Gardner's theory of multiple intelligences became one of my foundations. Human intelligence is not a one-dimensional capacity, as I.Q. tests presumed to measure, but it appears in many forms (verbal, mathematical, musical, spatial, social, physical, etc.) and in almost unlimited permutations. The educator's task is to aid students in developing their unique sets of intelligences and cluster them to meet the specific opportunities and roles their lives demand. A consummate basketball player has learned to combine physical/kinesthetic intelligence with his or her spatial, interpersonal, and even intrapersonal intelligences to make the deft pass, shoot the off-balance shot, motivate teammates, or psych out the opposition. And so it is with the concert pianist, the trial lawyer, or the gifted teacher. Whether the motivation is the passion to survive or the drive to excel, it is the urgency of the task that generates the energy and self-discipline to develop and harness the array of intelligences that are essential to mastering anything worthwhile.

As teachers, our job is to stimulate students' minds and motivations in whatever condition we encounter them, recognizing that there is surely more genius in any group of students than initially meets our eye. In a typical classroom, the other intelligences are usually expressed through each student's verbal ability. But where verbal intelligence is masked by a lack of language cultivation in literate and caring homes and good schools, brilliance in other intelligences can be especially difficult to identify and stimulate. This is one of the reasons that some of our "average" students turn out to be among our finest entrepreneurs, scientists, writers, and leaders.

But what do we know about professors who teach with unusual effectiveness? During my service as dean of Liberal Education at the University of Utah, I set out to find the most able teachers on my campus so that I could enlist them to design and teach courses in our core liberal education curriculum (that was required of all undergraduates). Over a period of years, I identified ten of these professors from across the academic disciplines and professional schools on our campus who were highly successful by multiple measures. They ranked perennially among the best on student course evaluations or (on a different survey) were most often cited by graduating seniors as having made the greatest difference in their education at the university. These two methods of identifying outstanding teachers rendered the same names only about half the time. I drew my group of ten from professors who rose to the top on *both* measures. Students rated them among the best at the conclusion of their courses and still held them in highest esteem at graduation.

Wondering what these colleagues might have in common, I invited each of them to lunch, one on one, at a café close to campus. We engaged in a conversation that I guided as subtly as possible with a series of questions about their teaching philosophies, life experiences, and personal beliefs. My work was aided or impeded, as one might judge, by knowing almost all of these scholars, some very well. Even so, when I look back over the series of conversations, some surprising conclusions jump out that seem particularly useful in thinking about what college teaching can be.

My consensus teaching stars were united in regarding each student as a valued human being who has important things to offer others. Neither vessels to be filled nor subjects to be served, every student was to them inherently interesting and worthy of attention and encouragement. Similarly, these teachers believed the ideas and information they taught were fundamentally important for their students to understand and potentially useful to their futures—as well as to society. If most teachers fall into one of two groups—those who teach students and those who teach subject matter—these professors straddled the divide and held the two sides of this equation in balance.

Perhaps for this reason, the faculty standouts I interviewed exhibited two other characteristics in common. Reflecting John Dewey's tenant that "Education is not a preparation for life, it is life itself," they regarded teaching as the most real of endeavors.[13] It was never a game to be played with a pea and three shells, with put-downs or one-ups, nor a test of authority, will, or status. As a result, these teachers were authentic and real in the classroom and outside it—being natural, approachable, and unthreatening. They were all mavericks by nature, resisting professorial affectations, socially defined expectations, and embracing the out-of-the-ordinary in both experience and taste.

These gifted teachers seemed to live comfortably on the margin between theory and practice, between established ways and emergent ideas, and between individual standards and community values. Rather than eschew ambiguity, they seemed to welcome situations brimming with it and, thus, empathized genuinely with students whose cultures, values, and lifeways contrasted with their own views or prevailing social norms.

These teachers did not profess answers, because they did not believe their teaching was about answers. For them, great questions about knowledge, truth, and goodness remained as intriguing and important as they had been in their own undergraduate years. Little wonder that they embraced each new class with the enthusiasm of potential discovery. They were still learning, and the less orthodox their students, the more likely a fresh question or new insight might appear.

In contrast to traditional student-professor paradigms, Walt Whitman's concept of "spiritual democracy" changed my thinking. (And it seems especially applicable to professors in the humanities and social sciences.)[14] I was drawn instinctively to Whitman's proposition that if I choose to regard every person I meet as my equal, including my students, I have created my own egalitarian republic and dwell within it. To the extent that this ethic of valuing others as equals becomes the norm within our classrooms, our institutions, and the whole body politic, our separate republics in spirit will merge and give life to the tangible political democracy for which we presume, with Dewey, to prepare our students.

I believe Whitman's notion of personally living the spirit of democracy is a necessary foundation for political and intellectual freedom. The wellspring of democracy rests within the heart and mind of individual students, professors, and citizens. Our fragile experiment with democracy in America, therefore, is poised precariously on the most intangible element of our existence: my conscience and that of others.

To encourage habits of careful argumentation and public engagement, I have pondered how I can best quicken my students' conscience—their capacity to hold self-interest in check and to suspend the destructive facets of ego expression. Every wisdom tradition and great religion has hallowed a few enduring ideas or ideals, and a surprising number of them are shared across cultures and traditions. Mortimer Adler wrote about six great ideas—too few by about half by my reckoning—which he grouped by western cultures (his intellectual bailiwick).[15] Three were central to Greek culture—goodness, truth, and beauty—and are ideas we judge by, while the French Revolution celebrated three others, liberty, equality, and justice, ideas that we act on. To these six, I believe we must add at least mercy and peace from the sacred texts of major religions around the globe.

These honorable ideals, when understood and internalized, can change the way students see themselves and how they understand those around them. But not necessarily. Encounters with actual social and political issues make the difference. Students can study multiple theories of justice and master tomes on just laws and unjust wars, but there is little evidence that any of this intellectual work prompts them (or us) to act in a more equitable and humane manner. That crucial step requires empathy. It depends on knowing people who suffer injustice or prejudice, reflecting on the sources of their pain, and truly sensing their feelings, motivations, and intentions.

To affect behavior, an idea or ideal must penetrate our rational minds and lay claim to our conscience. Once our heart gets involved along with our intellect, everything can change, usually (but not always) for the better. I see this principle at work in my students. Thomas Merton, Abraham

Maslow, and Ralph Waldo Emerson all described this transformation in similar terms. The highest purpose of education is to prepare each student for "ignition" by establishing the conditions and providing the materials that make flashes of insight possible. Learning is not a gradual progression. Better understood, it is characterized by long periods of plodding study that are punctuated by unexpected flashes of insight. Clearly, we teachers vary in our ability to set the conditions and provide the materials that predispose others for their leaps of understanding. But when these moments occur, they almost seem to happen without us. Sometime, perhaps, despite us.

William Perry, in his groundbreaking study of the interrelated nature of intellectual and ethical development,[16] demonstrated that "setting the conditions" for learning goes well beyond making wise and challenging assignments and providing an unthreatening environment to explore ideas and consider their implications. His research made it clear that the missing element in so much of college teaching is professors who are genuinely accessible to students as whole people in all their dimensions. This unguarded authenticity comes naturally to some but must more often be consciously developed as the norms of professorial role behavior give way to the personality of the teacher. By whatever means, becoming fully human in our classrooms, studios, and laboratories can be enhanced by getting out of the classroom with our students and by offering courses that extend across multiple semesters—involving academic year-long teaching and mentoring by the same professor. Whatever we can do to shed the role expectations of "professor" and become a genuine person with our students holds the potential to spur their overall development and nurture their own authenticity.

It matters to college students that they know their professors well enough to see that they struggle to live the principles they teach. What promises to change our students' behavior is witnessing a just act by someone they admire, seeing a merciful gesture (or benefitting from one), or absorbing the beauty of something both good and wholly unanticipated. It helps if a humanities professor's way of being reflects the ideas she or he teaches (though we may fall painfully short). Beyond the virtues we can model, each of us has the capacity to bring students into contact with other people who are exemplars of integrity, especially through the historical writing and creative literature we ask them to read and discuss.

Perils lurk, however, if students know only one person well who exemplifies mature ethical living and democratic virtues. Knowing just one such person can be intimidating because the student may infer that living only in that particular way can a satisfying life be achieved. Since none of us can become the same as another person, even if we wished to be, then relating productively to a single mentor may be intimidating.

What I try to provide every student, therefore, is access to, or at least a new awareness of, the variety of healthy models around them—among their teachers, friends, family, and other associates—who cleave to noble ideas in their own ways. If such people are present in their circles, they will unknowingly offer students the confidence to choose their own paths while drawing upon the fine qualities they observe in other's lives.

Note, too, that the personal models Perry believed are so vital to our development need not be living souls—or even real people. But they must be believable and engaging. The annals of history and literature are chock full of such figures. Their challenges and conflicts, and their tragedies and triumphs, are often described by historians in gripping detail. Further, novelists create characters that inspire, disgust, and inform us with their humanity and inhumanity. All these characters can serve as touchstones against which college students may strike their own actions and measure their own integrity.

Distilling Spirits

I retired early from the University of Utah to accept the presidency of my alma mater, Deep Springs College, where I served from 1995 through 2004.[17] Reflecting on this venture into institutional leadership and serious fund raising is the focus of another work, but I note here that this interlude added further to my understanding of the complexities and promise of liberal education. I continued to teach one course per semester with students of extraordinary ability and to benefit from working closely with them in the governance of the college itself. As rewarding as this was, by the end of my leadership there, I yearned to pay my dues at the other end of the spectrum of privilege.

I had known about Earl Shorris's multidisciplinary humanities course for low-income adults in New York City since 1997, and I hoped to develop something akin it when I returned to Salt Lake City.[18] I soon discovered that Jean Cheney at the Utah Humanities Council had the same idea, and she had already rounded up funding to launch such a course of study in which tuition, books, and child care were provided. Together with three other professors, we founded the "Venture Course in the Humanities." Westminster College agreed to serve as academic host for our program—providing transcripts for our successful students. Thus began another phase of my education.

Over the next decade, with only one staffing change, the five of us taught nearly 250 low-income, mainly mid-life adults who had never had the opportunity to attend college—and thought they never would. To be accepted into the program, they had to have graduated from high school or hold an equivalent GED, be able to read a newspaper with reasonable comprehension in English, and commit to two semesters of participation. Some were refugees from across the world, others homeless, and a few had served time in jail or prison. Most were women and people of color. All came to learn.

Over a span of two semesters, we offered a college curriculum that included American history, art history, literature, philosophy, and writing. None of our students could have afforded tuition or met the admission standards of an accredited college. Through our supporting foundations, we provided without cost the expense of tuition, books, and child care for every student. With this kick start, a surprising number of the students have gone on to complete undergraduate degrees or transformed their lives in other significant ways. And the five of us gained an education of our own as we learned to teach students less prepared but often more highly motivated than the undergraduates we typically teach.[19]

Running parallel with this teaching experience over the last dozen years has been my engagement with another annual two-semester course—this one for students at the opposite end of the spectrum of achievement—first-year Eccles Scholars at the University of Utah. Each year, about 30 students who receive these full-ride, four-year scholarships take my course titled "Ethics, Leadership, and the Humanities." Over two semesters we study the world's great religions, debate classics such as Camus's *The Plague* and Peter Singer's *Practical Ethics*, and confront the most pressing issues facing humans today. Among these students over the last several years have emerged a Churchill Scholar, a Truman Scholar, a Fulbright Scholar, a Rhodes Scholar finalist, and many who have been recognized with other distinctions.

Wrapping Up

It seems fitting to end by summarizing what I have learned about the *practice* of liberal education. What have I gained from 50-plus years of devotion to liberally educating undergraduates, most recently with two such utterly different student populations? Teaching is teaching. And at its best, improvisation plays a key role.

I have become known as "the professor who teaches with his mouth shut," perhaps for good reason.[20] The Socratic method works its magic in classroom environments devoted to liberal education, though work it surely requires. Drawing on a rich trove of personal experiences, a panoply of ideas and theories advanced by American transcendentalists, twentieth-century philosophers and psychologists, and my twenty-first-century colleagues, I follow a few simple principles to broaden the minds and embolden the hearts of my undergraduates.

Make it real. No academic concept or creative expression is beyond improvement by direct contact with the larger contexts within which we live. I try to bring the world into my classrooms and take my students outside the gates of academe—intellectually and physically. Student-led community projects related to the topics under study; engagement with local leaders in the arts, sciences, politics, and religion; class discussions of issues in these arenas that relate to course content—all of these connect theory with practice. And so can such simple devices as organizing peer feedback on student writing and requiring students to grade their own work before submitting it to me for my evaluation. I reserve full responsibility to decide on final grades, but find that, entrusted with the responsibility, students are often harder on themselves than I am. My purpose in asking students to grade themselves is to get them in a habit they will need to continue after graduation.

Know the students. The better I understand each student, the greater my appreciation for their struggles and the keener my ability to ask penetrating questions and encourage their responses. I cannot teach any course effectively without using journals as a primary writing requirement. Reading students' personal responses to assigned readings and class discussions offers me a window into each life that attunes my preparation for coming class meetings—as well as personal interactions outside of class. I make clear that no one should share personal details with me that might cause them discomfort, yet what they do write increases my empathy and lets me gage how well I am conveying the central ideas of the course.

Love the students. This follows naturally from knowing them well. They are *all* bundles of apprehension and hope, with gifts they barely comprehend. From the shell-shocked refugee to the celebrated mathematics recruit, each yearns for validation, rapport, and warmth. As a seasoned professor, I am uniquely positioned to understand and support their growth as human beings and scholars. In a society and world ravaged by anxieties, cynicism, and hate, my students give me hope. I am privileged to invest in their education. It is easy to love them.

Venture with students from the provincial to the universal. We talk in class about the joys of living in an increasingly wide world as our education unfolds. I taunt them all to risk fresh experiences outside their comfort zones, and I offer specific suggestion in one-on-one meetings or with personal messages or handwritten notes. Importantly, students need to know that they don't have to reject their points of origin in the process of becoming citizens of larger and larger communities. We all begin as parochials, whether we are reared in Tonopah, Nevada, or New York City.

Make connections for the students. Again, by knowing the students well, I become much more adept at creating links for them with other faculty, community resources, summer internships, and more advanced students. This element of teaching becomes richer with longevity—the longer one serves at a university and lives in its community, the greater the number and more varied the contacts we can provide our students. Even when we're relatively new, however, a penchant to forge connections for students pays dividends for us as well as them.

Trust the students. Preparing each one to become a free and responsible moral agent is a duty all professors share with respect to the content we teach—whether we believe we have a role in character development or not. (Being in the humanities, it is easy for me to believe I bear a larger responsibility here. But I don't.) At the least, we must prompt our students to consider the human implications—for good and ill—of the knowledge they are acquiring and the powers they are accruing as scientists, political theorists, journalist, actors, educators, or engineers. I hope, as well, that we are becoming increasingly sensitive to the roles they will play as citizens, parents, legislators, and leaders. Trusting students means granting them the space to make their own decisions. "Whatever you become, be a good one," Lincoln said, and it makes a superb mantra for my courses. Class discussions revolve around what "good" means when applied to a Christian, Muslim, Atheist, Democrat, or Libertarian. Initial reactions are often "the strictest," but students quickly shelve that idea in lieu of more nuanced interpretations.

Finally, I believe ethical responsibility comes naturally when we present students with generous and unfiltered information bearing on every issue they study, encourage them to consider as many points of view as possible, and then *give them room* to decide for themselves what course of action or interpretation is best. Their thinking is further stimulated by hearing each other wrestle with the problems at hand, and perhaps by the probing questions of a wise teacher, but the conclusion each reaches through this process will ultimately be her or his own. Through this method, students take ownership of their decisions and, therefore, assume the power to revise them as they learn more or conditions change. How better to prepare students, regardless of background, academic level, or natural gift, to take their places as citizens of a world that cries out for understanding, enlightenment, and principled leadership? How else to keep one's own curiosity, energy, and passion for teaching alive?

Back in the Galapagos Islands, Martin had shown me what I had struggled to learn as a professional educator. I must unleash the natural curiosity of my students, model the perpetual learning—and discipline—of the scholar, show courage in considering new ideas, and, above all, exude joy in the life of the mind. Even beyond knowledge and skill, attitudes may be the most enduring gift I leave my students.

Notes

1. Paulo Freire, *The Pedagogy of the Oppressed* (New York: Bloomsbury, 1970).
2. Thomas Jefferson, *The Portable Thomas Jefferson*, ed. Merrill D. Peterson (New York: Penguin, 1975), 435–36. Jefferson's failure to live up to his own ethical standards notwithstanding, his ideas and power of expression have inspired millions to strive to free their minds of inherent biases.
3. A related account of this story appeared in the *Chronicle of Higher Education*, December 9, 1992, http://www.chronicle.com/article/A-Gifted-Teacher-With-No/70504.
4. Ralph Waldo Emerson, "The American Scholar." In *Selected Essays* (New York: Penguin Books, 1982), 83–106.
5. Abraham Maslow, "Self—Actualizing People: A Study in Psychological Health," in *Motivation and Personality* (New York: Harper and Row, 1954), 149–180.
6. Another rendering of this address was published as the postscript to the book, *The Musician's Walk: An Ethical Labyrinth,* by James Jordan (Chicago: GIA Publications, 2006).
7. Thomas Merton, *Thomas Merton: Love and Living*, eds. Naomi Stone and Patrick Hart (New York: Harcourt Brace Jovanovich, 1985), 3.
8. Maslow used the term "self-actualized" as shorthand for a fully functioning human being, but the latter term is more explanatory and I prefer it.

9. Henry David Thoreau, *Walden and Civil Disobedience* (New York: Penguin Books, 1986), 375.
10. David A. Kolb, *Experiential Learning: Experience as the Source of Learning and Development* (Englewood Cliffs, NJ: Prentice Hall, 1984).
11. Aristotle, "Book II," in *Nicomachean Ethics*, ed. William David Ross (United States: Pacific Publishing, 2011), 13–721.
12. Some of the material in this section was drawn from my chapter on teaching American history in the Venture Course in the Humanities. See endnote 20.
13. John Dewey, *Democracy and Education* (New York: Macmillan, 1916), 239.
14. Walt Whitman, *Democratic Vistas and Other Papers* (London: W.J. Gage & Co., 1888).
15. Mortimer Adler, *Six Great Ideas* (New York, Collier Books, 1984).
16. William G. Perry, Jr., *Forms of Intellectual and Ethical Development in the College Years: A Scheme* (New York: Holt, Rinehart, and Winston, 1970).
17. Deep Springs figured prominently in my education and had a powerful influence on my educational philosophy. Before leading the college, I had also served two terms on its board of trustees. My biography of its founder and the philosophy and history of this unusual institution is the subject of my book, *The Electric Edge of Academe: The Saga of Lucien L. Nunn and Deep Springs College* (Salt Lake City: University of Utah Press, 2015). Deep Springs celebrates the centennial of its founding in July 2017.
18. For an account of Shorris's creation and teaching of the Clemente Course in New York City, see Earl Shorris, "On the Uses of a Liberal Education," *Harper's Magazine*, September, 1997. https://harpers.org/archive/1997/09/on-the-uses-of-a-liberal-education/.
19. For a full account of this Venture Course in the Humanities, see Jean Cheney and L. Jackson Newell, eds., *Hope, Heart, and the Humanities* (Salt Lake City: University of Utah, 2016).
20. Elaine Jarvik, "An Examined Life: U Professor Jack Newell Still Pushes Students to Think, and to Seek Experiences Beyond Academe," *Continuum,* Summer 2015, vol. 25, no. 1. https://continuum.utah.edu/features/an-examined-life/.

CHAPTER 6

The Conversation of a University

George Allan

Clutter

Universities claim to be educational institutions, but they are a lot of other things as well. Unfortunately, these other things have a tendency to crowd out the educational ones because they are more tangible—more visible, more vibrant—and with more immediate payoffs.

Sports teams are an obvious example, particularly high-visibility ones like football and basketball. Successful teams build strong student, alumni, and local area loyalties, considerable media attention, and significant income through television contracts, ticket sales, and responses to direct appeals for money. Less obvious but more significant is a university's support system, the groups that provide food, shelter, medical care, and various forms of personal counsel. Dorms and dining halls offer the comforts and convenience of living at home, classroom and laboratory facilities are at the cutting edge. The aesthetics of the campus, from the architecture of its buildings to the arrangement of its trees and flowers, give the campus an appealing aesthetic. The look and functionality of the university is thought to imply its quality, and positive expectations translate into satisfying experiences. Satisfied customers spread the word to potential customers, resulting in enrollment stability and increased selectivity, which translate into increased income.

G. Allan (✉)
Dickinson College, Carlisle, PA, USA

A. Stoller, E. Kramer (eds.), *Contemporary Philosophical Proposals for the University*, https://doi.org/10.1007/978-3-319-72128-6_6

There is also the question of who benefits from that income, since it is not necessarily the students. Indeed, one of the primary missions of a university is to further knowledge by supporting scholarly research. Some of this research is intrinsic, knowledge pursued for its own sake. Other research is applied, the understanding sought having an identifiable utility for some practical purpose. Research projects can be quite expensive, so much so that to support them the university is in constant need of external funds in order to supplement those derived from tuition, endowment, and general annual gifts. A few of these sources—governmental agencies such as NSF, NIH, or even NEH, and private charities of many kinds—provide research grants for intrinsic research, but the money they make available is small compared to what is provided by sources wanting results relevant to their practical aims: governmental agencies such as the Defense and State Departments, and private corporations hoping to create saleable products and services derived from the research results. Thus, one of the primary functions of a university has little or nothing to do with educating students.

There is a further sense in which a university's educational resources are not used primarily to educate its students. Many students enroll on a part-time basis, commute to campus daily, and/or do their course work online, while committing the majority of their time to a paying job or family care-giving or both at once. These kinds of students typically end up paying more per course credit than fully enrolled students, and they require fewer support services. Their parallel, the part-time faculty, are a good way for the university to reduce what it spends on teaching because these faculty typically receive entry-level salaries and are not eligible for fringe benefits or tenure.

All of these activities are quite legitimate university undertakings, but they are not what justifies a university calling itself an educational institution. Worthwhile as they may be, even necessary to the university's survival, they crowd out education. They undermine it by their attractiveness and by the confusion that tempts us to take them as educational even though they are not.

Actions

Obviously, I have been using the term "education" in a narrower sense than it is typically used. By constricting its meaning, I want to bring into focus the essential feature of education, its beating heart, the necessary condition for calling what faculty or students do an educational activity, the core on which the less constricted meanings of education depend. My aim in what follows is to explain what I understand this essential feature to be and why it is crucial that it not be confused with unessential features. It will be helpful to begin by distinguishing between practical purposes and the conditions constraining them.

An activity often confused with educating, because it is an important feature of what goes on in an academic course of study, is training. Training is a technique for providing someone with the information requisite to carrying out a kind of task. This information is composed of facts, methods for determining and manipulating them, and well-ordered frameworks for organizing them into systems. It also includes historical perspective, an account of how these facts have come to be understood as important. An academic discipline is such an informational structure. Its purpose is to understand something about the world and to devise the tools by which to grasp thoroughly and unambiguously what the things comprising that something are, then to distinguish them from all other things—Descartes' criteria of clarity and distinctness. On the basis of this information, a discipline is able to pursue its purposes more effectively: scientific disciplines to predict facts that have not yet occurred or been identified and aesthetic disciplines to devise works of art that disclose facts that have been long obscured or freshly made.

Actual things are inherently opaque and interdependent, so a discipline's facts are selective abstractions from those actual things. Along with the tools for their discovery and manipulation, they are functions of its purpose. The abstractions are justified by their adequacy to the achievement of that purpose. Hence persons trained in a discipline are experts, possessors of a special sort of information: an accumulated treasure chest of facts and the proper methods for acquiring and organizing them so that they can further the discipline's purpose.

Most institutions in a society are similarly purpose oriented. The members of an institution need to be experts in the methods and systems it utilizes, but they need not all possess the same kind or degree of expertise; a division of labor is typically appropriate. Consequently, an institution's members are usually organized hierarchically, based on the importance of their expertise to its purpose: presidents, owners, generals, and popes at the apex; provosts, CEOs, colonels, and cardinals lower down; assistant professors, day laborers, buck privates, and parish priests at the bottom. Michael Oakeshott calls an institution of this sort an "enterprise association," because "it is relationship in terms of the pursuit of some common purpose, some substantive condition of things to be jointly procured, or some common interest to be continuously satisfied."[1]

People come together to pursue a common purpose and form enterprise associations to do so. The purpose of a sports team is to win games, the purpose of a business to turn a profit, and the purpose of a political party to achieve control of the government. Of course, people can work for such an enterprise without allegiance to its purpose. They may work solely for the wages or as a temporary step toward a job with some other enterprise; they may work for glory or honor or out of loyalty to a purpose greater than but encompassing the enterprise's purpose. Whatever their reason for joining an enterprise association, it is crucial that they possess the training appropriate to furthering its ends. If they want to succeed, they must become skilled in the kind and level of expertise it expects from them.

Many kinds of training can be acquired on the job, through an apprenticeship arrangement or a pre-job training regimen paid for by the hiring enterprise. Other kinds of training can be learned at trade schools or through two-year community college programs. Businesses often require a baccalaureate degree or, after a few years' experience, advanced work in management or statistics or some other specialized field. Law, medicine, academics, and increasingly Silicon Valley-type jobs require an advanced degree and sometimes further work in a probationary status before a person is fully credentialed.

In short, most of us need to make a living, but to do so we need to become experts. And universities are usually a good place to acquire this training; the more so the more professional it is. Training is a part of any disciplinary study, although the jobs for which that training prepares a student can range from something quite specific like hotel management or quite general like comparative literature. My concern is not that universities train students for good jobs, since having an expertise and putting it to effective use are necessary for anyone to become a functional adult member of their society. But it is by no means sufficient. Students also need to learn the conditions under which the pursuit of their purposes is socially permissible. They need to recognize themselves as being members of what Oakeshott calls a "civil association," which he describes as "association in terms of moral considerations," by which he means conditions "not being instrumental to the satisfaction of substantive wants."[2] A civil association does not involve joining with others in order to achieve some shared purpose, but involves instead learning the proper conditions constraining whatever purposes one might pursue. Such conditions are moral in the sense that they apply to everyone in any situation.

An obvious example is learning the rules of a game. The purpose of a sports team is to win games. The players undergo the training needed to be experts in the position they play, in the expectation that if they and their team members are well trained they will achieve their goal, which is to win enough games to become the champions. On game day, they face off against another team which is also composed of players with similar expertise but a different purpose symbolized by their different-colored uniforms. This clash of parochial purposes will end with one team succeeding and the other failing, although failing only for that game, since another day will bring another game where again a clash of purposes will decide anew who is the winner and who the loser. The clash would be mayhem, a no-holds-barred battle between rival gangs, if the game only involved incompatible purposes. But it involves something more, and crucially so, for those purposes must be pursued in accord with the rules of the game. By participating in a sport, we belong not only to a particular enterprise association, our team and its particular purposes, but also to the civil association of all those who play that sport. It is an association in terms of the rules obligating anyone who plays its kind of game.

These rules favor no purpose. They are indifferent to the aims of the players and the hopes of their fans, but they make those purposes possible and the players' expertise necessary by laying down the conditions under which they can win. For without the rules, there can be no game at all. Hence players need to be versed in the rules of their game, and hence a game requires referees to enforce its rules and where necessary to punish those who violate them. Some rule violations are serious enough to be punished by excluding the violator from the game briefly, or until the game's end, or for multiple games. Some violations are punished in the form of fouls that hinder the violator's team or by which the opposing team receives a benefit. The violations of some rules are obvious, others require a referee's judgment, and some are instances of bad sportsmanship punished by the players themselves or perhaps by fan opinion. But to disdain the rules purposefully, violating them because they inhibit or block one's chances for victory, would be to undermine the integrity of the game itself, to win without deserving to, and is punishable with banishment from the game permanently.

At its most fundamental, these rules that are neutral to anyone's purposes are the kind that govern a nation, that constitute it a civil association in the literal sense. Such rules, constitutional and legislative, should be neutral to the private ends pursued by the various enterprise associations under its aegis. When they are not, when a legislative bill or executive decision becomes law without proper procedures having been followed, it is considered illegal, null and void. To implement it nonetheless would violate the conditions legitimating the government's authority to make and enforce the nation's laws. The bill or proposed edict need not itself be neutral; it might be biased, favoring some at the expense of others: lowering the capital gains tax or making it legal for same-sex couples to marry. However, it must adhere to procedural rules that are neutral. Only if appropriate hearings have been held, sufficient time for debate provided in committee and on the floor, a scheduled vote taken with the bill securing a requisite majority, will it then legitimately have become a law. Governments make choices among the conflicting aims of enterprise associations, creating winners and losers, or on occasion finding win-win compromises. A law may be unfairly biased, but if the rules have been properly followed, it is nonetheless a valid law.

The rules of civil association stipulate the limits of what can properly be done in a given social order, what citizens should or shouldn't do no matter what their goals, no matter how important their skills or impressive their status. These are, for a soccer team or a bridge club, for a town hall meeting or a nation, for a civilization or for all humankind, the conditions of living in community with others. They indicate the proper forms of action as such, the normative conditions of any kind of civil order, its moral code.

Practices

I have distinguished enterprise associations from civil associations and discussed how each involves rules that one needs to know in order to function effectively within the scope of its authority. In one instance, rules stipulate actions for achieving some parochial end, for accomplishing some specifiable outcome; in the other, rules are that in accord with which any action in pursuit of any end should be conducted. Each kind of rule-governed action has its appropriate "practice." Actions are what we do, practices are how we go about doing what we do. They are not actions but features of actions, not verbs but adverbs.

The rules governing an enterprise are what Oakeshott calls "prudential": "specifying useful procedures"[3] for relating agents "to one another in the substantive activity of choosing performances contingently connected with a common purpose or interest," rules they are advised to follow if they are to achieve their goal.[4]

Prudential rules stipulate the actions most likely to accomplish an identified purpose. They can be quite explicitly ethical. A society, for example, might be formed as an enterprise association, its aim to help its members lead good lives. Such a society would likely formulate an ethic involving rules that need to be followed to become such a kind of person, and these rules would certainly be taught since they are transmittable information. The good life, these rules might state, is a matter of seeking pleasure and avoiding pain: don't smoke; exercise daily; do unto others as you would want them to do unto you. Or they might state that the good life is a matter of following maxims that distinguish right actions from wrong ones: don't steal; honor thy father and mother; all persons have an inalienable right to life, liberty, and property.

It matters, however, how we go about our pleasure-seeking and pain-avoiding activities or how we go about following the course of action our ethical rule says is just. Prudential rules for being good or doing good involve teachable facts, but they are not reducible to those facts, for they also involve prudential practices, a way of going about doing what the rules of the enterprise say should be done, a style of behaving prudentially.

Willie Talos is a politician who knows how to get things done. You've got to get your hands dirty, he insists, that's the rule you have to follow if you are going to achieve anything. However, the question is not the dirt, says Willie, but how to use it properly. "It's dirt makes the grass grow. A diamond ain't a thing in the world but a piece of dirt that got awful hot.... It all depends on what you do with the dirt," whether you use it to make more dirt or use it to make something good.[5] For good is not something you simply have. "You got to make it ... if you want it. And you got to make it out of badness.... Because there isn't anything else to make it out of."[6] A good politician is not someone who has clean hands, but one who knows how properly to use the dirt that necessarily stains his or her hands.

We learn to swim by swimming. Having been instructed in the way to move our arms and legs, to hold our head and time our breathing, we need to get into the water and try to turn the instructions into a behavior. It's how we move our body through the water that turns thrashing around into awkward progression, which eventually becomes the smooth propulsion of an accomplished swimmer. Initially we attempt to imitate the instructions, which are composed of defined specific steps abstracted from a continuous process. We become a swimmer when we learn how to do that toward which those steps gesture: to propel ourselves through the water in the proper way one should when swimming. We need to keep trying to swim until we get it right.

If we are learning to play the piano, we can be taught the sequence of notes that must be played in performing a piece of music, the fingering to use in doing so, what the marks mean that indicate the duration of a note or chord, the tempo and volume of a sequence. Guided by this information, we can learn to play the piece and can even become proficient in playing pieces involving very difficult sequences. However, what distinguishes a musical artist, a virtuoso pianist, is the ability to grasp how those sequences of sound should be played so as to evoke the aesthetic meaning the composer intended them to convey or the pianist decides they should convey. What the notes are that should be played is obvious, and playing them without mistakes is a skill worthy of our admiration, but how the sequences of chords should properly be played, such that the piece is played in the right way, is an art. How a musical composition should be interpreted can only be discovered by trying to do so, until the right interpretation is achieved.

The civil associations within the scope of which enterprise associations pursue their ends are also guided by rules, ones that Oakeshott calls "moral" because they are "conditions in not being instrumental to the satisfaction of substantive wants."[7] They are like "prevailing winds which agents should take account of in sailing their several courses."[8] The moral practices comprising the ways by which these rules are implemented, those practices the effectiveness of which are essential therefore to civilized behavior, are what students need to acquire if they are to become educated. "What has to be learned in a moral education is not a theorem,"[9] "nor is it a rule …, but how to speak the language intelligently."[10] This shift from useful to moral, from achieving purposes effectively to acting appropriately, is fundamental since it is a shift from unessential features of education, however important they may be, to its essential feature. So it is important that we are clear about how moral practices differ from prudential practices.

Aristotle can be helpful here (*Nicomachean Ethics*, book 6). He distinguishes scientific activities (*theōria*) from productive activities (*poiesis*).

Scientific reasoning is concerned with universals; its purpose is to identify the unchanging realities that govern the uncertain world of ever-changing particulars. The practice that guides this kind of activity is wisdom (*sophia*): a person who reflects wisely will achieve excellence in thinking and is most likely to reach the goal of theoretical reflection, which is the contemplation of first principles. Productive activity, in contrast, is concerned with the ever-changing particulars that science seeks to transcend. Whether in the fine arts or the practical arts, its purpose is to identify the possibilities particulars have for yielding, through the artifice of human imagination and dexterity, resources for fulfilling our needs and assuaging our desires. The practice guiding these activities is skillfulness (*technē*): a person who works skillfully will achieve excellence as an engineer or an artist and is most likely to produce things of great utility or exquisite beauty. Both kinds of activity, scientific and productive, are those of enterprise associations. The practices that, when learned, make those who engage in these activities masters of their art are prudential. Scientific associations depend on scientists able to act wisely, to decide judiciously how best to formulate hypotheses that can be turned into verified theories. Associations of engineers or artists depend on people able skillfully to fashion from available resources products that serve their pragmatic or aesthetic purposes.

Aristotle also identifies a third kind of activity, that of doing (*praxis*). Doings are the actions by which members of a community conduct their mutual affairs. They are not making either theories or things; they are not making anything. Rather, they are realizing the social order which gives such practical pursuits meaning. The practice guiding one's civic activity is good sense (*phronēsis*). It is the practice of choosing sensibly to do those things conducive to the proper functioning of a moral community, ways in which its laws are formulated and constrained in a manner that best establishes a level playing field for enterprise associations of every sort to pursue their varied and often incommensurable ends. A person whose civic choices show good sense demonstrates thereby excellence in matters of governance and public service. Such a person is moral: virtuous neither as a thinker nor as a maker but as a citizen.

The salient feature of civic virtue is that it is intrinsically valuable. What is important is the character of the activity itself and not what results from it. In contrast, the point of engaging in scientific inquiry is not the thinking but the knowledge to which it leads: the addition of a new element to the periodic table, a theory of gravitation more adequate to the experimental data than Newton's, a proof that no consistent logical system can also be complete. The reason for making something lies not in the making but in what is made: the eulogistic poem, the skyscraper able to withstand a hurricane, the bumper crop of corn. But civilly is how people should interact within communities; it is the normative style of their social relationships. If the result is happiness for the participants, this comes as a by-product of their activities rather than as its goal, a retrospective judgment concerning the excellence of their civil intercourse in combination with the excellence of their theoretical and productive efforts and accomplishments. The purpose of *praxis*, of doing, is the doing itself.

Wisdom and skillfulness are prudential practices since they provide advisories on how best to gain verified knowledge or to create valuable objects, whereas good sense is a practice advising persons on how best to interact with others in determining and effecting those or any other purposes. The exercise of Aristotelian good sense is what Oakeshott means by a moral practice.

Practices, both prudential and moral, can be learned but they cannot be taught. They are not information to be found in books or on the internet or noted down during a lecture. They are not instructions to be followed or hypotheses to test. And yet being adept at the prudential practices appropriate to the pursuit of an enterprise association's goals, the know-how and not the know-what, is the difference between being a competent cog in its machinery and being knowledgeable enough and skilled enough to guide it toward the likely achievement of those goals. And possessing the moral practices appropriate to one's community, indeed to civil association of any sort, is the difference between being a resident of that community and being one of its responsible citizens.

Educating students, as opposed to only training them, is creating conditions that make it possible for them to learn how to become both effective leaders and good citizens.

Conversation

How do we learn how to do what cannot be taught? How do we learn to act prudentially or morally? Best, I'm convinced, through conversations. Through a process that can usefully be characterized as follows: you and I and some others are together; one of us poses a problem of some sort, which we think is important, with which we need or want or at least are willing to deal; we tentatively suggest things that might be relevant to the problem's resolution; we imagine possible solutions and ways to attain them; we decide to try one, clarifying as we go our aim and methods. It seems to work, or works but maybe not well, or it fails to work; we critique our results; we repeat the process with adjustments based on what we have learned or pose a different, now more interesting, problem for our consideration.

This rough sketch of a procedural model fits the standard scientific method of hypothesis formation and empirical testing, but it fits as well the process by which a work of art is created, a philosophical essay composed, a moral dilemma resolved. What I want to emphasize, however, is not what is done in each phase of such processes, but how it is done: how a scientist arrives at a fruitful hypothesis, how an artist recognizes the need to adjust a design, how a philosopher decides whether the argument will be convincing, how Sophie makes her choice, how a condition of civilized order is adjudicated. I also want to suggest that the "we" needs to be a group: the collaboration of the hypothesis replicated by other scientists, the solitary artist or recluse philosopher approaching a new work in the light of critical reactions to earlier ones, the citizen supporting or opposing the edicts of governmental agencies on the basis of judgments earnestly debated and sharp differences compromised. A reputation as wise or skilled or moral is the harvest of many occasions of others' responses to our decisions that have affected how we arrive at them.

I refer to the process of learning a moral or prudential practice as a conversation because it involves others and because it is open-ended. Prudential practices differ from moral practices, however, because the openness is for the sake of eventual closure. The conversation goes on, but its aim is, after a sufficient time, to reach closure, as when a scientific hypothesis is finally verified and becomes a theory, a painting is finished and finally sold, a choice is made at a point of no return. Fresh data can put an established theory in doubt, requiring further hypotheses. The artist paints the same subject matter again and yet again, never satisfied with any result even though the art world finds each painting a work of genius. The test of prudential practices is pragmatic, however, their worth the success of the closure they achieve. A prudential practice is wise or skillful if, over the long run, it works, if it serves well the methods by which the enterprise's purposes are achieved.

Moral practices, in contrast, are intrinsically open-ended because there is no outcome by which to measure them. They can be described only in vague generalities: acting fairly, honestly, respectfully, honorably, judiciously. It is foolish for us to think our current moral practices are sensible, because there is no fixed standard, no commonly agreed upon evidence, by which to be confident that we have become proficient in their exercise. We can agree that the evidence is sufficient to find the killer guilty of premeditated murder, but did the judge act judiciously in sentencing him to life imprisonment instead of death by hanging? Or did she act precipitously? What justifies our saying that her choice was arrived at properly, this particular choice in this particular case involving this particular person at this particular time? Is a parent acting wrongly when he angrily sends his eldest son to his room without supper for violating one of the household rules, the one about doing all one's homework before supper, even if the child is unapologetic for unidentifiable but real reasons? These are all questions with plausible but incompatible answers, calling for extended discussion and likely as not leading to no settled conclusion. They are open-ended questions requiring an appropriately open-ended practice for coming to a decision which we think proper even if it is not possible that it be definitive.

The classic paradigm for how one goes about learning how to act morally is Socrates' practice. The early Platonic dialogues are about defining a moral virtue: courage, friendship, self-restraint, piety, justice. Socrates is an adept at pointing out weaknesses in each of the definitions proposed, encouraging his interlocutors to come up with a better definition, probing in turn for its weakness. The dialogues end inconclusively, failing to come to a satisfactory answer, and the parties to the discussions then go their own way, some persisting in the beliefs Socrates has exposed as inadequate, some in a quandary not knowing what to believe. But more than an answer is at stake, for the question is whether those who took part in the conversation have become more courageous or supportive or temperate or pious or just. And whether, through reading the dialogue, we have.

Meno, for instance, comes to Socrates confident that he knows what virtue is but wanting to know whether it can be taught. After a long exchange with Socrates, he acknowledges that he doesn't know what he thinks he knows, that he actually has no idea at all what virtue is. What Socrates says of Meno's slave, while helping him discover that doubling the sides of a square quadruples its volume, applies also to Meno: "At first he did not know …, but then he thought he knew, and answered confidently as if he did know, and he did not think himself at a loss, but now he does think himself at a loss, and as he does not know, neither does he think he knows."[11] But, says Meno perplexedly, if we realize that we do not already know what virtue is, how can we ever come to know what it is? Socrates replies: "I myself do not have the answer when I perplex others, but I am more perplexed than anyone when I cause perplexity in others. So now I do not know what virtue is; perhaps you knew before you contacted me, but now you are certainly like one who does not know. Nevertheless, I want to examine and seek together with you what it may be."[12]

Knowing that we don't know, we search for answers, in the company of other searchers, settling for hypotheses not answers. As Meno and Socrates search together, Meno's responses shift slowly from "that is so" to "I think that is so," from "certainly" to "probably," from "yes" to "appears to be." His humility in the face of the task combined with his willingness "nevertheless" to proceed—to be "brave" and "not tire of the search," to be "energetic and keen on the search,"[13] in constant conversation with other seekers—shows Meno to have become, as was his mentor, virtuous. For virtue is an adverb, a way of acting that becomes an expression of our character through searching diligently for what we do not know and maybe will never know. Virtue is neither a course of action nor a rule; it is a moral practice. To be educated is to have become virtuous.

Conversation has many pedagogical forms, the most obvious of which is a discussion group in which the day's assignment is explored by students articulating interpretations of meaning or hierarchies of importance. They attempt to explain the supposed truth or falsity of truth claims about the proper way to manage hotels or decide beauty contests. They attempt to ascertain why soccer is truly the beautiful game or why the horror depicted in Picasso's *Guernica* is beautiful because it is true. The views of the conversants are critiqued and defended, dissected and expanded, until the bell rings and the students head off for another class exhausted, disgusted, exhilarated, or confused. But changed. Or not, of course, for I am describing a genuine discussion group and not an event in which the professor thinks lecturing is a form of discussing or in which students think discussing is an occasion to promenade their self-defined superiority.

Other pedagogical arrangements in similar but distinctive ways provide opportunities for conversation. In case studies, a problem situation is presented, and students are set to work figuring out what its particular dimensions are, and what facts and connections among facts seem important, what handles it has to grab onto, what routes there might be into its intricacies. Possible resolutions are then proposed and hypothetically applied, the likelihood of their success debated, and a best solution agreed on. This proposed solution is then compared to the one actually implemented by the organization that had found itself in the problematic situation, and the differences between them explored, with each student then writing up a white paper on the case.

Let me emphasize that the point of a case study is not the solution on which the students eventually agree, nor is it how close their decision comes to the one actually arrived at. What is important is how the students go about their analysis, how they choose certain data as relevant rather than other data, how they assess the quality of each one's contribution, and the extent to which their white papers are aware of these matters, able to assess the worth of their contributions to the group's final decision. Indeed, the really important thing about doing case studies is the degree to which students' moral practices, even more than their prudential practices, improve. Learning how to select, integrate, and assess what is at stake, recognizing when analysis is ripe for closure and when premature, is the point. To choose or invent case studies that are conducive to the development of the moral practices essential to critical thinking is the underlying educational challenge. Education is not about solving problems but about knowing how to get about doing so.

Laboratories and field studies, if they are problem oriented, can also provide opportunities for conversational inquiry. However, giving a student an unknown, one that is unknown to the student but known to the professor, is an artificially created problem because it has a correct answer awaiting discovery, like a detective finding the correct perpetrator of the crime. A genuine inquiry asks students to deal with an unknown for which there is not already a ready answer, for which a definitive answer may sometimes turn out not to be available for lack of adequate data or a clearly applicable theory.

Involving students in active faculty research projects is a powerfully effective way for them to learn inquiry. This is not easily done because the research is sophisticated beyond the student's level of expertise, with respect to both the requisite knowledge about existing studies relevant to the current project and the methodological techniques required. So faculty can be easily tempted to assign students gopher tasks or set them to work on unimportant subsidiary projects, the main value of which is to keep the students from getting in the way of the project's primary task. Substantive student involvement means finding ways for students, working alongside senior researchers, to make contributions that play an identifiable role in the research project—evidenced, in the sciences, by their names appearing among the authors of the project report or, in the humanities, by explicit information about the nature of their contributions in the publication's acknowledgments section.

When students work side by side with faculty, however junior their colleagueship might be, they learn not merely the appropriate rules of a discipline but also its proper practices. They learn to hypothesize like physicists do, mold clay on a potters' wheel like ceramicists do, generalize like philosophers do, dig deeply and with care like archeologists do. They learn to think like well-educated people do: imaginatively, systemically, critically—and open-endedly, their achievements always seen by them as needing to be corrected, enhanced, transcended. So teaching faculty need to be engaged in research and research faculty need to teach. And when that happens in the right ways, the university funding for research becomes a significant occasion for educating students.

The fundamental problem with conversations is that they need to take place in small groups if all the students are to take part. A conversation is not a spectator sport; the learning is in the conversing not the outcome. Outcomes are important, to be sure, and judging whether they are adequate, coherent, or even relevant is a crucial phase in the conversation. But learning how to inquire effectively, how to think like a scientist, artist, or citizen is not by learning outcomes but by learning how properly to go about getting to outcomes and how reasonably to judge them true or beautiful or good. A dozen students in a 50-minute equitably distributed conversation can each make only four one-minute contributions to the exploration of a problem. Add a few more students, and the conversation is for a portion of the class only a lecture, the smallness of the group irrelevant because the learning has become something taught and so could as easily have been taught in an auditorium.

Size is not the only difficulty, time is as well. For a conversation has no beginning, middle, and end. It starts when a perplexity is voiced and ends when the voices tire, and in the course of its explorations, it is liable to wander off along unexpected pathways into further perplexities. The conversation goes on until it has gone on enough. Socrates argues with Agathon and Aristophanes about the difference, if any, between comedy and tragedy, until his comrades are too drunk and too exhausted to continue. Socrates' last claim, "that authors should be able to write both comedy and tragedy: the skillful tragic dramatist should also be a comic poet,"[14] is left for further consideration at some other time. The conundrum of scheduling classes in an academic calendar is that they need somehow to be temporally open-ended if they are to provide an opportunity for students to learn a moral practice, to learn how to think and feel and act open-endedly. Nonresidential students, not living near one another nor eating in a common dining area, make the problem even worse because it is difficult for them to continue their discussion after class over coffee or a beer, or to start it afresh in someone's dorm room late at night.

Learning the moral practices that should govern any of our purposes best occurs in contexts where the purposes at stake in the learning don't matter much. The trouble with the "real world," the world outside the ivory towers of academe, is that the consequences of failing to achieving a purpose, or failing to recognize a purpose as inappropriate, are unforgiving, even a matter of life and death. Learning the proper constraints to our actions—what is appropriate even if not expedient, what is right even if an obstruction to reaching our goal, how we ought to proceed even if what we do has no payoff—means focusing on what, when learned, becomes a matter of our character, our style of acting, a habit of considering the conditions and not just the consequences of what we want or need.

It is by making mistakes about how to do what we do, how we select our goals and the means to their actualization, discovering what went wrong and why, leading to proposed changes thought to be more focused and informed, that we become more insightful judges of how properly to act. Yet it is one thing to receive a poor grade because one has arrived at a wrongheaded solution to a case study problem; it's quite another thing to destroy the firm's reputation because we could not resist fudging data to make our contract bid more attractive. Occasions in the university for learning how to shape purposive undertakings appropriately and how to become alert to the bite of the moral practices that constrain those purposes, even at the price of undermining them, need to be playful moments, through which students slowly develop the practices that will serve them well when the stakes are no longer trivial.

Children learn how to be adults by pretending they already are, baking imaginary cakes for their friends, dressing up in their parents' work clothes, or just in the high-heeled shoes or carpenter's belt that symbolize those clothes. Playing at being Mommy or Daddy, they try on adult behavior and thereby begin learning how to be what they will soon become. They practice the practices needed in their maturity. Students need to play at being archeologists or business executives, religious mystics or novelists, as a way to help them decide not merely how they want to be employed but how they want to live their lives in all its other aspects. They need to discover who they are and who they could become, but even more so they need to discover how they ought to become what they become. And the way to do this is not by looking up average annual salaries or googling for information about the kinds of jobs that will be needed a decade hence; nor is it ignoring a sense of their own dignity, their dreams and hopes, responsibilities and obligations, their sense of the demands of truth, the depths of beauty, and the lures of good. It is by developing character: learning how properly to go about finding local sites likely to harbor forgotten cultural artifacts, learning how judiciously to go about deciding which rules for using residence hall recycling containers will be best not merely for oneself but also best for the environment and for one's grandchildren, learning how humbly to go about disciplining one's body and mind until emptied of self-concerns, or learning how insightfully to write a first line that grabs the reader's attention. It is through these specific contexts that students begin to think sensibly about who they ought to be and what that might mean for what they do.

This kind of playfulness, where what the purposes pursued are takes second place to learning how to act appropriately in pursuing them, encourages the spatial and temporal expansion of our horizons. We are invited to try on others' ways. As children play at being adults, university students should play at being Greek or French by traveling to those countries for yearlong study programs where they have a chance of learning how to live as people in those countries live, the surprising complexity of this soon dawning, and the success of the study program measured by the students' awareness of the vast distance still remaining no matter how great their effort. The sojourn need not be physical. It can be in Socrates' Athens or Robespierre's Paris, traveling there by histories and novels, works of art and philosophic treatises, as indeed by those ways one can also travel to contemporary Greece or France. Learning how to trade one's culture for another is a lesson in humility, in realizing that a culture is all about its moral and prudential practices, and that these practices are tasks of a lifetime. What is learned by playing with the ways of strangers, coming to know them as friends even if not as family, develops the beginnings of an open-ended inviting style of thought and action, a depth and breadth of mind and heart that are the hallmarks of a civilized person.

Moral Universities

Our primary task as educators, therefore, should be to nurture neither learned scientists nor talented artists and artisans, but good citizens. Always, of course, the university needs to be teaching new generations of students to be scientists and artists, doctors and lawyers, soldiers, bakers, and candlestick makers. But these activities are not our primary task. Our communal life should not be guided by a science of society pointing the way toward some sort of ideal realization of the common good, nor should it be turned over to engineers and technocrats who would draft a program to get us from now to that ideal most expeditiously. Both alternatives have been suggested, but they presume a nation is an enterprise association and therefore that the nation's leader is a corporate CEO or five-star general, whose task is to lead us to the promised land or the classless society or a nation with a government governing least. The advocates of such national enterprises have dominated our politics over the last few centuries and have contributed tragically to the world's turmoil. But social good is neither a truth to be perceived nor a product to be engineered. It is an activity to be done, and its excellence lies in the adverbial character of the actions performed, in the moral capacity of persons to choose sensibly among complex and always changing possibilities.

We are properly educated only if we are conversant with the adverbial dimension of what we do. As enterprising associates, we need to know how to decide the manner of our purposings at the same time as we are determining our goals and methods, to develop a repertoire of prudential practices from which to draw in doing so. Practical success, however, is not enough. A civilized community is more than the sum of the enterprises at work within its boundaries. It is also, and essentially, a civil association. Only if we have learned how the moral conditions that constrain our enterprises function, learned them so well that they are the manner of our habits, the shape of our character, will our actions be marked by moral excellence. Just as our purposeful actions will be judged wise or competent if we are guided by appropriate prudential practices in choosing our ends and choosing means well suited to effect those ends, those actions will also be judged sensible if rooted not only in our cultural heritage but also in our natural heritage, in our sense of ourselves not only as Americans but also as human beings living precariously on a fragile planet. We cannot be taught to be moral, and yet unless we have learned how to act morally, we will not have been properly educated. Power in the hands of wise fools, no matter how competent they might be, is the bane of a civilization. A university that willfully graduates "sophomores" betrays the culture for which it was meant to be a bulwark.

A university education should provide understanding; it should provide technical competence; it should provide training in the skills required for making difficult choices among conflicting goods; and it should also provide instruction concerning ends worthy of pursuit. But a university should refrain from attempting to teach its students the one thing no one can provide another: a capacity for acting properly. The essence of a university lies not in what it teaches but in fostering an environment in which making the best choices is thought less important than learning the moral conditions for doing so. Oakeshott says it with metaphorical clarity:

> Most guides are confident that they know the way. The worst know only this; the best are those from whom we may learn also how to climb and are somewhat careless of the destination. And the marks of their teaching remain, even if long after we found ourselves to have learned what they never taught.[15]

Making the education of students primary is a serious matter because it is so problematic. It is hardly due solely to the failure of the universities that training and money raising rather than educating is their primary focus. Yet the universities by their misfocus are abetting the problem rather than addressing it. What to do is a conundrum, but how to go about figuring out what to do and how to go about doing it are matters the university can do something about. It can encourage the conversations and playful explorations that afford opportunities for its students to learn the moral practices of civilized society and for its faculty and staff—from president and deans to cleaning crews and food preparers and including alumni/alumnae and benefactors as well—to relearn or refurbish those practices in their own lives, both public and private.

Seeking ways to bring the development of people able to function morally back into focus as the properly beating heart of every university is an impenetrably difficult adventure to undertake. But undertaking it is the right thing to do.[16]

Notes

1. Michael Oakeshott, *On Human Conduct* (Oxford: Clarendon Press, 1990 [1975]), 114.
2. Michael Oakeshott, *On Human Conduct*, 122.
3. Ibid., 55.
4. Ibid., 115.
5. Robert Penn Warren, *All the King's Men: Restored Edition* (Boston: Houghton Mifflin Harcourt, 2001 [1946]), 66.
6. Robert Penn Warren, *All the King's Men: Restored Edition*, 359.

7. Michael Oakeshott, *On Human Conduct*, 122.
8. Ibid., 70.
9. Ibid., 78.
10. Ibid., 79.
11. Plato, "Meno," in *Complete Works*, trans. G. M. A. Grube., ed. John M. Cooper (Indianapolis: Hackett Publishing Company, 1997), 84a.
12. Plato, "Meno," in *Complete Works*, 80c-d.
13. Ibid., 81d-e.
14. Plato, "Symposium," in *Complete* Works, trans. Alexander Nehamas and Paul Woodruff, 223d.
15. Michael Oakeshott, *On Human Conduct*, 182.
16. Some of the ideas in this chapter were initially developed in *Rethinking College Education*, especially Chapter Four: "The Essence of a College." For more, see George Allan, *Rethinking College Education* (Lawrence, Kansas: University Press of Kansas, 1997).

PART III

Generalization: Reconstructive Proposals for the University

CHAPTER 7

Culture and the University: An Ecological Approach

Ronald Barnett

Introduction

In his now classic book, *The University in Ruins*,[1] the Canadian, Bill Readings, argued—among other things—that the link between culture and the university was severed some time back. Partly, he argued, it was a consequence of the retreat of the nation-state. Partly, too, implicit in his account, it was a consequence not just of the ways in which the university had been colonised by instrumentalism, but it was also a consequence of the succumbing of the university to extreme bureaucratisation (reflected in the empty idea of "excellence"). And partly, too, it was a result of a thinning out of culture in the wake of an advancing globalisation. "This is a crisis for the University … We are no longer excluded [from culture] because there is no longer any culture to be excluded from. … The global system of capital no longer requires a cultural content in terms of which to interpellate and manage subjects."[2] Was Readings right? *Has* culture been irrevocably been severed from the university?

Today, the very idea of plunging together the concepts of university and culture seems to be otiose. There *is* something of a literature that is interested in culture and the university but not in the sense I want to explore here. That literature is actually a mix of literatures, but they are

R. Barnett (✉)
University College London Institute of Education, London, UK

A. Stoller, E. Kramer (eds.), *Contemporary Philosophical Proposals for the University*, https://doi.org/10.1007/978-3-319-72128-6_7

united in being interested in the internal culture of universities. Issues that come into play are those of the "cultures" of academic disciplines, student "cultures" and the organisational cultures of universities. It will be noticed that in each case, the plural "cultures" is used. The implication is that researchers have recently taken their point of departure from a sense that the culture within the university exhibits itself in different ways, either across universities or within a single university. There is, by implication, nothing approaching a universal culture to which the university can ally itself or which might be commonly associated with the university. The other point is that, as already remarked, these cultures are internal to the university.

My focus here differs on both counts, however, namely, culture as significantly—in part at least—*external* to the university and as a *universal* entity. I shall argue that a positive idea of culture in relation to the university may be glimpsed, but it requires a new dual conception of this relationship. I shall sketch this picture by beginning from an idea of the ecological university and, accordingly, will argue for a university infused with an ecological culture.

Higher Education and Culture: The Seeming End of a Positive Idea

The very idea of putting culture and university together gives rise these days to a certain squeamishness. This situation is—at least in some places—of recent moment. In the UK, in 1963, a major national committee on higher education (chaired by Lord Robbins) published its report and identified therein, as one of four main aims of higher education, the transmission to students of "a common culture."[3] The implicit assumption was that there existed a common culture, into which students could be inducted. That idea, that there is or even could be a common culture—even if any validity attached to the notion—is now surely passé. Society in the twenty-first century is now fragmented, such that any talk of a common culture holds no water.

There is a further observation here. To speak of culture as such—without qualification and without differentiation (into "cultures," plural)—is to imply a reference to "Culture," with a capital "C," as it were. Implicitly, to speak of culture, unadorned by reference to particularities, is to smuggle in a supposition that there is such a thing as "Culture"; namely, that there exists a recognised set of significant symbols and meanings—and carriers of such symbols and meanings—within a society, and understood as constituting its culture. (In Western society, characteristically, such symbols and meanings have been presumed to be exhibited by its language in its most sophisticated forms (in its great novels or poetry) and in its music (especially its "classical" music, fine art and other great art forms. Opera, in drawing together all of these art forms, could be said to be the epitome of this sense of culture).)

In this vein, a more generous idea of culture was suggested famously by Ortega y Gasset as the foundation of the very idea of the university. "Culture is the *vital* system of ideas of a period," and it was a regret of his that "the contemporary university … has abandoned almost entirely the teaching or transmission of culture," understood as "the 'culture' of the age."[4] He went on to propose that "the primary function of the university is to teach the great cultural disciplines,"[5] and he went on to specify those that gave insight into the physical world (physics), organic life (biology), historical processes (history), social life (sociology) and the plan of the universe (philosophy). The essential idea here was a university "which teaches the ordinary student to be a cultured person … ."[6]

This whole idea—that it is meaningful to assume the presence of, and to refer to and promote, such a conception of culture, as a unified set of the "great" symbolic achievements of a society, and which had some universal validity—has surely fallen into a pit out of which it cannot escape. There were far too many question-begging assumptions in this promotional idea of culture. Who was to determine which symbols or artefacts or activities were to stand as a society's culture? Why should opera be placed ahead of dog racing or baseball (if, indeed, that was to be the order of preference)? Or even physics and philosophy ahead of plumbing and pottery? Such a sense of culture seemed, on inspection, to contain a hierarchy of preferences that could not stand by itself.

Inquiry into culture, not least in the context of education, therefore took two quite disparate paths. Some, a diminishing number, sought to hold to a positive view of culture. By "positive," I mean simply that there were those who considered that culture played a positive role in society and that, therefore, the task of education was to initiate pupils and students into that culture. This stance split two ways, between a culture being common in its being held commonly across society and a culture being common in its possessing edifying potential for a people in common. More fully, on the one hand, as intimated, some felt that a "common culture" could readily be identified that could be felt to bind a disparate society together; it was self-evidently obvious what constituted *this* culture. Others felt, to the contrary, that the culture that could play a positive role in society was but a portion of the total culture of and in society, and it was part of the task of educational institutions—especially universities—to identify and hold to that selection. Who was to make such a selection? It followed that only those possessed of refinement and taste, a cultured elite, were in a position to do so.

All of these positive views of the role that culture might play—and with it a place for education as a space for promulgating the culture so identified—ran into difficulty. Where, in society, lay any such common culture? Was the very idea not a mask for an elite to smuggle in its own definition as to what was to be included in the common culture? Perhaps this common culture was less a culture that was commonly present in society now but one that the elites felt should become common. This was, it might be suggested, the interpretation of culture implicit in the British Broadcasting Corporation (BBC) in its early days, in the 1940s and 1950s. In those days, the BBC could unashamedly determine the forms and content of its transmissions, which reflected choices as to the culture that it felt was suitable for the masses newly tuning into the national broadcaster. This was a high-to-low transmission of culture.

Critical Difficulties

But if those espousing a positive view of culture could quickly be felt to be suspect, more critical perspectives also ran into difficulty. In a sense, this side suffered from an embarrassment of riches, as the critical perspectives continued to proliferate over time and still continue today so to proliferate. Among the critical stances were—more or less—the following: as stated, a sense that any selection of a culture (to count as "the Culture" of a society) could not be legitimated without embarrassment; a sense, too, that any such cultural selection was a kind of social class imperialism, with the choices representing the cultural tastes of the upper classes; and a broad concern that any selection was both arbitrary and was bound to be unduly narrow. These critical perspectives did not stop there but continued to multiply. First, there emerged a sympathy for the culture of the manual or "working" classes, such that it was felt that there were to be found much of value there; at least, there was no good reason to neglect the cultural forms there.

Secondly, and radicalising that line of thought, there was no, and *could not* be any, kind of universal culture. Culture was the expression of the forms of life of the manifold social classes, ethnicities and communities. The key problem of culture was now turned around. It was no longer that of trying to detect some kind of pure universal culture but, to the contrary, of the relationship of the many cultures present in society to each other. Were they compatible or contradictory? Were there any overarching values or "imaginaries"[7] across them, or did they stand, Robinson Crusoe-like, in their own cultural islands, in effect voicing their own languages and mutually incomprehensible to each other?

It was in this vein that emerged such concepts as "multiculturalism" and "interculturality," giving birth both to a recognition of a mix of cultures present in society and to the hope—or was it a fear?—that those cultures might find some way of living with the "other" and recognising the "strangers" in their midst, and even extending "hospitality" to them. This set of critiques, in short, opened to a strident empathy with the culture of the other and was accompanied by a disinclination to judge (that one culture was superior to another).

But these critical perspectives were not and are not finished. There was a line of thought going back to the Frankfurt School of Critical Theory in which culture provided a crucial category and was a carrier of the double perspective offered by that school of thought. On the one hand, in its neo-Marxist leanings, culture was seen as a way of gentling the masses. The Frankfurt School saw in the "culture industry" an impoverishment, indeed a gross reduction of culture, especially as it was taken up by corporate interests.[8] Culture, in other words, here took on an ideological function, serving to close horizons and thought, in effect, to be a carrier—as we may put it—of a hermeneutic closure. This culture provided on emotional anaesthetics that prevented an opening to large and troubling horizons, of the kind that genuine art could provide. And this was the other perspective of the Frankfurt School in relation to culture.

If the first perspective amounted to a savage critical assault on what passed for culture, this latter perspective was emancipatory in its content and its hope. Here, culture was seen as a space for offering authentic and counter-cultural ideas, symbols and emotions that would provide a release from the balm of the immediately sensed world into a different world. "[a]rt ... can contribute to changing the consciousness of the men and women who could change the world."[9] This is why art and culture were so significant for the Frankfurt School for they provided a means of societal liberation. Indeed, this was crucial to the Frankfurt School, which had sought to provide a new Marxism. If the forces of production could not provide the means of salvation, then perhaps emancipation could be found in the cultural "superstructure" of society.

More recently, this critical perspective has itself been radicalised amid the globalised world of the twenty-first century. This critical perspective draws into itself a marked dual sensitivity, on the one hand, towards the cultures of the world and fuelled by a sense that definitions of culture have been impregnated with the sentiments of the powerful nations. Alternatively construed as a West-East polarity or, perhaps more commonly, as a North-South polarity (de Sousa Santos 2014),[10] the claim has emerged that the cultures of the East and/or the South are not only neglected but that it is assumed that those of the North and/or the West are the cultures that really matter. In short, there is a kind of tacit global cultural war, with the cultures of the North and/or the West attempting to impose their hegemony worldwide.

Academic Culture: Glimpsing It and Losing Sight of It

Of course, this brisk overview of "culture" would need to be considerably nuanced, not least because there have been cultural wars within the dominant cultures. Notoriously, in England, there arose in the early 1960s a violent argument over the "two cultures" as science and the humanities came to be portrayed. For C.P. Snow[11]—both a scientist and a novelist—one could not be considered to be cultured in modern society unless one was familiar with the second law of thermodynamics, the point being that science was so significant a set of meanings and frameworks that anyone not on the inside of it was culturally deprived. For the Cambridge academic and literary critic, F.R. Leavis,[12] it was Snow who was culturally destitute, being representative of the "technologico-Benthamite" hold on society which in turn threatened culture, the epitome of which lay not just in the English novel but in *The Great Tradition* exemplified by Austen, Conrad, Eliot and Hardy.

That internal debate over culture and its demarcation has been superceded by what might be termed the Eagleton-Scruton debate. For Eagleton, fully on top of all of the complexities of culture as just outlined and more besides, and for whom "culture" was "one of the two or three most complex words in the language,"[13] a proper stance in relation to culture was one of interrogation and critique. Precisely because it has been used as an ideological carrier of dominant interests and because its manifold forms were associated with different groupings and social strata, culture deserved to be investigated and its pretentions and thinness unmasked. For Scruton,[14] on the other hand, culture was still deserving of a more sympathetic treatment. The task of the critic was much more that of identifying and holding up its internal characteristics and qualities as a means of public and social edification. If Eagleton was the arch-critic of culture, Scruton was the arch-endorser, at least of culture "at its best and finest" (as it might be said).

A more dispassionate and less judgemental account of culture in the academic world derived from the work of Tony Becher. In 1989, he published *Academic Tribes and Territories*[15] which sought to analyse and differentiate the cultures of different disciplines. Two axes were identified—those of soft/hard and pure/applied—so forming a grid space within which individual disciplines could be located. Essentially, this approach played up the *epistemological cultures* of disciplines, as derived from academics' understandings of their own disciplines. Over time, not least through Becher's later collaboration with Paul Trowler, a richer and more nuanced illumination of academics' cultures has emerged, more sensitive to context and to the wide range of activities and roles that academics play out in their various "academic identities."[16]

Such an approach can be widened to include the "cultural scripts" of students, not least since universities may be enrolling heterogeneous cohorts of students drawn from many nationalities and ethnicities, with their diverse cultures. Such cultural eclecticism may well be celebrated through multicultural events on campus.

"Culture" and "University": A Communicative Option?

What, then, can we make of the juxtaposition of "culture" and "university"? Can a narrative be woven that brings the two concepts together in a substantial way? Perhaps the key questions are these: can it sensibly be said that the university should have a concern with or for culture, and, if so, what form might that concern take? In what way(s) might it be exhibited by the university? And would or could any such exemplification carry across the university's disciplines, or would it be confined to certain disciplines? Could there be a kind of universal—that is, a transdisciplinary—culture characteristic of the university as such?

A generation ago, Alvin Gouldner[17] came close to offering an answer to these questions. The university could be said and be seen to exemplify a "culture of critical discourse." In other words, the academic culture (or, at least, an academic culture) was not to be sought in particular kinds of knowledge and understanding (a la Ortega) but rather in ways of legitimately coming to know the world. It was to a communicative sense of academic culture that we should turn.

However, that culture, Gouldner implied, was being gradually usurped by an incipient academic culture that was much more technical and instrumental in character. This could have been read as a particular version of the "two cultures" debate. But in that case, true culture—the culture of critical discourse—was to be found only sparingly, if at all. It was more a matter of glimpsing the kind of culture that the academic life, at its best, exemplified. This was not, and perhaps could not be, a culture universally characteristic of universities.

Jürgen Habermas, in his monumental *Theory of Communicative Reason*, might be called in aid here. For Habermas precisely posited that there lay within rational discourse a universal set of conditions—"validity conditions"—that acted at least as a standard against which any discourse purporting to be rational could be judged. There was just a limited set of such conditions: sincerity, truthfulness and appropriateness. These were held to be presuppositions of a rational discourse.[18] The problem is that it was never entirely clear why just these and only these should be felt to constitute the validity conditions of a rational discourse.

What of argumentativeness, that is, of the disposition to proffer and pursue an argument? What of persistence, of the disposition to continue doggedly with a conversation? What of courage, namely, the capacity to enter a debate even when the argumentative tide is running in entirely another direction? What of the capacity to listen, to give and take, empathically to enter the ground of the other? And what of creativity, of an interest in rocking the boat and coming forward with ideas, perspectives and frameworks that might, in due course, not only come to constitute a new paradigm but open an entirely new way of understanding the world? And so perhaps one could go further, identifying conditions that seemingly have to be upheld if a *culture of rationality* is to be sustained within the university.

Keeping Culture and Reason Apart

As we go on, identifying positions that have been held either in relation to culture in general or in relation to academic culture, the ground continues to dissolve beneath us. There seems to be no stable surface here. And just such a sentiment could be held to be characteristic of the present age. Postmodernism, relativism, complexity theory, the metaphors of the liquid and of the ever-spreading but ever-disorderly rhizome and the concepts of disruption, instability and supercomplexity and even of "multiculturalism": all these and others speak to a fragmentation, an insecurity characteristic of modernity (a modernity that seemingly began at least a hundred years ago, at the dawn of the twentieth century if not earlier).

Against this background, it is no wonder that talk of culture can generate a frisson. Much better to avoid the subject altogether. If it has to be invoked, then let it be subject to a sense of and a respect being granted to many cultures; no demarcation or hierarchy here! And/or let it be subject to critique, and its pretentions and hidden interests lay bare. What purports to be culture will turn out, if we pursue it long enough, to be a set of interests in which one society or one social group or one set of disciplines or even one set of universities attempts to protect and advance its own (obviously superior) interests.

The logic of this stance when pressed turns ultimately into this stark position, that reason and culture are to be kept apart and that any project of reason—such as might be sustained by the university—should have no truck with culture as such. There is a legitimation of this position to be had. Ernest Gellner, in his book, *Reason and Culture*, observed that this was, in effect, Descartes' position. Salvation—or knowledge at least—was to be obtained by pure reason, a reason that deliberately eschewed anything that might contaminate the reasoning process. "In effect, [Descartes] proposed a programme for man's liberation from culture."[19] So perhaps this whole venture—here, in this chapter at least—is doomed from the outset. Clear blue water should be kept between reason and culture and, thereby, between culture and the university.

The University: A Cultural Void?

On the basis of the overview given here, therefore, it appears that the ideas of "university" and "culture" cannot be put together in any substantive way that is suggestive of a universal programme of action. There is no idea of culture that can serve as a basis on which universities might be orchestrated that can hold both across disciplines and across universities. Yes, it might be that individual universities might adopt their own ethos and individual disciplines or departments might exhibit a culture of their own. It might even be that a university administration might exhibit a particular kind of organisational "culture," perhaps with some dirigiste or even democratic flavouring. And universities might adopt policies that seek to be sensitive to the cultures of their international students (from across very many countries). But it is far from clear, on the account so far provided, that there is to hand anything that might serve as a universal set of principles or ideas that universities, qua universities, might feel obliged to attach themselves to, so far as the maintenance, let alone the advancement, of culture is concerned.

To put the matter another way, there appears to be nothing by way of a responsibility that befalls a university so far as culture is concerned. There seems to be no set of conditions that a university should fulfil so as to support, encourage and sustain a particular kind of culture that is characteristic of an institution that is termed a "university." There are, to put it starkly, no necessary cultural conditions that have to be realised in order to warrant the institutional title of "university." A position of "cultural pessimism" may seem to be warranted.[20]

This is a serious and a practical matter. Across the world, universities are proliferating. (There are around 26,000 institutions with the title of "university.") And in many nations, the title of "university" is a protected title; or, at least, certain conditions have to be satisfied in order that a university might receive public monies. It, therefore, is—or could seriously be felt to be—a matter of public policy as to whether it is felt some particular kind of culture attaches or should attach to any institution bearing the title of "university." This is the matter that must now occupy ourselves in the rest of this chapter: might there be *any* necessary conditions that attach to a university so far as its culture is concerned? Might it be justifiably felt that being a "university" is indicative of the presence of a certain kind of institutional culture?

The End of Culture in the University

The matter before us, therefore, is precisely one of "institutional culture." Our starting point, it will be recalled, was that of Bill Readings and his suggestion, his thesis indeed, that culture had slipped away from the university. On his analysis, it is as if putting "university" and "culture" together constitutes a category mistake. They can no longer be said to stand in any serious relationship with each other. In response, and on the basis of our review here, there could be said to be two options in front of us.

First Option: Readings Was Wrong Far from culture and university not, as it were, having relations with each other, there is the contrary. There is a surfeit of actual relationships. The culture of the academics, especially in their separate disciplines; culture as might be evident from a micro-study of academics in their daily lives; the culture of student life, in all its multicultural variety; organisational or managerial culture, in the ways in which a university is governed and organised and the power relationships it promotes; and even culture in the way in which a university disposes itself in the world, not least in its stance towards other nations: all these manifestations of culture are testimony to culture being present in the university in manifold ways. More, picking up the concept of "cultural capital" as bequeathed to us by Pierre Bourdieu,[21] it is evident that culture as held within and as bestowed by the university may be a source of power and influence in the wider society. Whether philosophy or nanotechnology or medicine or even computer science bestows the greater cultural capital is now a moot point. But such a question points only to there being a multiplicity of spaces of culture in the university. Readings, then, was wrong.

Second Option: Readings Was Absolutely Right The manifestations of "culture" just enumerated are only exemplifications of a thin culture. Readings, it might be said, was concerned with a culture in a much thicker sense. One might be tempted to suggest that the instances of university culture just identified are furnished by and through a sociological perspective. They are instances of actual social relationships and meaning structures between social groups, both within the university and in the institutional relationships between the university and the wider society. Readings, on the other hand, was concerned, it might be said, with a philosophical idea of culture. It was a sense of culture as representing some universal claims about the human condition and its place on Earth. Those claims might be held by a small group—an elite, a clerisy—and they might change over time (as Raymond Williams displayed in his magisterial analysis of *Culture and Society 1780–1950*).[22] Nevertheless, this sense of culture appeals to the possibility of there being a set of symbols or meanings that offered universal value. That the symbols or meaning structures or creative arts in question were valued in practice by a small group was immaterial. What was significant was the universal significance that such representations possessed. And it was precisely this sense of culture that was now in question in modernity.

Moreover, the suggestion that the university could be said to be associated with this idea of culture could hold no water. No legitimation was available. For Readings, that legitimation hole arose as a result of the loss of the nation-state. For culture offered a national identity, even if it had universal pretentions. That the university was "in ruins" was very much in part due to the dissolution of the tight connection between culture and the state.

It will have noticed that these argumentative paths—in the wake of Readings' thesis—lead to a similar conclusion, in a way, even though they start off in opposite directions. Both options, that Readings was right and was wrong, lead to the conclusion that the association of the university with what might be termed high culture or Culture with a capital "C" (as it were) is passé. And various options open. Culture in the context of the university can be critiqued (as a hidden source of power) or neutrally analysed (as a set of culture*s*, plural) or lamented over (as a loss); and yet other stances would be possible. The university is at once saturated with multiple interests and has become a multicultural space, *and* it has simply lost its unifying and motivating and, indeed, moral and universal force—except as a source of power via cultural capital. What is no longer possible is for culture to be identified, and heralded and lauded, and protected and deliberately advanced by the university. The foundations on which such a cultural project for the university could be established have—it seems—dissolved.

Overcoming Squeamishness

Culture—if it is anything—is a supremely value-laden human achievement. It is a way of sustaining society through those symbols and meanings and activities to which is attached the highest value. And the university as a major institution in society, and as a source of creativity in meaning systems, has—or at least had—a major responsibility in bringing intelligent minds into a first-handed engagement with such "culture." But such a value-laden and value-oriented function for the university has now been put in question and even been extinguished.

This reading has much on its side. The very term "culture" evokes a squeamishness in serious circles. At best, it has to be kept at arm's length. One cannot get too close to it (for it will disintegrate or be seen to an emperor without clothes). Or it will evoke a sense of unjustified exclusion (even if the very idea of culture implies membership of some kind of community) and even domination, whether within or across societies. And, in turn, the prospect that it can be put together with the idea of the university, in any programmatic vein, must generate even more frisson. Culture, as an idea, simply will not carry weight so as to inspire any kind of programme of action say, of the kind required, in helping a university develop its self-understanding or its perceived mission in the world.

In practice, universities seem to intuit this set of considerations. At least, we may speculate that the term culture will be seen to be barely evident in websites of universities around the world. The university seems to want to project itself as a culture-free zone, at best, holding itself out as a neutral space for warring contestants to work out their argumentative angsts. But I want to suggest some caution here. The idea of culture may yet have some substance even or especially in relation to the idea of the university. That, at least, is a prospect still worth exploring.

I shall start with an assertion. Far from it having no serious part to play in filling out the idea of the university, the concept of culture is both inescapable and essential. It is inescapable in that the university is an institutional space that is projecting meanings into society. Whether it acknowledges it or not, the university *is* a cultural site; and it is so not just in that it serves as a space for cultures to have their day (so to speak) but that it is—as it were—*agentically* cultural. And it so to a significant degree and it is so in multiple ways. All this deserves some unpacking.

An implication of its being agentically cultural is that the university has in front of it cultural choices. Which kind of culture does it wish to reflect within itself, as its dominant cultural mode, qua institution? Through which form of life, which values, which way of engaging with the world, does it wish to be known? Responses to such questions, if they are to carry water, need to have a generalisability to them. They cannot be answers that represent and extend the culture of particular groups or interests.

To start, let us make a distinction between the way in which a university might conduct itself internally and the way in which it might engage with the external world; and here, let us begin with its internal disposition(s).

It will be recalled that reference was made to Alvin Gouldner's idea of a "culture of critical discourse." This is surely a worthwhile starting point.

Here, we may say that the dominant culture of the university should take on such a character. That is to say, no assumption needs to be made as the empirical presence of such a culture. Whether universities do in fact disport themselves in this way, and would be seen to sustain such a culture, is a separate matter. Indeed, there is much evidence to suggest that universities often do not exhibit such a culture; but that is a separate matter. What is before us is the conceptual matter as to whether and/or in what ways it makes sense to bring the concepts of university and culture together, and in a normative spirit.

A way in here is to ask the question: does the university, qua university, have *any* responsibility in relation to culture? Are there aspects of culture that are necessarily to be observed if an institution is to live up to the appellation "university"? A first step is to press Gouldner's notion of a culture of critical discourse. This is a powerful concept in that it has, potentially at least, application across all disciplines and all academic-related activities of a university. It is, thereby, a universal in this context, to be understood to be part of what is meant by the term "university." To put it in another idiom, that of Alasdair MacIntyre, we may say that it is an "internal good" of the university.[23] Even though the university is an institution, it is associated with practices that bear the imprint of a culture of critical discourse.

But what might be meant by that phrase? It is far from being self-explanatory. A critical discourse is self-evidently one that is critical but in what way or ways? I shall assert that, for our purposes and as a first shot, a critical discourse is one that minimally favours conversations in which there is both expositions of ideas (understood broadly to encompass statements, musings, daring suggestions, explorations without definite outcomes, imaginative patternings of representations, orderly presentations of significant data, and so on) ***and*** a space in which such expositions can be evaluated. This deliberately open-ended formulation says nothing about the manner in which such presentations may be made nor, and even more importantly, about the manner in which such presentations may be critiqued. Such conditions are to be avoided, at least for the moment.

There is, however, an immediate problem with this "culture of critical discourse" approach, even if it is accompanied by a specification of the communicative conditions through which it might be realised. The problem is that this approach can all too easily lead to a debating society conception of the university. The university is understood to have a culture of reasonableness such that it can run internal debates effectively. It knows the rules of reasonable—and critical—discourse and cares about them and tries to uphold them. It offers a space of reason.[24] This is not without merit. Indeed, we have only to look at the news from campuses around the world to gain a sense of its contemporary pertinence. Not infrequently, speakers are "no-platformed," or university authorities are obliged to act in the face of threatened major disturbances, cancelling invitations to speakers whose presence is resented. Researchers are found to have manipulated data. And journal editors are seen sometimes to exert excessive control over papers that are published. So the university's pretensions to uphold a culture of critical and reason-oriented discourse need both philosophical legitimation and practical defending.

Such a set of reflections echoes T.S. Eliot's suggestion that, in fulfilment of their cultural function, universities "should stand for the preservation of learning, for the pursuit of truth and [so far as practicable] the attainment of wisdom."[25] However, this is a limited idea of culture in the context of the university. It is not unimportant; far from it. But it is unduly limited, being confined to an upholding of the university as a space for reason-based inquiry and communication. It is an idea of culture and the university that will appeal to lovers of debate—a not dishonourable tradition that harks back to the mediaeval disputations. But this would undersell the combination of "university" and "culture."

An Ecological Approach

One way of widening the narrative is to bring a third term into view, alongside "university" and "culture," namely, that of "ecology"—in short, to develop an ecological approach in comprehending the relationship between the concepts of university and culture.

Culture, I suggest, may be considered to be an ecosystem—or, at least, possess properties of an ecosystem. These properties include those of a system or set of entities that possess some degree of interconnectivity, some actual or potential powers of sustainability, a real presence in the world, its internal range and scope (its "diversity") being in jeopardy, being somewhat impaired or falling short of its possibilities, impinging on humanity and humanity being so implicated having, in turn, responsibilities towards the further flourishing of the ecosystem in question. Each of these characteristics of ecosystems is exhibited by culture, *and* each characteristic can be seen, too, to be in play in the relationship between universities and culture.

These aspects of culture and universities raise, in turn, some searching questions. For instance, what is the range of cultural entities that characteristically come into play in the university? What is the scope of culture as an ecosystem? The most significant of such cultural entities are surely those of symbol systems, exemplified in concepts, disciplines, languages and interpretative frameworks. To what degree, it may be asked, are these entities flourishing? Are they fecund? Are they as wide as they might be? Or are they unduly restricted? For example, the concern being evinced over the fate of the humanities suggest that there is at work within the academic world a kind of disciplinary-cultural imperialism, in which disciplinary work is being dominated by the STEM disciplines.[26] Or, to take another matter, questions may be asked about the character of academic life and its effect on the flourishing of symbols and frameworks. Might it just be that the sheer press of academic life in the twenty-first century is causing a shrinking of horizons, and a culture of safety, as academics—subject to audit and performance management regimes—are subtly encouraged to remain within current paradigms rather than seek to overturn them?

What, then, against considerations of this kind, would it be for a university to possess a concern for the cultural ecosystem in which it is implicated? Responses to such a question should distinguish between different manifestations of culture, in particular the (a) *cognitive*, (b) *practical*, (c) *communicative*, (d) *expressive* and (e) *material* domains. In (a) the cognitive domain, so as to encourage fecundity and a critical culture, conditions would include openness, sight of nomadic intellectual practices and disciplinary and cross-regional (North-South) generosity. In (b) the practical domain, such a university would be willing to "speak truth to power" and maintain its intellectual integrity. In (c) the communicative domain, a university would approach an open communicative structure, exhibiting a culture of truthfulness. In (d) the expressive domain, such a university would constitute itself as a space for expressive experimentation, for example (as some universities are doing), opening its grounds for public displays of sculpture and art. And in (d), the material domain, is the dominant cultural symbol to be that of the computer (and internet devices more generally), it having succeeded the book in this respect? Will the university connive in the end of the book?

The point here is that it is conditions and exemplifications such as these that may enable the university not merely to sustain its cultural ecosystem but to advance it. As implied, actually, there are several cultural subsystems here in which the university is implicated. And the ecological university will be concerned to play its part in advancing those regions of the cultural ecosystem in which it moves, either necessarily or potentially. A university necessarily moves amid languages, symbols and frameworks of understanding. It necessarily works through communication processes of various kinds and so exhibits a discursive culture. It necessarily is involved in cultural pragmatics—as we might term it—as it engages with the wider society. And in all of these sub-cultural domains, possibilities open in relation to which it possesses agentic powers. The ecological university will seek to bring its disciplines into contact with each other and so enliven its cognitive culture. It will be vigilant in looking out for ways in which its communication processes are being impaired, for instance, in the "no-platforming" of speakers.

But this ecological story of the university is by no means exhausted; and perhaps in a way it has barely begun. For now a quite different relationship between the university and culture comes into view, once an ecological perspective is entertained. The prospect opens—and it is a profound prospect—of a university taking on and coming to evince an *ecological culture.* Such a university would be a university that has a care for the many ecosystems in which it is implicated; certainly, as stated, the ecosystem of (i) culture itself but also the ecosystems—in particular—of (ii) knowledge, (iii) the wider social institutions, (iv) the economy, (v) persons (including students but persons more generally), (vi) learning (both at the personal and societal levels) and (vii) the natural environment. These are seven ecosystems that, together, constitute the *ecological hinterland* of the university. The ecological university not just has influence on these ecosystems—for all universities have such influence—but does so intentionally. Moreover, it strives, within its compass, to play its part in advancing each ecosystem, in enhancing the health and vibrancy of each one.

The ecological university can accomplish all this only through an ecological culture running through its institutional veins. This is a necessary condition of what it is to be an ecological university, that it cares about its total environment and seizes its agentic powers to realise its ecological leanings.

This is not just a metaphysical calling but plays itself out practically and imaginatively. Each university will have its own ecological possibilities, but they have to be worked at. They have to be envisaged and discerned and brought to fruition. Such a programme of action has to be realised throughout a university (if it is to warrant the title of "an ecological university"). It will, for instance, require a distributed leadership, in which pools of autonomy are granted throughout the university such that staff at all levels feel encouraged to be imaginative in discerning possibilities that succeed in advancing the university's ecosystems. For instance, it will seek to widen the public sphere, in taking students into experiential spaces, in advancing societal learning. It will bring disciplines into new relationships with each other. It will encourage new economic models based on imaginative conceptions of the "commons." And it will play its part in sustaining and even strengthening the natural environment.

To bring off a never-ending programme of these kinds calls for institutional energies that are themselves continually replenished; it calls for an internal culture of critical discourse; and it calls for ecological responsibilities to be felt throughout the university. In short, this university will be marked by a vibrant *ecological culture*. This culture will percolate the ecological university, calling for and generating a vital energy, and impart a stance of care and concern towards the whole world.[27]

Conclusions

Contemporary thinking about the relationship between the ideas of university and culture, and about ways of exemplifying that relationship, has run into the sands, a situation that seems to be self-acknowledged. One looks in vain to see any serious and positive account of that relationship, and one looks in vain to see mention of "culture" in universities' accounts of themselves and their aspirations. That cupboard is distinctly bare. It is as if that very juxtaposition—of "culture" and "university"—brings on only nervousness or embarrassment, or both. Ortega's effort to locate a cultural mission of the university in certain disciplines now seems to be passé.

There have been some efforts in the recent past to glimpse anew such a relationship, but they have tended to be doubly thin conceptualisations. On the one hand, it wasn't clear as to the extent that they were intended to be descriptive of a veneer of cultural presuppositions at work deep within universities. On the other hand, it wasn't clear as to the extent they were intended to be suggestive of possible programmes for universities: were they to apply to all disciplines? Were they intended to apply not just to the large research ("world-leading") universities but also perhaps to all universities? Such uncertainties and difficulties are entirely explicable, given the frisson that accompanies any claim as to Culture, with a capital "C" so to speak. With what authority dare one attempt to demarcate a sphere labelled "Culture" with the disregarding of other possible ways of life—even of academic life—that might be involved?

My argument here has been that such thinness and such doubts are not necessary stances and positions in relation to universities and culture. To the contrary, I have suggested that a bold and affirmative conception of that relationship may justifiably be held and advanced. The tack I have taken is to look towards "the ecological university" (as I have termed it), and this idea plays out at *two levels*. Firstly, the ecological university would take an interest in itself as *a space of culture*, in the five ways intimated here (communicative, cognitive, practical, material and expressive). Secondly, the ecological university would itself exemplify a particular culture, *an ecological culture*. This would be a culture of concern for the world in all of its manifestations, especially as manifest in the ecosystems in which the university is especially implicated.

These ecosystems range well beyond the natural environment; and I have identified seven such systems, which together constitute an ecosphere of the university. The characteristic culture of the ecological university, accordingly, would be one of active—and even proactive—concern for that total ecosphere, with the university playing its part. This culture would ooze through the veins of the ecological university, potentially present in all of its parts. It would enliven the university, orient it in the world and enable it to hold steady when all around is in chaos (as is the case in some jurisdictions in the world). This culture is not a nice add-on, but is the essence of the ecological university.

Notes

1. Bill Readings, *The University in Ruins* (Cambridge, MA and London: Harvard University Press, 1997).
2. Bill Readings, *The University in Ruins*, 103.
3. *Higher Education: Report of the Committee appointed by the Prime Minister under the Chairmanship of Lord Robbins 1961–63* (HMSO: London), 7, para 28.
4. José Ortega y Gasset, *Mission of the University* (London: Kegan Paul, Trench, Trubner and Company), 44, 47.
5. José Ortega y Gasset, *Mission of the University*, 58.
6. *Ibid.*, 73.
7. Charles Taylor, *Modern Social Imaginaries* (Durham and London: Duke University, 2007).

8. Theodor Adorno and Max Horkheimer, *Dialectic of Enlightenment* (London: Verso. 1989 [1944.]), 120–67.
9. Herbert Marcuse, quoted in: Charles Masquelier, *Critical Theory and Libertarian Socialism: Realizing the Political Potential of Critical Social Theory* (New York and London: Bloomsbury, 2015), 65.
10. Boaventura de Sousa Santos, *Epistemologies of the South: Justice against Epistemicide* (Abingdon and New York: Routledge, 2014).
11. C.P. Snow, *The Two Cultures and a Second Look* (Cambridge, UK: Cambridge University Press, 1978 [1959]).
12. F.R. Leavis, *English Literature in our Time and the University* (London: Chatto and Windus, 1969).
13. Terry Eagleton, *The Idea of Culture* (Oxford and Malden, MA: Blackwell, 2000), 1.
14. Roger Scruton, *Modern Culture* (London and New York: Bloomsbury, 2006).
15. Tony Becher *Academic Tribes and Territories* (Stony Stratford: Open University Press/Society for Research into Higher Education, 1989).
16. Tony Becher and Paul Trowler, *Academic Tribes and Territories: Intellectual Enquiry and the Culture of Disciplines* (Buckingham: Open University Press/Society for Research into Higher Education, 2001); Paul Trowler, Murray Saunders, Veronica Bamber, eds., *Tribes and Territories in the 21st Century: Rethinking the Significance of Disciplines in Higher Education* (Abingdon and New York: Routledge, 2014).
17. Alvin Gouldner, *The Future of Intellectuals and the Rise of the New Class* (Basingstoke: Macmillan, 1979).
18. Jürgen Habermas, *The Theory of Communicative Action*, Volume 1 (Cambridge, UK: Polity, 1991), 99.
19. Ernest Gellner, *Reason and Culture: New Perspectives on the Past* (Oxford, UK and Cambridge, MA: Basil Blackwell, 1992), 13.
20. Oliver Bennett, *Cultural Pessimism: Narratives of Decline in the Postmodern World* (Edinburgh: Edinburgh University, 2001).
21. Pierre Bourdieu *Homo Academicus* (Cambridge, UK: Polity, 1990).
22. Raymond Williams, *Culture and Society 1780–1950* (London: Penguin, 1966).
23. Alasdair MacIntyre, *After Virtue: A Study in Moral Theory* (London: Duckworth, 1985), 194.
24. David Bakhurst, *The Formation of Reason*. (Chichester, UK: Wiley, 2011).
25. T.S. Eliot, *Notes Towards the Definition of Culture* (London: Faber and Faber, 1962 [1948]), 123.
26. Martha Nussbaum, *Not for Profit: Why democracy needs the humanities* (Princeton and Oxford: Princeton University Press, 2010).
27. Ronald Barnett *The Ecological University: A Feasible Utopia* (Abingdon, UK and New York City: Routledge, 2018).

CHAPTER 8

Education for Citizenship in an Era of Global Connection

Martha Nussbaum

In 424 BC, the great ancient Greek comic playwright Aristophanes produced his comedy *Clouds*, about the dangers of Socrates and the "new education." A young man, eager for the new learning, goes to a "Think Academy" near his home, run by that strange notorious figure Socrates. A debate is staged for him, contrasting the merits of traditional education with those of the new discipline of Socratic argument. The spokesman for the old education is a tough old soldier. He favors a highly disciplined patriotic regimen, with lots of memorization and not much room for questioning. He loves to recall a time that may never have existed—a time when young people obeyed their parents and wanted nothing more than to die for their country, a time when teachers would teach that grand old song, "Athena, glorious sacker of cities"—not the strange new songs of the present day. Study with me, he booms, and you will look like a real man—broad chest, small tongue, firm buttocks, small genitals (a plus in those days, symbolic of manly self-control).

His opponent is an arguer, a seductive man of words—Socrates seen through the distorting lens of Aristophanic conservatism. He promises the youth that he will learn to think critically about the social origins of apparently timeless moral norms, the distinction between convention and nature. He will learn to construct arguments on his own, heedless of

M. Nussbaum (✉)
University of Chicago, Chicago, IL, USA

A. Stoller, E. Kramer (eds.), *Contemporary Philosophical Proposals for the University*, https://doi.org/10.1007/978-3-319-72128-6_8

authority. He won't do much marching. Study with me, he concludes, and you will look like an intellectual: you will have a big tongue, a sunken narrow chest, soft buttocks, and big genitals (a minus in those days, symbolic of lack of self-restraint). Socrates's self-advertisement, of course, is being slyly scripted by the conservative opposition. The message? The new education will subvert manly self-control, turn young people into sex-obsessed rebels, and destroy the city. The son soon goes home and produces a relativist argument for the conclusion that he should beat his father. The same angry father then takes a torch and burns down the Think Academy. (It is not made clear whether the son is still inside.) Twenty-five years later, Socrates, on trial for corrupting the young, cites Aristophanes's play as a major source of prejudice against him.

Should a liberal education be an acculturation into the time-honored values of one's own culture? Or should it follow Socrates, arguing that "the examined life" is the best preparation for citizenship? Almost 500 years later, in the very different culture of the Roman Empire of the first century AD, the Stoic philosopher Seneca reflected on this same contrast, creating, in the process, our modern concept of liberal education.

Seneca begins his letter by describing the traditional style of education, noting that it is called "liberal" (*liberalis*, "connected to freedom"), because it is understood to be an education for well-brought-up young gentlemen, who were called the *liberales*, the "free-born." He himself, he now announces, would use the term "liberal" in a very different way. In his view, an education is truly "liberal" only if it is one that "liberates" the student's mind, encouraging him or her to take charge of his or her own thinking, leading the Socratic examined life and becoming a reflective critic of traditional practices. (I say "him or her" not just out of contemporary political correctness: Stoic philosophers of the first century AD wrote at length about the equal education of women and defended the view that women as much as men should lead the examined life.) Seneca goes on to argue that only this sort of education will develop each person's capacity to be fully human, by which he means self-aware, self-governing, and capable of recognizing and respecting the humanity of all our fellow human beings, no matter where they are born, no matter what social class they inhabit, no matter what their gender or ethnic origin. "Soon we shall breathe our last," he concludes in his related treatise *On Anger*. "Mean-while, while we live, while we are among human beings, let us cultivate our humanity."

In the contemporary United States and Europe, as in ancient Athens and Rome, higher education is changing. New topics have entered the curricula of colleges and universities: the history and culture of non-Western peoples and of ethnic and racial minorities within the United States, the experiences and achievements of women, the history and concerns of lesbians and gay men. These changes have frequently been presented in popular journalism as highly threatening, both to traditional standards of academic excellence and to traditional norms of citizenship. Readers are given the picture of a monolithic highly politicized elite who are attempting to enforce a "politically correct" view of human life, subverting traditional values and teaching students, in effect, to argue in favor of father-beating. Socratic questioning is still on trial. Our debates over the curriculum reveal the same nostalgia for a more obedient, more regimented time, the same suspiciousness of new and independent thinking that finds expression in Aristophanes's brilliant portrait of the old education and in the defense by Seneca's contemporaries of the old-style liberal education in a time of rapid social change.

But we can defend many of the changes in traditional models of liberal education as a response to the challenge of Socrates and Seneca, and I shall argue that it is this paradigm we should consider, as we think about what is well done and not well done in contemporary reforms of liberal education. In fact, by and large, the changes that we witness are attempts to follow Seneca's advice to cultivate our humanity. Seneca's ideas of cultivated humanity and world citizenship have had a large influence on modern democratic thought, through Thomas Paine and other writers who were steeped in Stoic ideas. And these ideas have long been at the root of our aspirations, as we construct a higher education that is not simply preprofessional but a general enrichment and a cultivation of reasonable, deliberative democratic citizenship.

Today's universities are shaping future citizens in an age of cultural diversity and increasing internationalization. All modern democracies are inescapably plural. As citizens within each nation, we are frequently called upon to make decisions that require some understanding of racial and ethnic and religious groups in that nation, and of the situation of its women and its sexual minorities. As citizens, we are also increasingly called upon to understand how issues such as agriculture, human rights, ecology, and even business and industry are generating discussions that bring people together from many different nations. This must happen more and more if effective solutions to pressing human problems are to be found. But these connections often take, today, a very thin form: the global market that sees human lives as instruments for gain. If our institutions of higher education do not build a richer network of human connections, it is likely that our dealings with one another will be mediated by the defective norms of market exchange. A rich network of human connections, however, will not arise magically out of our good intentions: we need to think about how our educational institutions contribute to that goal.

The new emphasis on "diversity" in college and university curricula is above all, I would argue, a way of grappling with the altered requirements of citizenship in an era of global connection, an attempt to produce adults who can function as citizens not just of some local region or group but also, and more importantly, as citizens of a complex interlocking world and function with a richness of human understanding and aspiration that cannot be supplied by economic connections alone. In this attempt, the humanities—often viewed as useless and equally often viewed with suspicion, as scenes of subversion—play a central role.

The systems of university education in Europe have a disadvantage from the point of view of implementing my proposals. All colleges and universities in the United States offer approximately two years of "liberal education" (sometimes also called "general education") in many subjects before asking students to focus primarily on a major subject for another two years.[1] They do this out of the conviction that higher education is not simply preparation for a career but a general enrichment of citizenship and life. Thus, every undergraduate, whether focused on business or mathematics or art history, will take whatever basic required courses the university sees fit to require. This of course is not the situation in Europe, where for the most part (Scotland being a partial exception) students simply study one or perhaps two subjects and are admitted to the university in order to pursue that subject. Moreover, professional courses such as law and medicine in the United States are offered only as second degrees, after the candidate has already received a bachelor's degree in some other subject, whether history or philosophy; in Europe students enter such courses directly. So here is another source of humanistic richness in the professional education of US students that is absent from most European universities.

It is particularly difficult for a system structured in the European way to integrate new forms of study, such as women's studies and the study of race.[2] Most students do not want these to be their major subject, because they do not lead to many job opportunities. Most often, they are sought out, in the United States, as either basic required courses or so-called elective courses, that is, courses where the student has some latitude to roam outside the major subject. In Europe, it has been exceedingly difficult for programs in these areas to get established. In both England and The Netherlands, I know that people in women's studies feel extremely marginal at most major universities, because the structure of degree programs does not include them, or, if it does, few students want to make the major commitment of doing an entire degree in that area. But short of that, students have little access to those subjects, and the programs are typically more helpful to faculty doing interdisciplinary research than to students.

Ultimately, I believe, the universities of Europe will need to think about adding a segment of general "education for citizenship" to the curriculum, in order to realize the goals that I shall outline here. I shall return to that theme in my conclusion. But now let me proceed with the ideas themselves.

In *Cultivating Humanity*, I have argued that three capacities, above all, are essential to the cultivation of humanity in today's interlocking world. First is the capacity for critical examination of oneself and one's traditions for living what, following Socrates, we may call "the examined life." This means a life that accepts no belief as authoritative simply because it has been handed down by tradition or become familiar through habit, a life that questions all beliefs and accepts only those that survive reason's demand for consistency and for justification. Training this capacity requires developing the capacity to reason logically, to test what one reads or says for consistency of reasoning, correctness of fact, and accuracy of judgment.

Testing of this sort frequently produces challenges to tradition, as Socrates knew well when he defended himself against the charge of "corrupting the young." But he defended his activity on the grounds that democracy needs citizens who can think for themselves rather than simply deferring to authority, who can reason together about their choices rather than just trading claims and counter-claims. Like a gadfly on the back of a noble but sluggish horse, he said, he was waking democracy up so that it could conduct its business in a more reflective and reasonable way.

This norm of deliberative democracy has not been fully realized in our modern democracies, any more than it was in ancient Athens. As I write this, the American controversy about the election continues, and one may observe the extent to which mere rhetoric and the attempt to sway public opinion dominates over all attempts to reason clearly and well. Good reasoning can be found on both sides, and at many levels. But so often the dominant concern of both journalists and politicians is for how things "play," for "spin," rather than for the quality of ideas and arguments. There are some philosophers, notably Alasdair MacIntyre, who see in our situation a defect of modernity itself, and who hold that things were much better in ancient Greece, when we had a secure grasp of an end for human beings imposed by authority on all citizens. I think that MacIntyre is quite wrong here, both about the Greeks and about us. The Greek democracy had just the same problems that we have: that is why Socrates's mission was necessary. Nor does the solution to those problems require abandoning the Enlightenment's commitment to self-critical reason, or the commitment to pluralism and toleration that is at the heart of our modern ways of life. Political deliberation can proceed well in a pluralistic society—if citizens have sufficient respect for their own reasoning and really care about the substance of ideas and the structure of arguments. The responsibility for instilling these values lies with our institutions of higher education.

I believe that for this reason instruction in philosophy is an indispensable part of higher education. Of course, it can't be just any type of philosophy course. Large lecture classes are not very much use, because the main purpose is to give students practice in analyzing and constructing arguments in a Socratic fashion. What is crucial is plenty of opportunity for interchange between faculty and students, and many writing assignments, carefully evaluated with ample comments. More or less useless, in my view, are required courses where lectures are given to a huge number of students, who have no opportunity to discuss or to write papers, and evaluation is based on a multiple-choice examination. This is not Socratic philosophizing, this is unhelpful regurgitation.

Many American universities and colleges, however, have been able to construct curricula that require all students to take one or two courses in philosophy. (Often this is an excellent source of employment for talented PhD students, who are either teaching assistants in such courses or in some cases teach sections of the courses on their own.) Let me mention just one example of the effects of such required courses, a student named Billy Tucker at a business college named Bentley College in Waltham Massachusetts. Tucker went to Bentley because he planned to focus on marketing and did not want a more general academic education. On the other hand, the college wisely requires two semesters of philosophy from all students and hires enough faculty to keep class size around 25 students per faculty member. Tucker encountered a very gifted teacher, originally from India, named Krishna Mallick. Mallick began with the trial and death of Socrates. (I met Tucker at my fitness center, where he was working behind the desk, reading Plato's *Apology* and *Crito*.) She also showed a film about Socrates, and the combination really grabbed the imagination of this young man, intelligent but lacking in confidence about his own intellect. He thought it was so odd that Socrates did not escape from prison when he had the chance, but died for the activity of arguing. This example stung his imagination, and he got more and more interested in the course, which continued by presenting the basics of formal logic, so that students could then discover examples of valid and invalid reasoning in newspaper editorials and political speeches. Tucker did really well on this and was amazed to discover that he actually had a good mind—he had thought he was not that kind of person. Finally, the course assigned students roles in debates about issues of the day that were to be staged before the class. Tucker was puzzled to discover that he was assigned to argue against the death penalty, although he actually supports it.

Tucker told me that this experience gave him an entirely new attitude to political debate: he had never understood that you can argue on behalf of a position that you do not hold yourself. Now he is more likely to see political argument as a process of searching for good answers, rather than just a way of making boasts and establishing your status. Now he knows how to ask what assumptions both sides share, where their differences really lie, and what the structure of each argument is. As you can guess, I think that this result is exactly what Socrates was after, and an exceedingly important result, in a democracy where most people learn their norms of political rhetoric from the rhetoric of talk radio. I believe that such abilities can be cultivated in many different types of classes, but that philosophy does the best job of educating the mind in this way—if taught with sufficient attention to the student's starting point, and with sufficient imagination and creativity. The important thing is that students need to be made active, and I must emphasize that the proposals I am making are no good at all in the absence of resourceful creative teaching that really respects the mind of the pupil.

But now to the second part of my proposal, citizens who cultivate their humanity need, further, an ability to see themselves as not simply citizens of some local region or group but also, and above all, as human beings bound to all other human beings by ties of recognition and concern. As I have already said, the world around us is inescapably international. Issues from business to agriculture, from human rights to the relief of famine, call our imaginations to venture beyond narrow group loyalties and to consider the reality of distant lives. As Seneca and the ancient Stoics knew, we very easily think of ourselves in group terms—as Americans first and foremost, as human beings second—or, even more narrowly, as Italian-Americans, or heterosexuals, or African-Americans first, Americans second, and human beings third if at all. We neglect needs and capacities that link us to fellow citizens who live at a distance, or who look different from ourselves. This means that we are unaware of many prospects of communication and fellowship with them, and also of responsibilities we may have to them. We also sometimes err by neglect of differences, assuming that lives in distant places must be like ours and lacking curiosity about what they are really like. Cultivating our humanity in a complex interlocking world involves understanding the ways in which common needs and aims are differently realized in different circumstances. This requires a great deal of knowledge that American college and university students rarely got in previous eras, knowledge of non-Western cultures, of minorities within their own, of differences of gender and sexuality.

As I have said, Americans face particular dangers in this area. On the one hand, we have been thinking about internal minority traditions for a long time, and to some extent we have succeeded in understanding our nation as a multicultural society, where the contributions of different groups all make a difference. I shall return to that point later. But on the other hand, Americans, unlike most citizens of Sweden, are tremendously ignorant of the other nations of the world. They have little factual knowledge and little curiosity. Institutions of higher education have a crucial role to plan in combatting these cultural vices. So, as I describe this part of my proposal, I shall focus on teaching involving non-Western cultures, although I shall later return to the role of learning about internal minorities.

Education for world citizenship has two dimensions: the construction of basic required courses that all students take (part of the "liberal education" or "general education" component of a US university education) and the infusion of world-citizenship perspectives in more advanced courses in the different disciplines. Let me give one example at each level, making my description concrete enough to give you an idea of the actual classroom experience.

At Scripps College, in Pomona, California, the balmy climate and the lush campus sometimes make studying difficult. As a visitor from Chicago, I feel like getting outside as quickly as possible. Nonetheless, the freshman class, consisting of 250 women, crowds the lecture hall, with eager energy and expectation. Their freshman core course is about to meet, to discuss feminist criticisms of the international human rights movement as a false Western type of universalism, and responses that other feminists have made to those criticisms, defending the human rights movement against the charge of Westernizing and colonizing. (That's what I am there to do.) Called "Culture, Values, and Representation," this course, required of all first-year university students, replaced an earlier required course on Western civilization course that had gotten tired and diffuse. It studies the central ideas of the European enlightenment—in political thought, history, philosophy, literature, and religion. (The staff is drawn from many different departments; instructors take turns giving lectures, and each leads a section.) The study of the Enlightenment is then followed by critical responses to it: by formerly colonized populations, by non-Western philosophy and religion, by Western postmodernist thought, including feminist thought. The course then turns to responses that can be made to those criticisms.

This course obviously does not provide a systematic investigation of even one non-Western culture, but it sets the stage for inquiry and questioning. Its clear focus, its emphasis on cross-cultural debate and reasoning, rather than simply on a collection of facts, and its introduction of non-Western materials through a structured focus on a single set of issues, all make it a valuable introduction to further questioning on these issues. Above all, the course has merit because it plunges student's right into some of the most urgent questions they will need to ask today as world citizens: questions about the universal validity or lack of validity of the language of rights, the appropriate way to respond to the legitimate claims of the oppressed. I like this course so much that I have imitated its structure in a seminar that I will soon be conducting for leaders of business and industry at the Aspen Institute in Colorado.

Pedagogically, this course gives a good model of how to deal with large class size without diluting instructional quality. The lectures themselves, of course, do not involve much faculty-student interaction—although a dramatic and problem-oriented lecturing style can do a lot to involve students and prevent passivity. But there is at least one discussion section every week, led by a faculty member, and the sections have around 15 students. There are also very regular writing assignments. Students thus are rendered active participants in the working out of the ideas of the course, and the open-ended structure of criticism and reply indicates to them that these are ongoing problems in human life that they will have to approach as best they can, rather than closed issues to which some knowing intellectual has found a solution. The spirit of questioning carries over into the informal life of the campus. Because all students take it, discussion of its questions fills the dining halls and residences.

Another important aspect of the course's success that needs comment is its interdisciplinary character. Faculty from many different departments are brought together and given financial support to work on the course during the summer, exchanging ideas and getting one another's disciplinary perspectives. Such financial support for development of new ideas in a deliberative interdisciplinary framework is crucial to making the course as rich as it is.

Now let me turn to a program that aims to affect more advanced course in each of the disciplines. Again, I begin with a description of what faculty are actually doing.

At St. Lawrence University, a small liberal arts college in upstate New York, the snow is already two feet deep by early January. Cars make almost no sound rolling slowly over the packed white surface. But the campus is well-plowed, even at Christmas. In a brightly lit seminar room, a group of young faculties, gathering despite the vacation, talk with excitement about their month-long visit to Kenya to study African village life. Having shared the daily lives of ordinary men and women, having joined in local debates about nutrition, polygamy, AIDS, and much else, they are now incorporating the experience into their teaching—in courses in art history, philosophy, religion, women's studies. Planning eagerly for the following summer's trip to India, they are already meeting each week for an evening seminar on Indian culture and history. Group leaders Grant Cornwell from Philosophy and Eve Stoddard from English talk about how they teach students to think critically about cultural relativism, using careful philosophical questioning in the Socratic tradition to criticize the easy but ultimately (they argue) incoherent idea that toleration requires us not to criticize anyone else's way of life. Their students submit closely reasoned papers analyzing arguments for and against outsiders' taking a stand on the practice of female circumcision in Africa.

Again, notice that the success of this program requires interdisciplinary discussion and financial support. The unique travel component was very important to these faculty but is probably not absolutely indispensable. What is indispensable is the time to sit together and read and work together, learning how the problems of a region of the world look from historical, economic, religious, and other perspectives. Each faculty member will ultimately go on to incorporate this knowledge into the standard course offerings in his or her field. Thus, economics now offers a course on "African Economies." Art history offers a course focused on representation of the female body in African art. Philosophy offers a course in cultural relativism and the critique of relativism. Biology offers a course in AIDS and the African experience. These courses enrich standard course offerings in each of the departments.

These same two levels need to be considered when we consider what students should learn about minorities and previously excluded groups in their own nation. Once again, the basic courses that all students take should contain a new emphasis on the diversity of the nation's own population.

Thus, in many American universities, discussions of US history and constitutional traditions now contain a focus on race, the changing situation of women, and the role of immigration and ethnic politics that would have been previously unknown. At the same time, courses in each of the disciplines must increasingly incorporate and are incorporating these perspectives. Literature courses increasingly focus on works by women and expressing the experience of excluded racial minorities; economics, art history, biology, religious studies—all these can find ways of confronting students with the reality of a multi-ethnic and multicultural society. Even in disciplines as traditional as the Greek and Roman Classics, we now study the lives of women in the ancient world, and the role of slavery in ancient economies, something that both promotes a richer understanding of the past and facilitates good deliberation about modern problems.

As I remarked earlier in countries where university curricula have a firm disciplinary focus, it will not be easy to incorporate the "general education" part of my proposal. That may happen over time, but it is possible right now to think of ways in which each of the separate disciplines may prepare students more adequately to see themselves as citizens of a multicultural and diverse society, in a multinational interdependent world.

This brings me, in fact, to the third part of my proposal. Citizens cannot think well on the basis of factual knowledge alone. The third ability of the citizen, closely related to the first two, can be called the narrative imagination. This means the ability to think what it might be like to be in the shoes of a person different from oneself, to be an intelligent reader of that person's story, and to understand the emotions and wishes and desires that someone so placed might have. The narrative imagination is not uncritical: for we always bring ourselves and our own judgments to the encounter with another, and when we identify with a character in a novel, or a distant person whose life story we imagine, we inevitably will not merely identify, we will also judge that story in the light of our own goals and aspirations. But the first step of understanding the world from the point of view of the other is essential to any responsible act of judgment, since we do not know what we are judging until we see the meaning of an action as the person intends it, the meaning of a speech as it expresses something of importance in the context of that person's history and social world. The third ability our students should attain is the ability to decipher such meanings through the use of the imagination.

This ability is cultivated, above all, in courses in literature and the arts. Preparing citizens to understand one another is not the only function of the arts in a college curriculum, of course, but it is one extremely important function, and there are many ways in which such courses may focus on the requirements of citizenship.

Many courses in literature and the arts cultivate this sort of imagination, and many standard and familiar works thus prepare students to understand the situation of people different from themselves. But there is also reason to focus on the incorporation of works that confront students vividly with the experience of minority groups in their own society and of people in distant nations. The moral imagination can often become lazy, according sympathy to the near and the familiar, but refusing it to people who look different. Enlisting students' sympathy for distant lives is thus a way of training, so to speak, the muscles of the imagination.

This point was vividly put by Ralph Ellison, one of America's great novelists, in his novel *Invisible Man*. In an introduction to a reissue of the novel in 1981, Ellison explicitly links the novelist's art to the possibility of American democracy. By representing both visibility and its evasions, both equality and its refusal, a novel, he wrote, "could be fashioned as a raft of hope, perception and entertainment that might help keep us afloat as we tried to negotiate the snags and whirlpools that mark our nation's vacillating course toward and away from the democratic idea." This is not, he continues, the only goal for fiction; but it is one proper and urgent goal. For a democracy requires not only institutions and procedures, it also requires a particular quality of vision, in order "to defeat this national tendency to deny the common humanity shared by my character and those who might happen to read of his experience" (xxvi).

Let me show you a bit of how Ellison's novel does this, by commenting on its opening paragraph.

A voice speaks to us, from out of a hole in the ground. We don't know where this hole is—somewhere in New York, it appears. It is a warm hole, and full of light; in fact, there is lighter in that hole, we are told, than on top of the Empire State Building, or on Broadway. The voice tells us that he loves light, and he can't find much of it in the outside world. Light confirms his reality. Without light, and that is to say virtually always in the world above, he is invisible, formless, deprived of a sense of his own form and his "vital aliveness."

> I am an invisible man. No, I am not a spook like those who haunted Edgar Allan Poe; nor am I one of your Hollywood-movie ectoplasms. I am a man of substance, of flesh and bone, fiber and liquids—and I might even be said to possess a mind. I am invisible, understand, simply because people refuse to see me. Like the bodiless heads, you see sometimes in circus sideshows, it is as though I have been surrounded by mirrors of hard, distorting glass. When they approach, me they see only my surroundings, themselves, or figments of their imagination—indeed, everything and anything except me. Nor is my invisibility exactly a matter of a biochemical accident to my epidermis. That invisibility to which I refer occurs because of a peculiar disposition of the eyes of those with whom I come in contact. A matter of the construction of their *inner* eyes, those eyes with which they look through their physical eyes upon reality.[3]

Ellison's novel concerns a refusal of acknowledgment, a humanity that has been effaced. From its very opening, however, the work itself goes to work undoing that refusal of recognition, alluding as it does so to its own moral capacities. The refusal to see the Invisible Man is portrayed as a moral and social defect but also, more deeply, as a defect of imagination, of the inner eyes with which we look out, through our physical eyes, on the world. The people around the Invisible Man see only various fantastic projections of their own inner world, and they never come into contact with the human reality of his life. *Invisible Man* explores and savagely excoriates these refusals to see, while at the same time inviting its readers to know and see more than the unseeing characters. "Being invisible and without substance, a disembodied voice, as it were, what else could I do? What else but try to tell you what was really happening when your eyes were looking through?" In this way, it works upon the inner eyes of the very readers whose moral failures it castigates, although it refuses the easy notion that mutual visibility can be achieved in one heartfelt leap of brotherhood.

The novel's mordantly satirical treatment of stereotypes, its fantastic use of image and symbol (in, e.g., the bizarre dream-like sequence in the white paint factory), and its poignant moments of disappointed hope all contribute to Ellison's democratic end, linking the novel's sources of pleasure to its sources of insight.

One could go on much further about this wonderful work. But my point is that we need to educate the eyes of our students, by cultivating their ability to see complex humanity in places where they are most accustomed to deny it. Defeating these refusals of vision requires not only a general literary education but also one that focuses on groups with which our citizens' eyes have particular difficulty.

Although one may certainly add a literary component to courses in many different disciplines, from law to philosophy, I think that here the "liberal education" part of the US system has a special strength, enabling all students to get a common imaginative awakening through confrontation with carefully chosen literary works. It is very difficult to see how students bound for careers in business and industry, for example, will get such a training from courses in those disciplines alone.

Our campuses educate our citizens. This means learning a lot of facts, and mastering techniques of reasoning. But it means something more. It means learning how to be a human being capable of love and imagination.

We may continue to produce narrow citizens who have difficulty understanding people different from themselves, whose imaginations rarely venture beyond their local setting. It is all too easy for the moral imagination to become narrow in this way. Think of Charles Dickens's image of bad citizenship in his novel *A Christmas Carol*, in his portrait of the ghost of Jacob Marley, who visits Scrooge to warn him of the dangers of a blunted imagination. Marley's ghost drags through all eternity a chain made of cash boxes, because in life his imagination never ventured outside the walls of his successful business to imagine the lives of the men and women around him, men and women of different social class and background. Scrooge is astonished at the spectacle of his old friend wearing this immense chain. "I wear the chain I forged in life," he tells Scrooge. "I made it link by link and yard by yard. I girded it on of my own free will, and of my own free will I wore it." Trying to deny what he is hearing, Scrooge, terrified, blurts out, "You were always a good man of business, Jacob." "Business," the Ghost dolefully intones. "Mankind was my business. Charity, mercy, benevolence was all my business." (Here in Dickens's own Christian way he is directly alluding to Seneca's ideas of cultivated humanity and to related ideas of mercy and benevolence.) Then, turning to Scrooge, the Ghost asks, "Don't you feel the weight of the chain you bear yourself?" "My chains!" Scrooge exclaims. "No no." And then, in a smaller voice, "I am afraid."

Scrooge got another chance to learn what the world around him contained. During that fateful night, he got what we might call a belated liberal education, traveling to homes rich and poor, to a lighthouse on the sea, to the poverty of his own clerk's home only a mile or so away in Camden town in North London, but a very long mile indeed, the mile that divides rich from poor. We need to produce citizens who have this education while they are still young, before their imaginations are shackled by the weight of daily duties and self-interested plans. We produce all too many citizens who do drag cash boxes around with them, whose imaginations never step out of the counting house. But we have the opportunity to do better, producing Socratic citizens who are capable of thinking for themselves, arguing with tradition, and understanding with sympathy the conditions of lives different from their own. Now we are beginning to seize that opportunity. That is not "political correctness," that is the cultivation of humanity.

Notes

1. Strictly speaking, the course of study is rarely linear in this way. Usually students begin study of the major subject early, in the first or certainly the second year; and in the third and fourth years, they do not study only one thing but continue to take some basic required courses and other "elective" (optional) courses outside their major.
2. For helpful discussion of this issue, I am very grateful to the University of Humanistic Studies in Utrecht, the Netherlands, which sponsored a conference on these ideas in 1999. This University is the closest thing, in Europe, to an American liberal arts college, with a five-year humanistic curriculum integrating many different subjects.
3. Ralph Ellison, *Invisible man*. (New York: Random House, 1992).

CHAPTER 9

An African Theory of the Point of Higher Education: Communion as an Alternative to Autonomy, Truth, and Citizenship

Thaddeus Metz

Introduction

Much philosophy of higher education in the English-speaking literature has addressed the appropriate *final ends* of a higher education institution such as a university with a significant public dimension (whether substantial state funding or influence on civil society), that is, it has considered what such an institution ought to aim to achieve for its own sake and not merely as a means. In addition to being of intrinsic philosophical interest, a comprehensive conception of the final ends of higher education would have major implications for a variety of more specific educational issues, such as what kind of independence a university or lecturer should have, which research to discover and disseminate, what to teach, how to teach it, and whom to include among academic staff and the student body.

In this chapter I seek to advance enquiry into the point of a public higher education institution (from now on merely "university") by drawing on ideals salient in the sub-Saharan African philosophical tradition. There are relational, and specifically communal, values prominently held by African thinkers that I use to ground a promising rival to the dominant

T. Metz (✉)
University of Johannesburg, Johannesburg, South Africa

A. Stoller, E. Kramer (eds.), *Contemporary Philosophical Proposals for the University*, https://doi.org/10.1007/978-3-319-72128-6_9

contemporary Western, and especially Anglo-American, accounts of what a university ultimately ought to strive to achieve, which focus mainly on autonomy, truth, and citizenship. My aims are not merely comparative, contrasting an Afro-communal approach with other ones that have been more globally influential, but also substantive. Although the theory of a university's point that I articulate and defend has an African pedigree, I work to show that it should be taken seriously by a global audience, for plausibly capturing a variety of intuitions and claims that are widely shared.

To show that the Afro-communal account of higher education's final ends merits consideration is of course not to demonstrate that it is the best or even that it is better than the characteristically Western philosophies with which I contrast it in this chapter. My aims are the limited ones of arguing that the African view is strong, even by "non-African" lights, in some areas where major competitors appear to be weak, and that it also does not suffer from some weaknesses that one might have initially thought.

Another limit of this project is that I do not bring out the African credentials of the philosophy as much as some readers would find useful. I do indicate how it naturally follows from some statements of important sub-Saharan thinkers, but do not do the work of showing that their statements, in turn, are indeed a function of worldviews and ways of life indigenous to the African continent, especially south of the Sahara desert.[1]

In the following section I spell out an ethic informed by African thought, according to which just policies are those that treat people's capacity to commune with respect (2). Then, I apply this ethic to the final ends of higher education, identifying five major ones and noting some of their implications for policy and practice (3). I next contrast these communal final ends with those of autonomy, truth, and citizenship, arguing that the latter have gaps that the former help to fill (4). I conclude by briefly summarizing and reflecting on the argumentative strategy of appealing to characteristically African values when addressing a largely Western audience (5).

An Afro-communal Ethic

When writing on Africa, one is expected to note the variety of long-standing languages and cultures, which historians and sociologists would sensibly address in their particularity. From a philosophical perspective, however, it can be reasonable to work at a more general level, noting recurrent African values, that is, ones that have been common over a long span of time and a wide array of space on the continent and that are not as prominent in many other philosophical traditions such as the Western, Chinese, Islamic, Hindu, and so on. At least when contemporary African philosophers have written about moral matters, they have tended to focus on a small handful of distinctive values taken to be fundamental in the sub-Saharan context.

Specifically, some philosophical articulations of sub-Saharan values take life-force, roughly, an invisible energy that has come from God, as basic to African ethical thought.[2] Frequent, too, is the idea that a moral person is at bottom one who interacts in certain positive ways with human beings and imperceptible finite agents such as the not-yet-born and ancestors, those who have died but are thought to continue to live on earth and to guide the clan they had founded.[3] Other thinkers have deemed the common good, practices that would leave no one's well-being unaddressed, to be foundational.[4]

I merely note these strands of ethical thought here, lacking the space to argue that they are not the best interpretation of the African tradition. I must rest content with providing a prima facie plausible alternative interpretation of it, one that I believe would be of particular interest to a global audience of philosophers of higher education, educational theorists, and policy-makers. According to my favoured reading of sub-Saharan morality, it is secular and relational. Roughly, from this perspective, communal relationships with human persons (and certain animals) are what merit pursuit for their own sake, whereas discordant ones are to be avoided (unless necessary to prevent a greater discord). In this section, I expound this ethic, applying it only in the following sections.[5]

Communion

To begin to get a sense of what communal, or harmonious, relationship involves for sub-Saharan thinkers, consider the following statements:

> Every member is expected to consider him/herself an integral part of the whole and to play an appropriate role towards achieving the good of all.[6]
>
> Harmony is (to be) achieved through close and sympathetic social relations within the group.[7]
>
> (T)he purpose of our life is community-service and community-belongingness.[8]
>
> If you asked ubuntu (the southern African Nguni word for personhood or virtue—ed.) advocates and philosophers: What principles inform and orga-

> nise your life? ... the answers would express commitment to the good of the community in which their identities were formed, and a need to experience their lives as bound up in that of their community.[9]
>
> (The African value of cohesion includes–ed.) living a life of mutual concern for the welfare of others, such as in a cooperative creation and distribution of wealth....(and) feeling integrated with as well as willing to integrate others into a web of relations free of friction and conflict.[10]

These quotations, by philosophers, theologians, intellectual historians, and other kinds of thinkers from Nigeria, Kenya, and South Africa, are of interest for two reasons. One is that they suggest that a certain kind of relationship is to be pursued as an end, not merely as a means. Another is that they specify the nature of this relationship, in terms of two logically distinct facets. On the one hand, there is what I call "identifying with" others or "sharing a way of life" with them, that is, as per the quotations above, considering oneself part of the whole, being close, belonging, being bound up with others, and feeling integrated. On the other, there is "exhibiting solidarity" with others or "caring for their quality of life," namely, achieving the good of all, being sympathetic, servicing, being committed to others' good, and being concerned for others' welfare.

More carefully, it is revealing to understand identifying with another (or being close, belonging, etc.) to be the combination of exhibiting certain psychological attitudes of "we-ness" and cooperative behaviour. The attitudes include a tendency to think of oneself as a member of a group with the other and to refer to oneself as a "we" (and not merely as an "I"), a disposition to feel pride or shame in what another member does, and, at a higher level of intensity, an emotional appreciation of the other's nature and value. The cooperative behaviours include being transparent about the terms of interaction, allowing others to make voluntary choices, acting on the basis of trust, adopting common goals, and, at the extreme end, choosing for the reason that "this is who we are."

Exhibiting solidarity with another (or acting for others' good, exhibiting concern for their welfare, etc.) is also usefully construed as the combination of exhibiting certain psychological attitudes and engaging in helpful behaviour. Here, the attitudes are ones positively oriented towards the other's well-being and include a belief that the other merits aid for her own sake, an empathetic awareness of the other's condition, and a sympathetic emotional reaction to the empathy. And the actions are not merely those likely to be beneficial, that is, to meet the other's needs, but also, in the ideal case, are ones done for that reason and for the sake of making the other a (morally) better person or for the sake of communal relationship itself.

I call the combination of identity and solidarity so defined "communion" or sometimes "harmony." I tend to abjure the word "community," in part because it is used in a variety of ways and in part because it might suggest the (Western) communitarian view that appropriate norms are determined by a group's attitudes or culture. In contrast, the African ethic is meant to be an objective standard by which to determine whether a group's norms are appropriate, that is, whether it has some moral reason to change its attitudes or culture so that people are treated as special in virtue of their capacities both to be communed with and to commune.

Respect for the Capacity to Be Party to Communion

Supposing the capacity to commune confers a dignity on us, sometimes honouring it will include actions that seek to promote actualization of the capacity, that is, that are expected to foster communion. However, the ethic I advance does not say to promote communal relationships as much as possible wherever one can in the long run, as per agent-neutral consequentialism; it rather says to treat people with respect in virtue of their natural capacity to relate communally, both as subjects and objects. This principle is deontological or agentrelative, in at least three major ways.

First, honouring communion, or people insofar as they can be party to it, means first and foremost exhibiting it in oneself. One is more to relate communally than to enable or prompt others to do so.

Second, actual communal relationships of which one is a part have some priority relative to merely possible relationships one could have (and the actual relationships of others). To honour communion means in the first instance sustaining one's own ties, even if cutting off extant ones is foreseen to result in marginally more communion for oneself (or elsewhere in the world). Such is a philosophical reconstruction of the special obligations often accorded to kin in traditional African societies[11] and intuitively accepted by many in the West (and especially the Confucian East). Note that giving priority, when it comes to positive obligations to aid, to those related to oneself does not mean that strangers count for nothing[12]; instead, by the present ethic, everyone with the ability to exhibit communion has a dignity that must be respected, but those who have been in communion are entitled to more of one's help.

Third, to honour the capacity for communion entails that it is normally wrong to seek to realize it, including among one's own relations, by using a discordant means against innocents, where discord consists of relationships that are the opposites of communal, that is, acting on an "us versus them" attitude, subordinating, harming, and doing so consequent to hatred, cruelty, or the like. It is wrong to seek to advance identity and solidarity in the long term by being divisive or exhibiting ill-will in the short term (when unnecessary to rebut an initial discord[13]).

To see some of the prima facie appeal of this ethic, consider its implications for the nature of wrongdoing, on the one hand, and of what justice requires from public institutions, on the other. The relationship of identifying with other people in combination with that of exhibiting solidarity with them is basically what English speakers mean by "friendliness" or even a broad sense of "love." Hence, this African moral theory implies that wrong actions are, very roughly, those that are not friendly. Wrongdoing, in respect of innocents, is a matter of either failure to commune with them, and so being indifferent to others, or, worse, discordance. What makes acts such as killing, coercing, deceiving, exploiting, cheating, breaking promises, and the like typically impermissible is that they are (extremely) unfriendly, indeed, ways of prizing the discordant relations of division and ill-will. As one scholar of African ethical thought has summed up, "immorality is the word or deed which undermines fellowship"[14]; wrongness is more or less behaviour that treats innocent parties as separate and inferior, subordinates them, is expected to harm them, and is done consequent to indifference or cruelty. This explanation of wrongdoing differs from familiar Western appeals to failure to promote well-being in the long run, degradation of autonomy, violation of what would be agreed to in a social contract, or disobedience of God's commands, the most prominent principles in the modern era.[15]

With regard to the normative ground of public policy, the utilitarian believes that institutions ought to enhance subjective well-being, and the Kantian believes they should protect and enhance people's autonomy. In contrast, the adherent to communion contends (roughly) that institutions ought to commune with those they influence in the first instance and then also enable others to commune with each other. This approach entails that conditions such as these are to be prized: a state that meets the needs and promotes the virtues of its residents; a business that forgoes some profits so as to strengthen ties with stakeholders; a school in which class, gender, and racial divisions are overcome with a national identity; a populace that is cohesive in the sense of being disposed to trade and cooperate across political, religious, and ethnic lines; and a household in which adult romantic relationships are evenhanded and stable and in which children are reared with wisdom. It is not merely the effect on well-being or the treatment of autonomy that matters, from this perspective, but centrally the quality of the relationships as friendly. This ethic, too, merits consideration when thinking about how to organize a society.

The Communal Final Ends of a University

This section applies the African ethic from the previous section to the context of public higher education. Supposing that the basic duty of a moral agent (including an institution[16]) is to treat individuals respectfully in virtue of their natural abilities to commune and to be communed with, which ends should a university pursue for its own sake? This section argues for five major ones.[17]

Foster Socio-economic Well-Being

The Afro-communal principle prescribes respecting relationships of identity and solidarity, where solidarity is roughly a matter of people helping one another for each other's sake. If a university, or the government funding it, is required to act for the sake of people in a certain territory, then a major part of doing so will be a matter of seeking to improve their socio-economic conditions. A university is in a good position to do that by imparting skills to help run a modern economy and by promoting scientific knowledge that would facilitate technological spin-offs and predictions of natural events. Fostering what many would call "development" is a justifying aim of a university—that is, it is a good reason to set one up and keep it—in the light of the nature of a university and the costs of maintaining it.

Another dimension of advancing socio-economic well-being is directing it largely towards the worst off and not so much towards those already flourishing. Public higher education ought to strive to help students from lower economic classes acquire the qualifications needed to compete for jobs and other positions and to obtain the rewards that are attached to them. Treating people as equals in virtue of their abilities to be communed with and to commune means that an agent with substantial resources, such as a university, has strong moral reason to assist those from poor backgrounds who otherwise would not have a chance to acquire the education essential to engage in interesting work that is well paid. If a state university did not yet exist, then the government would be failing to exhibit solidarity with the poor and would alienate them from itself. And if a state university did exist but did not accommodate those from economically disadvantaged backgrounds, then it would be doing the same. To avoid these moral problems, a state university must be created and maintained in order to ensure that citizens have an equal opportunity to become qualified for jobs.

In practice this would mean adopting familiar practices such as providing financial aid of various sorts and possibly remedial classes. It would also likely mean that a university may not accept only the "very best" applicants in purely meritocratic terms. Instead, it would have to make allowance for those whose preparation for tertiary education has not been ideal, at least for reasons of class and other structural matters beyond their control. So, for example, a public university might accept the best applicants from schools across a demographic range; it might draw on the top ten percent of schools in wealthy neighbourhoods and in poor ones, even if the top ten percent of the latter were not as well prepared as the top 11–20 percent of the former.

Furthermore, fostering equal opportunity in a robust way informed by a requirement to care and share would mean meeting several broader needs of students, supposing that a university's finances and other resources permitted. For instance, if students lacked enough food to concentrate on their studies and to remain healthy, a university would have some obligation to provide it. If students were unfamiliar with the professional norms of a labour market, a university would have a duty of some weight to help them obtain internships, to teach them how to construct a c.v., and to give them advice about how to interview. For a third example, students from impoverished backgrounds and from cultures at odds with middle-class lifestyles could be entitled to counselling, support groups, and the like, in order to adjust to a university environment in the first place.[18]

Promote Virtue

The solidarity element of the communal ethic instructs a moral agent to act for the sake of others, and, while part of acting for another person's sake is making her better off, say, in terms of meeting her needs, another part is making her a (morally) better person. Part of honouring communion is enabling other people to be good at communing, and, so, part of what a state university ought to be intrinsically striving for is helping others to improve their character.

Notice that this aim is not reducible to merely teaching university students about ethical views, say, by conveying propositional knowledge of utilitarianism, Kantianism, virtue ethics, or even the present, Afro-communal ethic. The primary aim would instead be to enable students to improve their moral decision-making in day-to-day life. It would mean a curriculum and pedagogy oriented towards imparting not merely an abstract apprehension of moral claims or controversies but also some moral wisdom and sound practice. The aim would not be so much *moral education*, an orthodox focus on belief formation, but more *education for morality*, an orthopraxy. On this score, a university might teach students, say, how to become more aware of their implicit biases, how to identify and deal with conflicts of interest, and how to become more attuned to other people's points of view and feelings.

Although the communal ethic in principle entails that public higher education ought to strive to enhance people's virtue, in practice its reach would probably be limited. In light of some reasonable empirical claims, a university should perhaps not adopt the final end of developing virtue insofar as that is very thick, for example, involves doing the right thing for the right sort of reason or exhibiting all the apt kind of emotions, such as being glad when others flourish. There is likely not the time and other resources available for a university to make students better people in the above senses, if it is going to realize the aim of teaching them intricate knowledge and refined skills in fields such as chemistry, medicine, economics, metaphysics, sociology, and engineering. In theory, a government could tack an additional six or 12 months onto the bachelor's degree, but most students—and governments—already find higher education expensive and something to streamline on the road to economic productivity.

Although a university probably cannot foster much virtue understood in terms of certain *attitudes*, it is in a good position to advance it when it comes to performing *actions*, including those with some expressive dimension. For instance, university pedagogy could work to incorporate what are often called "communities of practice,"[19] where students would learn by collaborating with others to realize shared goals. Relationships of sharing a way of life and caring for others' quality of life are more likely to be realized in the context of joint, public activities than isolated assignments done or prepared for at home in which students are competing against each other for grades.[20]

Furthermore, enabling people to excel at the right sort of job, meaning one that would contribute positively to others' good, would be a significant way to impart moral virtue. If the state must treat people as having a dignity because of (in part) their capacities to be cared for and to care for others, then it must care for each of them by enabling them to work at jobs in accordance with their particular abilities and inclinations to care for others. Indeed, the central meaning of work in traditional African cultures was to realize oneself by labouring in ways that would support one's (extended) family and the broader society.[21]

Support Culture

The previous sub-sections argued that the solidarity element of the communal ethic entails that a university must care for people's quality of life in the economy, understood not in terms of whatever the market calls for, but rather relationally, in terms of enabling students to obtain fulfilling, well-paying jobs and to engage in work that improves others' lives. Turning to the identity part of communion, it requires publicly funded higher education to assist people in sharing a way of life, which includes the protection, interpretation, and transmission of a culture. Those lacking a common culture tend neither to think of themselves as a "we" nor to coordinate their action in pursuit of shared ends. Interpreting the world in similar or at least familiar ways, something a university is in a key position to enable, would foster a strong sense of togetherness and common values. In practice, this might mean that a university should favour the culture of a large majority, but the ideal would be to foster ways of interpreting life with which nearly everyone in the state's territory could identify.

There is something wrong when a music department in an African university is focused largely on Western classical music, or when a literature department in a Japanese one addresses mainly works in English. Instead, there is intuitively some moral reason for a university to engage with the culture in which it is set—where that culture could be quite heterogeneous or admit of competing interpretations—which a demand to prize communion *qua* shared way of life well explains. As is explained below, to focus on local ways of life need involve neither an undue restriction on students' liberty to explore other cultures nor some kind of chauvinism.

One might wonder what the difference is between fostering socio-economic well-being and supporting culture, for is not the latter one way of doing the former? As construed here, and as the literature is best interpreted, well-being (or "development") has less to do with the "intangible" heritage of language, tradition, and aesthetic expression, and more to do with "concrete" goods such as nutrition, education, healthcare, shelter, communications, transportation, and electricity. These are distinct considerations, underwritten by largely differential facets of the value of communion.

Facilitate Cooperation

This end is another dimension of identifying with others. Sustaining a culture is only one way of treating people's capacity to share a way of life with respect; there are additional ways to foster the coordination of behaviour and the adoption of common or at least compossible ends. There are certain policies that, when routinely enforced by the state or otherwise adhered to, would enable people to avoid interfering with one another and would foster joint projects. Key examples are certain Constitutional laws, good governance policies, principles for resolving conflict, and rules to regulate debate, all of which a university could readily impart to its students.

Note that universities could teach students about cooperative participation not merely theoretically but also practically. For example, universities might do more than they normally do to include students in decision-making bodies and disciplinary hearings. From this standpoint, a university Senate ought not to consist merely of full professors and senior managers and should include not just one or two student representatives. Instead, it ought to include many students, at the very least to watch as observers, to learn how to share opinions, to disagree constructively, and to forge consensus. In addition, when students are charged with violating university rules, such as by cheating on a test, it would be useful to have other students participate as ones who collect the evidence, ascertain guilt or innocence, and make recommendations about how to respond to the infractions, ideally by sentencing guilty parties to perform kinds of labour that would persuade other students not to cheat.

Note that cooperation is usually a precondition for the moral worth of supporting culture; there would not be a genuine *sharing* of a way of life if a culture were foisted on people without their having freely chosen it for themselves. The Afro-communal ethic gives some principled weight to a common lifestyle, but not one forced onto others à la colonialism or patriarchy.

Rectify Injustice

The rectification of injustice, say, from colonialism, is unlikely to be the sole justifying aim of public higher education, for that would oddly entail that a university should be closed down once compensation for cultural, psychological, and economic losses had been made. However, if a state's assault on a people's way of life, self-esteem, and ability to compete had been extreme, then, as an essential part of respecting people in virtue of their capacity to commune, one intrinsic aim of a university would be to effect redress and more generally do what is likely to repair the broken relationship.

Part of effecting redress could be seeking to correct for competitive disadvantage in the form of affirmative action for those whose socio-economic situations had been wrongfully worsened in a way that made it difficult for them to obtain the education needed to compete for positions. Another facet of effecting redress is likely to involve seeking to make up for epistemic injustice, that is, finding ways to do right by people insofar as they had been treated discordantly in respect of their ways of interpreting the world. In the first instance, and most easily, this would mean changing the curriculum to include neglected or denigrated works. However, a complete form of epistemic redress might call for much more. In the ideal case, a university would reflect on respects in which its current practices (perhaps unintentionally) occlude engagement with suppressed cultures. For example, it is far from clear that the way for a university to honour an oral culture that has been historically disadvantaged is merely to include written texts by those who had come from that culture but were educated elsewhere. Indeed, the best route would probably be for those from this culture, if not to give guest lectures, then at least to give their opinion to university instructors about how they could best honour it, and not for instructors to decide on their own what this might involve.

In sum, if one finds attractive the idea that right acts are those that respect (people's capacity for) relationships of identity and solidarity, then one should think that a university ultimately ought to aim to foster well-being, promote virtue, support culture, facilitate cooperation, and rectify injustice. Having specified these five distinct final ends for a university that appear justified by the Afro-communal ethic, a natural question is whether there is some ranking to be made of them to guide decision-making in cases where they conflict. Above it was suggested that the good of culture normally cannot come at the cost to cooperation, that the value of a common way of life depends on it having been chosen, but there are likely other situations when a policy would advance the realization of one final end but retard that of another. For example, sometimes a dimension of culture, perhaps concerning medical practice, would thrive in a certain respect only at the cost to well-being. Although contextual, political judgement is often what is required in these contexts, some more general moral considerations about how to balance competing values might be available.[22]

Contrasts with More Western Final Ends

This section compares the communal final ends from the previous section with those of autonomy, truth, and citizenship, salient in the contemporary Anglo-American and more generally Western tradition of thought about the final ends of public higher education. Part of the purpose is simply to point out similarities and differences between the African approach and the more Euro-American-Australasian ones, but another part is to argue that the former approach merits consideration as a rival to the latter.[23]

Autonomy

Broadly speaking, the contemporary Western moral and political philosophical tradition is liberal, at least to a degree that no other long-standing tradition around the world is. That means that recent works in the philosophy of higher education by those from the West have tended to prize human, that is, individual, rights and more generally civil liberties to live as a person sees fit.

More specifically, a recurrent theme has been that at least one major (if not the) point of higher education should be to protect, develop, or respect the individual's capacity for self-governance. Often the language used is that of "autonomy," with John White, for instance, having contended that a university ought to enable people to satisfy desires upon which they have reflected.[24] Others speak of "critical thinking" or "rational enquiry,"[25] the thought being that a university ought to foster students' abilities to think for themselves and guide their lives in the light of the deliverances of their intellectual faculties.

Much of what friends of autonomy value is plausibly captured by the concept of cooperation that is inherent to communion as conceived above. Cooperating by definition means not coercing, deceiving, exploiting, or otherwise manipulating another person. In addition to including these "negative" dimensions of autonomy, it also includes its more "positive" ones, such as being able to express oneself to others, to be assertive, to negotiate, and the like.

However, there are differences between the two concepts of being autonomous and relating communally, and where there are, the Afro-communal view is competitive. For example, a characteristically African perspective would (somewhat rhetorically) ask the friend of autonomy for what this capacity should be employed. A procedural focus on the individual reflecting, selecting, and pursuing ends on the face of it lacks the theoretical resources to account for the idea that some ends are substantively more worthwhile than others (beyond the end of respecting others' ends). Should one autonomously or upon rational reflection choose to spread ignorance as opposed to knowledge of facts fundamental to human nature, or choose to count how many blades of grass are on a quad rather than improve others' health, or choose to engage in self-destructive behaviour such as cutting oneself instead of developing aesthetic talent to create art objects that please others? There is nothing within the mere concept of self-governance that can provide grounds to favour the latter ends relative to the former ones. It is reasonable, however, to suppose that a university ought to orient students towards the latter ones.

Those partial towards liberalism or individualism might ask whether one should truly be deemed morally obligated to use one's autonomy for the sake of others. It is indeed typical of an African approach to contend that with freedom comes responsibility[26] and, specifically, responsibility to others. By the communal ethic, one roughly has a duty to come closer to others (who are innocent), not to remain distant. We are not merely to "pursue our own good in our own way" (as per John Stuart Mill) but, roughly, to pursue others' good in our own way.

That said, it does not obviously follow that one may rightly be forced to participate with and aid others. One's having a duty to commune is one thing, and others having a right to make one do so is another. Furthermore, it is intuitively justified for a public higher education institution to insist that its expensive resources be spent on students not merely so that they can remain isolated from and indifferent towards others' way of life and quality of life but rather so that they can learn how to contribute to society. The communal principle captures this intuition about how students should exercise their decision-making better than an appeal to autonomy, which is open about which choices they are to make (apart from not degrading others' choices).

Another dimension of the contrast between autonomy and communion is whether moral education is appropriate for young adults, particularly those at a university. While in the West debate rages about whether to educate with the aim of imparting virtues (at least those that do not appear essential for sustaining a liberal polity),[27] there is no real debate about that among those in the African tradition, with the present interpretation following suit. Treating people with respect in virtue of their capacity to commune means helping them to develop and realize this special, moral capacity. Alternately, insofar as communion includes solidarity, one is to make others not merely better off but also better people, by helping them to become more virtuous.

Truth

A second final end prominently advanced by Western philosophers of higher education is truth or knowledge for its own sake, which is shorthand for a variety of epistemic goods that might include mere justified belief, that is, belief that could be false and so not strictly speaking knowledge. Somewhat recent lengthy defences of this conception of a university's point are an essay by Edward Shils, in which he argues that the basic aim of a researcher should be to discover truths about fundamental matters,[28] and a book by Gordon Graham, in which he contends that intellectual reflection, particularly the understanding of certain topics, is a good that a university ought to pursue for its own sake.[29]

Also worth mentioning are classic works such as Edmund Husserl's Vienna Lecture contending that the European intellectual tradition is uniquely and desirably characterized by a propensity to adopt what he calls "a purely 'theoretical' attitude" that is "thoroughly unpractical"[30] and of course John Henry Newman's claim in *The Idea of a University* that higher education ought to teach (although, interestingly, not strive to discover) certain kinds of knowledge for its own sake.[31]

Those who maintain that truth is a proper final end of public higher education need not deny that epistemic goods are often likely to have beneficial consequences for society. They instead tend to claim that epistemic goods would merit pursuit even in the absence of practical benefits, or at least that, even if practical benefits were a necessary condition for justifiably spending resources on the pursuit of epistemic goods, the latter should be much of a university's *aim*, what it should be striving to achieve.

The communal ethic can capture much of what drives the truth seekers. On the one hand, the solidarity dimension of communion will naturally prescribe scientific and other empirical enquiry of the sort likely to improve people's quality of life, while, on the other, the identity dimension makes good sense of engagements with local culture, for example, philosophy, literature, and the arts.

It might seem as though the Afro-communal theory does better than a strict concern for truth at capturing the rightful concern of public higher education with culture. Quite often truth or knowledge is understood in terms of propositional claims, *that* something about the world is the case, but it does not appear that being familiar with, say, Shakespeare's works or having learned to play the piano is reducible to that. It is, however, open to the adherent to knowledge for its own sake to broaden her conception of what counts as knowledge. In addition to knowing that certain claims are true, she could plausibly contend, as Jonathan Adler apparently has,[32] that the point of a university includes the impartation of know-how such as piano playing and knowledge by acquaintance such as learning the content of a poem.

So, an interest in knowledge for its own sake appears, upon reflection, to be able to account for the idea that a university ought to foster culture. In contrast, it appears difficult for the adherent to communion to account for the idea that a university ought to pursue certain kinds of "blue-sky" or "pure" knowledge that is not expected to facilitate either identity or solidarity. Consider, for example, cosmological questions such as whether there is a black hole at the centre of every galaxy or what the ultimate fate of the universe will be and historical questions such as what killed the dinosaurs or how fishes evolved into terrestrial creatures. Answering these questions is unlikely either to improve people's quality of life, whether understood in terms of meeting their needs or making them more virtuous, or to enhance the local culture or otherwise facilitate the sharing of a way of life. Of course, answering these questions could indirectly and unforeseeably foster communion, but, then, a university ought to devote its resources to answering other kinds of questions that are more likely to do so.

There are many in the African philosophical and more broadly intellectual tradition who would "bite the bullet" and deny that public higher education should in fact advance knowledge that is unexpected to promote the sharing of a way of life or the caring for people's quality of life (or some other facet of what is good for people).[33] There is a noticeably pragmatic strain to characteristic sub-Saharan approaches to knowledge, according to which it ought ultimately to meet people's needs, including ones as social-moral beings. Traditional African education has valued *wisdom*, roughly understood as what fosters communion between people. In contrast, Western education has been much more centred on discovering and conveying abstract truths and has done so centrally by fostering competition between enquirers.[34] Although the latter sort of approach has often ended up producing technologies that have improved people's quality of life, Western higher education has not sought it out mainly in the expectation of that outcome. It has instead tended to prize knowledge for its own sake, frequently produced in ways that have put distance between those seeking to learn new things.

It is hard to deny that a university should be pleased were its researchers to use its resources to succeed in discovering the fate of the universe, even if that had no concrete social benefit. This author's inclination is therefore to revise the understanding of what it means to improve someone's quality of life so as to account for the aptness of some "pure" cosmological, historical, and similar enquiries.

Suppose that one's life is worse, the less meaningful it is, and suppose, too, that one's life is less meaningful, the more one is misguided about one's environment.[35] There is something to be pitied about members of Heaven's Gate, who killed themselves in the belief that only suicide would take them to a spacecraft trailing the Hale-Bopp Comet that would, in turn, carry them to paradise. The reaction of pity is well explained (in part) by the idea that ignorance of the fundamental nature of reality undercuts meaning in life and hence the sort of life one has reason to lead. If part of caring about people's good is indeed a matter of enabling them to live meaningfully, and if that depends on understanding certain objective truths about the world, then the communal account can provide an account of why a university should advance knowledge of them.

In fact, the appeal to the human good of meaning might do a plausible job of explaining precisely which "pure" knowledge a university ought to pursue. After all, there are many objective truths that would be utterly impractical to seek out, for example, knowledge of completely coincidental correlations. A promising criterion to identify which knowledge should be pursued for its own sake is whether it would make people's lives more meaningful to have.

In sum, it appears that a concern for communion can capture much of what drives the interest in truth, and, furthermore, note that it can do so without being overly narrow. It has been tempting for those who believe that the job of a university is to pursue knowledge for its own sake to deny that it should perform other functions, such as promoting equal opportunity, at least when they would come at some cost to knowledge.[36] However, it is surely the case that a state must do what it can to enable people to become qualified for jobs, including those who might not be superlatively qualified due to historical injustice for which it is responsible, and public higher education is the natural way for it to do so. Communion makes sense of that intuition, as well as the further ideas that public higher education also ought to do things such as facilitate cooperation between people and promote their virtue as social beings.

There are a variety of final ends to be pursued and to be balanced as the circumstances require, not merely the goal of truth, and it is implausible even to think that truth should be the overriding goal that must come first before all other considerations, which may come second but only at no cost to it ("lexical priority"). One theoretical advantage of the communal view is that it captures the multiplicity of appropriate final ends for a university under a single (albeit complex) concept.

Citizenship

A third common account of what the central (even if not sole) final end of public higher education ought to be is citizenship, specifically, active membership in a democratic polity. This approach has been notably championed by Martha Nussbaum,[37] on which this section focuses as a powerful representative.[38]

For Nussbaum, the central aim of a university in societies that have constitutions and widely accept the idea of human dignity should be to cultivate democratic and global citizenship. Such an end includes three major elements, for her.

First, a good citizen is critical, meaning that she is one who does not defer to authority, peer pressure, or the like. She instead is inclined to evaluate policies in the light of their rationality, to be confident enough to voice a dissenting opinion, and to use her creativity to advance justice.

Second, a good citizen is cosmopolitan, that is, one who is not merely self-regarding in her interests and who is not merely aware of her own way of life. She rather seeks to advance the public good and is knowledgeable of a wide array of cultures, including different religions, languages, and socio-economic policies.

Third, a good citizen is respectful of, and concerned for, other people, by which is meant that she is one who is not emotionally crippled in the sense of being unable to see others as equals or to sympathize with them. In contrast, she can and does view others as having a dignity that requires her to exhibit compassion for their inner lives.

Like the appeal to communion, this conception of citizenship is complex and so on the face of it is able to make sense of a plurality of final ends for a university, including, as is well known, a key role for the humanities and liberal arts. Nussbaum aptly denies that citizenship is the sole end of education, acknowledging that education also ought to prepare people for employment.[39] She also accepts that education can be important for fostering meaning in people's lives, but she appears to deny that public higher education should serve that function in a democratic society that includes reasonable disagreement among citizens about conceptions of the good life.[40]

The Afro-communal view entails that a state ought to protect people's human rights and ought to be (consensually) democratic, for these are ways of treating people's capacity to relate cooperatively and helpfully with respect.[41] So, it entails that Nussbaum is correct to contend that one "way of assessing any educational scheme is to ask how well it prepares young people for life in a form of social and political organization,"[42] specifically one that is a Constitutional democracy and applies to people with different backgrounds.

However, the appeal to communion entails that citizenship, as Nussbaum and other liberal democratic philosophers in the West conceive of it, should be tempered in certain ways. There is a plausible middle path in between, on the one hand, being utterly unfamiliar with, or contemptuous of, other cultures (parochialism) and, on the other, educating students about a wide variety of cultures and leaving it up to them which interpretations, values, and aesthetics they will adopt (cosmopolitanism). A third way, prescribed by the African ethic, is to give some priority to understanding and enriching local culture (insofar as it has been freely chosen), while not remaining ignorant of other cultures. The African ethic of honouring communion entails giving additional moral weight to existing communal relationships, and so it would indeed be incumbent on a university not only to inform students of their duty not to radically upset norms central to the community's freely chosen self-conception but also to focus on transmitting, interpreting, and developing these norms.

It does not follow that education about culture should simply be a matter of ensuring students mimic a given society's past. Being concerned for the good of students entails not utterly restricting their knowledge to that of a circumscribed culture, particularly in a globalized world in which even rural communities have to engage with a wide array of foreign people, policies, and institutions. It is implausible to think every culture at a particular moment is optimal, or even adequate, for the welfare of all the people who participate in it. So, the injunction to exhibit solidarity with others, an independent facet of communion beyond identifying with them, gives a university reason to inform students about the rest of the world and not to quash student doubt about the propriety of an existing way of life.[43]

The other major way that the friend of communion would question citizenship as the central final end of higher education is by noting that it is implausibly narrow, even when conjoined with the independent end of fostering employment. First off, many believe that a university is a place to find alternative, minority viewpoints, even ones that might lead one to question Constitutional democracy. It would not be inapt for a university to enable students to consider the desirability of living under, say, a benevolent dictatorship of the sort that Confucian political philosophers routinely support, where political rulers are chosen on merit, not by majority rule.

Secondly, note that Nussbaum and others in favour of higher education for citizenship intend this approach to apply only to societies that are already Constitutional democracies. Surely, though, there would be a major role for public higher education in other kinds of societies, and then not merely to train a labour force. Citizenship educationists might reply that the major aim of a university in such societies would be to enable people to transition to Constitutional democracy, but that is implausible. Even if there were no hope of autocracy falling away, there would intuitively be important roles for a university to play beyond qualifying people for jobs. Specifically, according to the communal ethic, there would remain these important ends: facilitating cooperative interaction in day-to-day life, sustaining culture, promoting virtue, and perhaps enabling understanding insofar as that contributes to the human good of a meaningful life.

Higher education is not something for the state to allocate primarily as a means to enable people to act as citizens in a state with a particular distribution of political power. The political is one dimension of the interpersonal, but it is reasonable to think that a comprehensive or substantially large conception of a university's final end would focus on more than just the former and would capture much of the latter. Whereas good citizenship is a matter of the governmental roles of voter and advocate for justice, communion can also be manifested in the non-political contexts of being a romantic partner, friend, parent, neighbour, worker, colleague, mentor, therapist, manager, consumer, and member of a board. Voting takes place only once every several years; one's vote has virtually zero effect, while writing letters to the editor or lobbying a political party is only marginally more effectual; and one's odds of becoming someone with any real political power or influence are extremely low. In contrast, since communion can be displayed in a variety of everyday roles, and since a university is in a good position to foster communion, it is often in a position to make interventions that will greatly improve people's lives. And it is reasonable to think that the prospect of making a substantial difference to others' lives is something that would—perhaps alone—justify the costs of setting up and maintaining a university.

Conclusion: The Relevance of Africa to Global Thought about Education

This chapter has drawn on ideas salient in the sub-Saharan African philosophical tradition to spell out a theory of the point of public higher education. According to it, the basic aim of the state should be to respect individuals insofar as they are capable of communing and being communed with, where communion consists of relationships of identity and solidarity. Honouring people for their ability to commune, applied to a university, means that it should strive to foster well-being, promote virtue, support culture, facilitate cooperation, and rectify injustice. These final ends were contrasted with those more prominent in contemporary Euro-American-Australasian reflection on higher education, in particular, those of promoting autonomy, truth, and citizenship. Although the chapter did not argue that the Afro-communal ends are more defensible than the more Western ones, it did provide reason to take the former seriously as correctives and rivals to the latter.

Notice how the chapter sought to defend the African approach: it did not appeal to intuitions and claims that only those who had already accepted that approach would hold. Instead, the chapter aimed to defend the communal theory of what a university should be striving to achieve by making arguments that could be expected to have some prima facie appeal even to those who had not considered such a relational approach before.

The implicit view here is that different cultures tend to have insights into different facets of morality and that, specifically, the African philosophical tradition has highlighted the goods of relationship in ways that the Western one has not. Westerners, including Western *theorists*, routinely appreciate the values of identity and solidarity, but Western *theories* of higher education by and large neglect these values, often treating them merely as a means towards the practical end of self-governance (at either the individual or political level) and the intellectual end of understanding nature. The reflection in this chapter suggests that in order to capture in a principled manner the variety of ends that a university plausibly ought to aim for, a characteristically African conception of communal relationship has much to offer, even to philosophers working in other traditions.[44]

Notes

1. Which has been undertaken elsewhere, for example, in Thaddeus Metz, "Toward an African Moral Theory" (rev. edn), in *Themes, Issues and Problems in African Philosophy*, ed. Isaac Ukpokolo (London: Palgrave Macmillan, 2017), 97–119. Note that in claiming that certain relational values have been salient among indigenous sub-Saharans does not suggest that they are utterly unique to them. There are probably some similarities with the values of other native peoples, on which see George Silberbauer, "Ethics in Small-scale Societies," in *A Companion to Ethics*, ed. Peter Singer (Oxford: Blackwell, 1991), 14–28.
2. For example, Noah Dzobo, "Values in a Changing Society: Man, Ancestors, and God," in *Person and Community; Ghanaian Philosophical Studies, Vol. I*, ed. Kwasi Wiredu and Kwame Gyekye (Washington, D.C.: Council for Research in Values and Philosophy, 1992), 223–240; and Laurenti Magesa, *African Religion: The Moral Traditions of Abundant Life* (Maryknoll, NY: Orbis Books, 1997).
3. For example, Bénézet Bujo, "Differentiations in African Ethics," in *The Blackwell Companion to Religious Ethics*, ed. William Schweiker (Malden, MA: Blackwell, 2005), 423–437; and Munyaradzi Felix Murove, "The Shona Ethic of *Ukama* with Reference to the Immortality of Values," *The Mankind Quarterly* 48 (2007): 235–241.
4. Most prominently Kwame Gyekye, *Tradition and Modernity: Philosophical Reflections on the African Experience* (New York: Oxford University Press, 1997), and "African Ethics," *Stanford Encyclopedia of Philosophy*, ed. Edward Zalta, https://plato.stanford.edu/entries/african-ethics/ (2010).
5. Some of the paragraphs in this section have been cribbed from Thaddeus Metz, "An African Theory of Social Justice: Relationship as the Ground of

Rights, Resources and Recognition," *Distributive Justice Debates in Political and Social Thought*, ed. Camilla Boisen and Matt Murray (Abingdon: Routledge, 2016), 171–190, "Replacing Development: An Afro-communal Approach to Global Justice," *Philosophical Papers* 46 (2017): 111–137, and "The Ethics and Politics of the Brain Drain: A Communal Alternative to Liberal Perspectives," *South African Journal of Philosophy* 36 (2017): 101–114.

6. Segun Gbadegesin, *African Philosophy* (New York: Peter Lang, 1991), 65.
7. Yvonne Mokgoro, "*Ubuntu* and the Law in South Africa," *Potchefstroom Electronic Law Journal* 1 (1998): 15–26 at 17.
8. Pantaleon Iroegbu, "Beginning, Purpose and End of Life," in *Kpim of Morality Ethics*, ed. Pantaleon Iroegbu and Anthony Echekwube (Ibadan: Heinemann Educational Books, 2005), 440–445 at 442.
9. Gessler Muxe Nkondo, "*Ubuntu* as a Public Policy in South Africa," *International Journal of African Renaissance Studies* 2 (2007): 88–100 at 91.
10. Dismas Masolo, *Self and Community in a Changing World* (Bloomington: Indiana University Press, 2010), 240.
11. On which see Anthony Appiah, "Ethical Systems, African," in *Routledge Encyclopedia of Philosophy*, ed. Edward Craig (London: Routledge, 1998).
12. A criticism made by Penny Enslin and Kai Horsthemke, "Philosophy of Education: Becoming Less Western, More African?" *Journal of Philosophy of Education* 50 (2016): 177–190 at 186.
13. Although respecting others insofar as they are capable of communion means not aiming to foster it by being discordant with those who have themselves respected communion, it can mean directing discordance towards those who have misused their capacity to commune, if it is necessary to get them to stop or to compensate their innocent victims.
14. Peter Kasenene, *Religious Ethics in Africa* (Kampala: Fountain Publishers), 21.
15. There have of course been some relational strains in the Western tradition, including the ethic of care, certain appeals to loyalty, and some kinds of communitarianism. Even here, however, there are important differences between these views and the Afro-communal moral theory. For one, communion includes not merely caring for others' quality of life but also sharing a way of life, a distinct way of relating not often thematized by care ethicists. For another, the concept of human dignity is central to the African tradition and grounds a kind of impartiality that is rare to encounter in Western forms of relationalism, particularly those appealing to bonds of loyalty and social identity. By the communal ethic, everyone has a dignity in virtue of the capacity to be party to communal relationships, even if those with whom we have in fact communed are entitled to greater aid.

16. If the reader is uncomfortable with the idea of an institution being an agent distinct from the individual human persons who compose it at a given time, then she may read the duty as binding on all the individual members.
17. This section draws on some ideas first published in Thaddeus Metz, "The Final Ends of Higher Education in Light of an African Moral Theory," *Journal of Philosophy of Education* 43 (2009): 179–201, and "An African Egalitarianism: Bringing Community to Bear on Equality," in *The Equal Society*, ed. George Hull (Lanham, MD: Rowman & Littlefield, 2015), 185–208.
18. Many of these programmes are in fact undertaken by public universities in South Africa, even if not to an adequate degree due to limited resources.
19. Etienne Wenger, *Communities of Practice: Learning, Meaning and Identity* (Cambridge: Cambridge University Press, 1998).
20. For more on this point, see Thaddeus Metz, "Communitarian Ethics and Work-Based Education: Some African Perspectives," in *Learning, Work and Practice*, ed. Paul Gibbs (Dordrecht: Springer, 2012), 191–206 at 198–200.
21. On which see Bénézet Bujo, *The Ethical Dimension of Community*, trans. C. N. Nganda (Nairobi: Paulines Publications, 1997), 164.
22. For some suggestions, see Metz, "The Final Ends of Higher Education in Light of an African Moral Theory," 185–193.
23. It is common for theorists to maintain that behind the different global moralities are different ontologies. One frequently encounters the suggestion that Western societies hold an atomist metaphysics that grounds an individualist approach to ethics, whereas African and Asian societies adhere to a holist metaphysics that grounds a relational approach to ethics. Although there have been these historical associations, for reason to doubt that a certain ontology necessitates a particular sort of morality, see Thaddeus Metz, "Questioning African Attempts to Ground Ethics on Metaphysics," in *Ontologized Ethics*, ed. Elvis Imafidon and John Bewaji (Lanham, MD: Rowman & Littlefield Publishers, 2013), 189–204.
24. John White, *The Aims of Education Restated* (London: Routledge, 2010). See also Richard Norman, "'I Did It My Way': Some Thoughts on Autonomy," *Journal of Philosophy of Education* 28 (1994): 25–34, and several contributions to Roger Marples (ed.) *The Aims of Education* (London: Routledge, 1999).
25. For just a few examples, see Israel Scheffler, *Reason and Teaching* (New York: Bobbs-Merrill, 1973); Harvey Siegel, *Educating Reason: Rationality, Critical Thinking, and Education* (New York: Routledge, 1988); and John Mearsheimer, "The Aims of Education," *Philosophy and Literature* 22 (1998): 137–155.

26. See, for example, Bujo, "Differentiations in African Ethics," 432–433; Robert Birt, "Of the Quest for Freedom as Community," in *The Quest for Community and Identity: Critical Essays in Africana Social Philosophy*, ed. Robert Birt (Lanham, MD: Rowman & Littlefield, 2002), 87–104; and Polycarp Ikuenobe, *Philosophical Perspectives on Communalism and Morality in African Traditions* (Lanham, MD: Rowman and Littlefield, 2006), 51–87, 265–287.
27. See, for example, Elizabeth Kiss and J. Peter Euben (eds) *Debating Moral Education: Rethinking the Role of the Modern University* (Durham, NC: Duke University Press, 2010). For clear critics of moral education beyond some contributors to that volume, see Mearsheimer, "The Aims of Education"; Jonathan Adler, "Knowledge, Truth, and Learning," in *A Companion to the Philosophy of Education*, ed. Randall Curren (Malden, MA: Blackwell, 2003), 285–304; and Stanley Fish, *Save the World on Your Own Time* (New York: Oxford University Press, 2008).
28. Edward Shils, "The Academic Ethic," repr. in *The Calling of Education: The Academic Ethic and Other Essays on Higher Education*, ed. Edward Shils and Steven Grosby (Chicago: University of Chicago Press, 1997), 3–128.
29. Gordon Graham, *Universities: The Recovery of an Idea, 2nd edn* (Exeter: Imprint Academic, 2008).
30. Edmund Husserl, "Philosophy and the Crisis of European Man," trans. Quentin Lauer, http://www.users.cloud9.net/~bradmcc/husserl_phil-cris.html (1935).
31. John Henry Newman, *The Idea of a University* (repr. New York: Longmans, Green, 1907).
32. "Knowledge, Truth, and Learning," 287.
33. Cited and critically discussed in Thaddeus Metz, "Higher Education, Knowledge for Its Own Sake, and an African Moral Theory," *Studies in Philosophy and Education* 28 (2009): 517–536.
34. For more on this contrast, see Thaddeus Metz, "Values in China as Compared to Africa," in *The Rise and Decline and Rise of China*, ed. Hester du Plessis (Johannesburg: Real African Publishers, 2015), 75–116 at 96–99, and "How the West Was One: The Western as Individualist, the African as Communitarian," *Educational Philosophy and Theory* 47 (2015): 1175–1184.
35. See my *Meaning in Life: An Analytic Study* (Oxford: Oxford University Press, 2013), esp. 204–205, 209–210, 213–215, 229–230.
36. For instance, Edward Shils, "'Render unto Caesar ...': Government, Society, and the University in Their Reciprocal Rights and Duties," in *The Calling of Education: The Academic Ethic and Other Essays on Higher Education*, ed. Edward Shils and Steven Grosby (Chicago: University of Chicago Press, 1997), 177–233.

37. Martha Nussbaum, *Not for Profit: Why Democracy Needs the Humanities* (Princeton: Princeton University Press, 2010).
38. A similar view is advanced by Elizabeth Anderson, for whom the main point of higher education is to enable people to advance social justice conceived in terms of improving the economic lot of the worst off and taking advantage of political and civil liberties. See her "What Is the Point of Equality?" *Ethics* 109 (1999): 287–337 and "Fair Opportunity in Education: A Democratic Equality Perspective," *Ethics* 117 (2007): 595–622.
39. Nussbaum, *Not for Profit*, 9.
40. Ibid., 9.
41. Argued in, for instance, Thaddeus Metz, "Developing African Political Philosophy: Moral-Theoretic Strategies," *Philosophia Africana* 14 (2012): 61–83.
42. Nussbaum, *Not for Profit*, 9–10.
43. For this point and some additional ones about the aptness of focusing on local culture, see Thaddeus Metz and Joseph Gaie, "The African Ethic of *Ubuntu/Botho*: Implications for Research on Morality," *Journal of Moral Education* 39 (2010): 273–290 at 279–280.
44. For written comments that have led to some substantial improvements in this essay, the author is grateful to Eli Kramer and Aaron Stoller.

PART IV

Return to Experience: Reconstruction Put into Practice

CHAPTER 10

Remaking the Academy: The Potential and the Challenge of Transdisciplinary Collaborative Engagement

Danielle Lake, Amy McFarland, and Jessica Jennrich

Closing the gap between public education and the public, addressing "real" community problems in "real" time, and preparing students to meliorate intractable social problems are—and have been—consistent challenges for institutions of higher education. Increasing tuition costs, shrinking public budgets, instantaneous around-the-clock access to information, and massive open online classes also challenge conventional academic structures. In truth, however, concerns about the role of higher education and it's disconnect from public needs are not new. A persistent lack of focus on social literacy, local and global policy, public action, and collaboration within higher education impedes the ability to view—let alone effectively address—the complex, interconnected, systemic challenges we are facing across the globe. Indeed, the dominant structures, processes, and cultures within higher education present serious barriers to our ability to collaboratively address these public problems.[1]

D. Lake (✉) • A. McFarland • J. Jennrich
Grand Valley State University, Allendale, MI, USA

A. Stoller, E. Kramer (eds.), *Contemporary Philosophical Proposals for the University*, https://doi.org/10.1007/978-3-319-72128-6_10

We argue higher education can better respond to these challenges by more fully committing itself to not only (1) *collaboratively* generating and disseminating knowledge and skills but also by (2) connecting the production of knowledge to its use, (3) fostering the capacity for these practices, and (4) operating as a boundary-spanning space, working to train students as boundary spanners (people who cross worlds, drawing together stakeholders across difference in order to address social challenges).[2] Indeed, we believe this is the purpose of higher education. This chapter explicates this philosophic approach to higher education, documents how we have instantiated it at our own institution, and highlights the lessons learned. In particular, we suggest feminist pragmatism, the movement towards public engagement,[3] and the field of transdisciplinarity[4] offer a vision for—and effective approach to—collaborative engagement. When taken together and applied in the academy, these fields offer a vision, path, and set of tools for remaking the academy as a place where collaborative engagement work is not only supported and promoted, but integrated into the very framework and culture of the institution itself. As a part of these commitments to more fully engage in inclusive and collaborative practices, this chapter was not only imagined and coauthored by three university stakeholders across various positionalities (two are tenure-track faculty located in different spaces at the university and one is the director of the Center for Women and Gender Equity), it was also reviewed and affirmed by a learning community from across the university.

After explicating our own philosophic commitments, we document how we have put these commitments into practice through the creation of a unique and diverse learning community. For instance, our community was envisioned as a catalyst for not just procedural changes but also structural and cultural changes intended to support collaborative teaching and learning. It included participants from across the campus representing diverse positionalities and roles. With a commitment to learning-by-doing, participants harnessed the vision above, developed a plan to advocate for change, and began to implement changes designed to better support and incentivize collaborative engagement. This approach allowed us to test our philosophic commitments, exploring how a feminist pragmatist approach, the public engagement movement, and the call for transdisciplinarity might generate particularly promising opportunities for bridging divides and fostering connections along various dimensions and scales. We conclude by noting that creative and collaborative advocacy across university and community divides can be an effective approach along a couple of dimensions: it can "disrupt and dismantle" the existing hegemony within university structures ***and*** create new models that recognize, resource, and reward collaborative engagement, bringing this work to the forefront of the university.[5] But first we say a bit more about why many of the dominant culture and structures of higher education are detrimental to our collective future.

What, More Precisely, Is the Problem with the Dominant Structures, Processes, and Culture of Higher Education?

While the STEM subjects have been important in our quest for understanding and solving complex problems (e.g., space travel, antibiotics), many of our shared problems cannot be resolved through formulas, technological innovation, or expert intervention. Think, for instance, of the long-standing issues surrounding poverty, religious intolerance, food justice, and racism. Technological intervention or expert innovation cannot resolve such issues. Given the pressing need to address "wicked" public problems—diabolical, intractable, systemic, interconnected messes like those noted above[6]—collaborative, courageous, and creative engagement is needed. Defined as "authentic reciprocity in partnerships between those working at colleges and universities and those in the wider community,"[7] collaborative engagement has the power to contextualize, apply, and thereby extend and enhance academic research so it can be put to use to meliorate such public problems. This approach would help develop the connection between the academy and community needs that has consistently been criticized as either absent, haphazard, or self-serving. Indeed, according to Keeler et al. the world literally "cannot afford to wait decades more for universities to provide infrastructure and foster the culture needed to turn ideas into action. If we want science to serve society and the planet... we must take responsibility for institutional innovation."[8]

On the other hand, we recognize that collaborative work can increase the demand on faculty, staff, students, and the community. Not only are the demands already high, but more than half of faculty are part-time and nontenure track, which necessarily impacts the ability of those faculty to instantiate collaborative engagement in their work efforts.[9] Indeed, community engagement thought leaders have concluded that such burdens have operated as powerful barriers towards substantive and sustainable institutional change.[10,11] We agree and argue that collaborative engagement efforts are often stymied precisely because they are an "addition to" current structures and demands within the academy. Attempting to force collaborative engagement initiatives into a structure and culture resistant to and disdainful of this work will not generate the kind of deep, pervasive, and integrated change being called for.

To be fair, the academy is not a "singular entity" (as George Allan in this volume notes); there are collaborative departments, disciplines, and research teams, but these "micro-communities" are still too rare and their reach too narrow (see Ronald Barnett's piece). Academics often fail to cross the hall to converse with one another, and—when they do—they often talk *past* one another instead of *with* one another, compete instead of collaborate, deconstruct instead of build upon. We suggest committed stakeholders focus on generating more diverse, collaborative, and activist-oriented micro-communities. Given our own experiences we believe such efforts can help to infuse collaborative engagement throughout higher education.[12]

A Philosophy, a Movement, and a Bridge to the Collaboratively Engaged Academy

We have found three fields particularly relevant to reimagining higher education so it operates as an effective boundary-spanning space for collaborative engagement: feminist pragmatism, the recent public engagement movement, and transdisciplinarity. Feminist pragmatism articulates the philosophic commitments behind the move towards collaborate engagement, but it is not widely recognized within the academy. The recent movement within higher education towards public engagement offers a pathway forward via a community of practice. Publicly engaged scholars offer some practical tools for re-envisioning scholarly work as a holistic endeavor connected to our lives and communities. Transdisciplinarity, as the academic framing of a feminist pragmatist approach, helps scholars and teachers see how they might move along a path towards publicly engaged scholarship, supporting not just the current generation of engaged scholar-practitioners but also more established scholars. Thus, we next briefly document the merits of these fields and show how operating from the intersections between them can be an effective catalyst for change in the infrastructure, procedures, and culture of academic institutions.

The Philosophy: Feminist Pragmatism

As a philosophy dedicated to addressing complex, social problems, feminist pragmatism is uniquely placed to support on-the-ground ameliorative efforts. Emerging in the 1990s, this strand of feminist philosophy is grounded in the core concepts of pragmatism: fallibilism, experimental and context-bound action, public engagement, and integration. Seeing collaborative reflective praxis as critical for addressing shared social challenges, feminist pragmatists are committed to the iterative movement between theory and action.[13] They also deliberately employ feminist critiques, enhancing and instantiating pragmatist notions of narrative and activism. Like other forms of feminism, feminist pragmatism reminds us that philosophy is inherently embodied and activist focused and should thus always acknowledge the need for narrative, other ways of knowing, and for addressing systemic problems of power.

In addition to harnessing philosophy in order to address on-the-ground social challenges, feminist pragmatists have also sought to recover women who were a part of the emergence of pragmatist thought/action and yet left out of the canon. Prior to the emergence of this approach, the most celebrated forms of American pragmatism largely came from *within* the academy through figures like John Dewey, William James, George Herbert Mead, and Charles S. Peirce (considered the founders of pragmatism). Feminist pragmatists retrace this same time period—the late nineteenth and early twentieth century—from *outside* the academy, capturing the social activist work of women enacting unique versions of this philosophic approach to social justice from other spaces. By doing so the field captures important critiques of traditional pragmatism, democracy, diversity, education, and social action, offering a wealth of resources for feminist philosophers, working activists, and practitioner scholars seeking to address social injustice.[14]

This form of philosophy provides a grounded approach for meliorating the barriers, risks, and constraints encountered by those attempting the work of collaborative engagement within dominant structures. Feminist pragmatism offers a viable vision for higher education that honors whole selves (not just our intellectual development but social and emotional development as well) and diverse communities. In contrast, the academy still often neglects to recognize the assumptions and value commitments under which it operates, the public nature of its work, and the value of other forms of knowledge construction (i.e., indigenous, community, and holistic knowledge). Given that these dominant practices have endured for hundreds of years in the United States and that, in general, institutions of higher education have the resources to reimagine themselves, this lack of self-reflexivity is particularly disheartening.[15]

Directly influenced by feminist pragmatists of the time, John Dewey's educational philosophy offers a strong initial vision upon which many have built. He argues the goal of academic inquiry, indeed the purpose of higher education as a whole, is not endless knowledge production but the resolution of problems. He advocates for an education that fosters creative capacity, recommending we design our institutions so they foster such habits in all persons.[16] This approach prompts academics to consider how our policies and practices are and should be experiments in action, subject to revision if and when they no longer serve a wide range of interests.[17] Feminist pragmatists add to this a focus on diversity, dialogue, and reciprocity,[18] challenging the idea that experts should have an authoritative say "by deliberately seeking to involve those for whom the situation was problematic or disadvantageous in the first place."[19] According to this approach, we need to ***reimagine*** and ***reposition*** the expert, designing a more limited, fallible, and engaged position that navigates between spaces.[20]

A host of education reformers, philosophers, and activists have taken up this call over the years. Experiential learning researcher David Kolb notes that the "process of socialization into a profession" tends to instill not simply "knowledge and skills but also a fundamental reorientation of one's identity" that is "pervasive," leading to a certain "standard and ethics" and a clear-cut way to "think and behave."[21] He argues higher education needs to develop the "whole person," encouraging "creativity, wisdom, and integrity."[22] Through such adaptive flexibility, we can move towards integration and counteract the tendency towards isolated professionalism. Parker Palmer further supports Kolb's work by providing a vision for resisting this negative socialization process. We can resist the pressure towards adverse performativity, through "integrity,"[23] through acknowledging that the "things I teach are things I care about—and what I care about helps define my selfhood."[24] Palmer's explanation of successful teaching as a practice infused by authenticity that educates others as well as enriches himself illustrates how to open space for whole selves: share our lived experiences, value authenticity, and model passion; doing so is likely to spark active engagement despite the constraints of the academy.

In addition to practicing strategies for inspiring wholeness, advocacy work encouraging the academy—as a public institution designed to serve public needs—to give primacy to public participation and pursue research linked to social and political change is needed. According to activist philosopher—and feminist pragmatist—Grace Lee Boggs, the "conditions of postindustrial society especially challenge educators to reexamine conventional assumptions and to create a new community-based, person-centered model of education."[25] Indeed, she says we need to go beyond educational reform; "we need a *paradigm* shift." She argues that it will be through the revolution of our educational models that we can imagine and enact a better future.[26] Instead of becoming public intellectuals, experts have set themselves apart. Academics need to "transcend the 'value-neutral' ideology of expertise by explicitly anchoring research to the interests of particular interest groups and to the processes of political and policy argumentation in society." Such outreach would make implicit assumptions explicit, make public otherwise hidden practices, and encourage those involved to "speak for themselves."[27]

Thus, feminist pragmatism makes it clear that there is a need to reimagine and restructure the processes, policies, and infrastructure of the academy. Higher education policies and practices discourage academics from paying attention to one another (let alone the public), fostering misunderstanding.[28] Such systematic processes also promote technical and obtuse language discouraging public involvement.[29] A number of recent national initiatives have recognized these barriers and are currently working to enact a collaborative approach. Such approaches have shown some promise for shifting higher education towards collaborative engagement. We argue that public engagement—explored next—is that paradigm shift.

The Movement: A (Re)New(ed) Demand for Publicly Engaged Scholarship

In large measure, the incoming generation of scholars and students seek to enact what we have defined as a feminist pragmatist approach: resisting the notion that their identities must be segmented, that academics must be trained in customary, disciplinary theories, or that knowledge must be produced in traditional non-narrative ways.[30] Instead of choosing between public or private, the community or the individual, rationality or sentiment, publicly engaged scholars acknowledge the value of both and bring their whole selves to their work. They are more interested in "remaking the academy" than "making it" in the academy.[31] By bridging the boundaries that divide and reimagining what counts as valuable knowledge, they become agents of change. By engaging in this work with others, they also train resilient agents of change: those with the capacity, flexibility, and courage to engage in self-authorship.[32]

Publicly engaged scholarship upholds a feminist pragmatist approach by seeking to empower all stakeholders to become cogenerators of knowledge with scholars.[33] It encourages a pedagogy that enacts reciprocity and shifts power so students are no longer "entirely beholden to the 'authoritative other,' encouraging the integration of the 'subjective self.'"[34] Publicly engaged scholarship thus challenges conventional notions of the "peer" in the peer-review process; it extends the audience for scholarly output; and it expands upon the notion of expertise.[35] This movement opens pathways for enacting a feminist pragmatist philosophy within higher education; it responds to concerns about the relevancy of the university; it creates a community of like-minded individuals seeking change and creates space for sharing stories and tools designed to support collaborative efforts.

This approach, however, is risky. Although the commitment to serving the public good is becoming increasingly recognized by institutional administrators, the existing structures of the university continue to house a "narrow environment unaccepting of many ways of knowing and different habits of being."[36] The hierarchy of acceptable forms of scholarship and audiences for such scholarship has proven to be difficult to subvert. For example, within the academy, there exists a belief that the values of rigor and collaboration "are antagonistic."[37,38] Collaboratively authored professional publications are often met with skepticism from colleagues, particularly in the humanities, and tenure and promotion guidelines have historically valued single-author publications more highly than coauthored ones. This attitude remains even in institutions that formally recognize the value of collaboration.[39] Devoting time and energy to such scholarship puts at risk one's ability to complete traditionally recognized scholarship more likely to ensure tenure and promotion.[40] This problem is pervasive throughout academia, both in the United States and in other countries—with some scholars calling engaged work "career suicide."[41] They note that "academic career pathways [are a] challenging obstacle to any university's attempts to be responsive."[42] Privileging individualism at the expense of collaboration is not a problem confined to faculty. In the classroom, group work is frequently met with disdain from students, and unapproved student collaboration is considered plagiarism and academic dishonesty.[43] Individual work is the norm—in both our professional expectations of staff and faculty and the expectations of students.

Despite the university structures that continue to privilege individual, disciplinary work, students' academic experiences are enhanced by integrated, engaged, collaborative scholarship and teaching by many types of knowledge co-creators. Although research on specific objectives is lacking, increased retention and college completion rates are positively related to civic engagement in the classroom.[44] In addition, learning that draws upon personal experience encourages the reconstruction of narrowly framed customs and unreflective values, expanding students' ethical framework. Considering this, the movement towards public engagement must renegotiate academic spaces to meet the needs of a wider variety of stakeholders, opening opportunities for all to bring their whole selves to their work rather than segment their identities and experiences to fit the existing models within academia. By recreating the academy as an institution that not only supports and resources but actively rewards working with the community towards the public good, universities strategically challenge concerns about their relevancy in today's "Information Age." Public engagement provides students, scholars, and community members with critical opportunities to work across traditional boundaries and—by doing so—build the capacity and resiliency needed to address wicked problems. However, academics need a language to frame their work in a way that is understood by traditional academics and academic structures. Transdisciplinarity, explored next, offers a bridge for getting there.

The Bridge: Transdisciplinarity

As we've seen, collaborative efforts to address complex, shared problems are stymied by higher education's primary commitment to disciplinary expertise and departmental review. Expecting disciplinary departments—as they are currently structured—to address social, political, environmental, and economic messes is most likely a mistake for a number of reasons: (1) faculty tend to lack training to do this work and support in applying their findings, (2) disciplinary frameworks often address complex problems from a narrowly framed perspective (without paying attention to place specificities and context), and (3) pressures towards publication and grant funding prioritize narrow, short-term outcomes. In contrast, incentivizing transdisciplinary, context-sensitive initiatives encourages faculty to engage the public with a purpose, more consistently connect with one another across their divergent areas of expertise, and collaboratively design more flexible, responsive curriculum.

The term "transdisciplinary" emerges from international discussions about the need to move between and *beyond* the disciplines in the 1970s. Broadly defined, transdisciplinarity captures the movement between one's home base and the larger world (whether one's home is an academic department, center, non-profit, or other entity). While some scholars more narrowly define transdisciplinarity as the integration of insights across disciplines (an inward framing), others emphasize the need to begin in and with the problems of our surrounding community.[45] We engage with the latter definition, believing this outward framing provides a pathway towards "authentic" engagement: a process that seeks to empower "citizens, as well as administrators and political leaders" to "initiate and have an equal role in determining processes, agendas, and issues."[46] In contrast to traditional academic and research goals aimed at simply producing or assessing knowledge, transdisciplinarity expands the commitments under which scholars and researchers work: requiring collaboration across institutional divides aimed at meliorating complex, pressing problems.[47]

With this framing in mind, we argue transdisciplinarity provides a flexible epistemological and ethical framework as well as a set of tools and infrastructural models academics can latch onto as they move towards genuinely collaborative work.[48] As an *epistemology*, it emphasizes problems "on the ground," practical reasons, and all kinds of knowledge cultures (community and place-based knowledge, cultural knowledge, etc.), expanding who and what counts. As an *ethos*, transdisciplinarity commits us to "value process over structure, uncertainty over equilibrium, evolution over permanency, and individual creativity over collective stabilization."[49] It focuses attention on changing problematic situations, collaborative engagement, transformative learning, and contributing to useable knowledge. As a series of flexible and iterative, *participatory processes*, transdisciplinarity encourages a community of practice, expanding the range of others scholars are in dialogue with.[50]

With this framing in mind, we suggest transdisciplinarity might just be the vision behind which academics can rally, a moniker for expanding and connecting the purpose of higher education (to not only study and educate about our shared problems but also help prepare for and collaboratively address these problems) with the language of the academy.[51] According to Robert Frodeman, "it is the transdisciplinary moment" that will mark "the end of the era of peer control." It is the siren's call that "threatens to truly change things."[52]

We next show how we ourselves tried to enact these recommendations across our own institution.

Instantiating Our Commitments: Collaborative Engagement Learning Community

The What, Why, Where, When, and How

With this philosophic framework, national movement, and set of processes in mind, we attempted to enact collaborative engagement through a unique and diverse "learning community" at our own institution. Learning communities at our institution are grant-funded, faculty-only spaces sponsored by the campus Faculty Teaching and Learning Center. Traditionally, the center provides a small stipend and administrative support in order to bring a group of faculty together around pedagogical issues of interest.[53] Participants meet regularly throughout the semester, discuss relevant readings, consider how they might apply the knowledge gained, and, ultimately, author a brief report shared with the center documenting any group outcomes. Our own group deconstructed this typical learning community in a number of ways. For instance, we intentionally sought out participants from across the campus representing diverse positionalities, including students, directors and staff of the centers for social justice (including the Center for Women and Gender Equity director), adjunct, affiliate, tenure-track and tenured faculty (from departments such as liberal studies, art and design, and the Honors College), administrators (including the director for community engagement), as well as boundary-spanning individuals who have moved between different roles within the university (former university community partners, alumni, and support staff).

This community was envisioned as a means to spark discussion for and actions towards cultural and structural changes intended to better support collaborative teaching and learning. To work towards these goals, we met ten times over the course of the academic year, read and discussed *Publicly Engaged Scholars: Next-Generation Engagement and the Future of Higher Education*,[54] wrestled with how we might apply the text to our own institutional experiences, and worked towards envisioning new models and structures. Our objective was to identify barriers and opportunities to collaborative engagement and then imagine, advocate for, and enact ways for staff, faculty, administrators, current and former students, and community members to engage equitably and be legitimized as thriving scholars. We also sought to act on our conclusions.

Our learning community was surrounded by a larger set of recent transformations towards civic learning and community engagement across the university. The 2016–2021 university strategic plan highlights the importance of engagement, prioritizing increases to community-based learning experiences. In addition, a community foundation grant sparked funding matches by the university's colleges to create six "Engaged Departments" over a three-year period.[55] The university president also signed Campus Compact's civic action plan,[56] sparking the creation of teams across campus working on documenting and leveraging engagement activity. It has yielded a 21-page civic action plan. The creation of university-wide distinguished engagement awards, a community partnership showcase, and a faculty colloquia series on community-based learning also emerged over the same academic year. Efforts are also underway to explore the pursuit of Carnegie Community Engagement Classification.[57] These recent changes at the university are all promising. However, this community identified definite gaps between the *call* for change and the infrastructural, procedural, and cultural support needed to support collaborative engagement.

The institutional context within which our learning community operated posed challenges. With over 25,000 students, our institution is a large, public, liberal arts university located in the Midwest. Our institutional demographics reflect our state demographics with 82% of our student body identifying as white. In addition, approximately 30% of our students are first-generation college students.[58] In order to uncover the regional implications of historical segregation, support efforts to increase diversity, and work towards the empowerment of marginalized voices, we sought to keep such contextual factors at the forefront of our work.

Committing ourselves to learning-by-doing, to a reflexive praxis of engagement, we ultimately developed recommendations and advocated for change both on- and off-campus. For example, instead of staying housed in safe and convenient like-minded spaces, we met throughout the academic year in several spaces, including the student center, the Honors College, and off-campus in the community. We co-presented our work and gathered feedback from a student-led Teach-in and the Indiana Campus Compact Service Engagement Summit. The inclusive makeup of the community, its activist nature, the intentional moving between spaces, and its outreach efforts were all markedly different from the standard learning community approach. As we show next, these practices helped us define, enact, and thereby test the commitments noted above.

Initial Findings

From Barriers and Risks to Opportunities: In line with the national research on the challenges to collaborative engagement within the current structures of higher education, the learning community identified institution-specific risks surrounding the lack of preparation for students, staff, and faculty and the potential of harm to the community. In addition, the community noted that engaged faculty risk their work will be perceived as "less than," as service, and as suspect. The community also identified institution-specific barriers including a lack of collaborative spaces for engaging in this work (both virtual and physical), a lack of resources, and a lack of time. It was noted that faculty need assistance in locating, developing, and sustaining partnerships over time and staff and community partners need assistance to improve the capacity for information generated to be utilized without increasing full-time faculty and staff responsibilities.

On the heels of developing this list of barriers and risks, the community also considered how these issues were opportunities for transformation. Thus, we simultaneously developed a list of recommendations for addressing these challenges, including the creation of:

- Inclusive and ongoing training opportunities (where community, staff, and student voices are legitimized)
- Resources (e.g., fellowships, co-teaching grants, release time, student work study, community partner stipends, etc.)
- Collaborative positions designed to span the boundaries between these spaces (e.g., community coordinators, transacademic interface managers, boundary spanners, epistemediators, transdisciplinary managers, etc.)[59]
- Curriculum (collaboratively designed, facilitated, and assessed)
- Spaces for collaboration (virtual and physical)

From General Recommendations to Prioritized and Actionable Next Steps: We then transformed these general recommendations into a list of prioritized actionable next steps by discussing national best practices in the field and how we might enhance on-campus efforts already underway. In order to successfully advocate for the enhancement and recognition of collaborative engagement and transdisciplinarity, we also connected each of our "prioritized action recommendations" to the new university strategic plan (see appendix). In just a few short months, tangible on-campus changes have already emerged. For instance, the creation of one-page visual pathway flyers describing opportunities for student curricular, co-curricular, and community engagement with various social justice issues (both across and beyond the institution) has been crafted, the development of a preparatory collaborative engagement course is now underway, and opportunities for student ambassadors and leaders, as well as mechanisms for legitimizing community expertise on campus, are emerging. By next briefly explicating these changes, we hope to both validate the merit of our inclusive and activist approach and offer potentially useful examples for the reader.

1. *Visualizing Pathways*: Visual one-page flyers inspired by Carleton College's Pathways program[60] are now in development. These online and on-paper one-page brochures are intended to help students visualize ways they can leverage their interest in particular social justice issues by engaging their passion via curricular, co-curricular, and community opportunities. Such visual pathways can help students pursue opportunities across traditional divides, develop networks of support, and increase the chances of long-term and collaborative engagement projects; they, in essence, open opportunities for incoming students to become boundary spanners. Indeed, by distributing the visual pathways to a wide range of key stakeholders on- and off-campus (i.e., on-campus advisors, housing directors, resident associates, the social justice, career, counseling and service-learning centers, local non-profits, and governmental bodies), their impact and their inclusiveness can expand. We believe the development of these visuals is particularly valuable given that the current gaps between the curriculum, co-curriculum, and the community are often stark and the connection between these spaces still an undertheorized issue.[61]
2. *Connecting the Curriculum and the Co-curriculum and Supporting Student Readiness* (An Interactive Civic Engagement Training Module): Additionally, the Social Justice Centers (the Center for Women and Gender Equity; the Lesbian, Gay, Bisexual and Transgender Resource Center; the Office of Multicultural Affairs; Disability Support Services and Campus Interfaith Resources)

revamped an electronic learning tool originally designed to train students in the Center for Women and Gender Equity who were preparing to engage in gender justice civic engagement projects. The re-design generated a collaborative, intersectional social justice module that contextualizes engagement through a university-lens and intersectional framework. Beginning in the fall of 2017, this module provides students with initial exposure to these issues, training around the challenges and opportunities of engagement, and—upon completion—provides civic engagement opportunities focused on gender, racial, queer, disability, interfaith, and other social justice issues in the community. Further, the training itself serves as an excellent tool for instructors to introduce the idea of reciprocal civic engagement preparation from an intersectional lens while also introducing the Social Justice Center to students. As an online, interactive, multimedia experience co-created by on- and off-campus stakeholders, this module aligns with a range of best practices and can serve a wide-variety of students on- and off-campus. It is ADA compliant, shares stories from our own community, and visualizes engagement across our campus.

3. *Preparing Students and Engaging Community* (A Collaborative Community Prep Course): To address the challenges confronted by a lack of preparation for community engagement, the learning community also envisioned and drafted a community-based learning (CBL) 101 course focused on the what, the why, and the how of CBL. As a co-designed and co-taught course, it would help students explore the various reasons for collaborative engagement from across diverse perspectives and consider different approaches, best practices, as well as inherent challenges. The course would also require students situate themselves: what are their own values, biases, and perceptions in relation to various groups? The creation of such a course aligns with developmental theory and best practices around scaffolding student engagement opportunities,[62] thereby reducing the risks, challenges, and barriers for not just students but all stakeholders. The community generated a course proposal, shared it with interested parties across campus, and elicited feedback. With input the initial proposal has evolved into a course under development focused on the ethical challenges of engagement and activism. We have also advocated for community-based instructors

by talking with administrators about possible job descriptions and compensation strategies that recognize the role of the community partner as a co-educator.[63]

4. *Connecting Students, Staff, and Faculty Through Social Justice Workshops*: At the same time members of this community have spearheaded efforts to create cohesive social justice trainings that meet the needs of the university's co-curricular needs; foster connections between staff, faculty, and students; potentially get students out of the classrooms; and open up an array of future opportunities for students to engage. Traditional co-curricular expectations have been a consistent source of stress for faculty and students, requiring they find and attend on- and off-campus events that align with course objectives and their schedules. The establishment of social justice workshops allows instructors to request engagement opportunities on a day, time, and at a location that fits within their schedule and that align with their course objectives. Delivered by staff of the Social Justice Centers, workshops engage students in issues around "intersectionality," "microaggressions," "gender-based violence," and a range of others. In just one semester the number of workshops offered has doubled and two additional training programs are underway that will foster student leadership and workshop capacity.
5. *Fostering Student Leaders* (Student Ambassadors): The community recognized that opportunities to not just get students involved but also keep them involved was essential. To address this gap on our own campus, we recommended a student ambassador program; such programs legitimize student expertise, foster student leadership and peer mentorship, build capacity, and provide credit and funding (legitimizing sustained engagement).[64] Students working as ambassadors within the Social Justice Centers will receive training and a modest stipend to create and conduct two trainings each semester that speak to the experience of being students with multiple identities in the classroom. The second initiative underway targets students who answer an open call offered at the beginning of the fall semester and attend a training session to co-facilitate workshops alongside Social Justice Center staff. Additional, formal opportunities for students to become ambassadors through the curriculum—as teaching assistants, community liaisons, and project managers—are also being pursued.

6. *Modeling Collaborative Engagement and Creating New Processes* (Prototyping an Inclusive Activist Learning Community Model): Finally, we note that the creation of the community itself is a concrete change in university structures and processes. At the outset of our learning community, the Faculty Teaching and Learning Center had no mechanisms for including staff, students, community partners, or administrators in such communities. Indeed, interested faculty are required to apply to be a part of such communities, and the system in place does not allow students or community partners to submit an intention to participate. There is now a precedent of inclusive learning communities at our institution.

Taken together, the six emerging initiatives highlighted align with research findings on effective interventions for supporting collaborative engagement at the institutional level, leveraging on-campus resources, and empowering local stakeholders. According to Driscoll, the most foundational support metrics for collaborative engagement include ensuring that clear language is embedded into the mission, strategic plan, and marketing materials of the institution.[65] In reflecting on the fruitfulness of this learning community, we note that many changes occurred in large measure because of the passion and dedication of its members. In the end, it was our collective willingness to leverage our own power, space, and relationships with others that often led to the changes outlined. To sustain engagement efforts, further changes to university structures are needed. As Driscoll further notes, the budget and infrastructure must legitimize and supports such efforts and faculty development processes must be implemented.[66] Given the transitory nature of the student body and administration, sustaining such change tends to require strong faculty support and the transformation of university policies (including refining hiring, tenure, and promotion guidelines).[67]

Concluding Thoughts and Recommendations

In just one academic year, our collaborative, transdisciplinary advocacy efforts contributed to imagining and creating mechanisms for shifting isolated, expert-driven teaching, research, and service towards a recognition of the need for collaborative engagement. Our efforts not only disrupted some of the existing hegemony within university structures, they also helped to create structural, procedural, and cultural changes needed to sustain genuinely valuable collaborative engagement. As one initiative among others, it opened (limited) space for reconsidering the paradigms under which higher education functions. On this front, the boundary-spanning space and activist orientation of the group fostered opportunities for the expansion of narrow frameworks as well as flexible and quick responses to roadblocks (indicators of cultural transformation). The learning community also served as a framework from which to discuss the barriers to collaborative engagement in teaching, scholarship, and service with faculty and administrators alike.

We conclude by suggesting that the identification of barriers and risks across disparate positionalities needs to be accompanied by the tough, collective work of imagining a way forward and the even tougher work of advocating for change; and we reconfirm that the frameworks outlined above provide the philosophic underpinning, pathway, and tools for doing this work. By leveraging key tenets emerging from a feminist pragmatist approach, the movement towards public engagement, and transdisciplinary practices, the reader can help bring collaborative engagement to the forefront of the university,[68] providing opportunities for transformation to emerge from within, across, and between divisions instead of from "on high" or from "outside" (catalyzing structural and procedural changes). In our experience, this approach creates a flexible model for effective action, encouraging the reader to:

- Create and incentivize inclusive collaborative opportunities
- Contextualize the challenges to collaborative engagement at one's institution by identifying barriers, challenges, and risks from different positionalities (ensuring that student, community, staff, and administrative perspectives are heard as well as faculty voices from across different stages and spaces of the university)
- Move beyond the identification of challenges towards imagining new structures and processes
- Link these recommendations to the mission, vision, and values of possible strategic partners
- Develop a plan for sharing insights and leveraging feedback into subsequent revisions (understand one's findings as a living document)
- Engage the community in open-minded activism.

We thus recommend the reader consider how they might respond to their own institutional challenges by implementing any of the ideas and strategies outlined, noting that such efforts require we recognize the value of building relationships across divides, opening new pathways, and celebrating "small wins," in place of holding out for more radical formal change.

To the extent that diverse and activist learning communities open space for transdisciplinarity and shift the momentum behind theory-driven, classroom-bound practices and habits towards collaborative and active learning, they can be affirmed as a fruitful point of entry for shifting current practices. Their very existence opens opportunities for pressing against the culture of one's institution; their focus on including diverse positionalities increases the likelihood of understanding the barriers and risks to this work more holistically; their experiential, activist approach increases the chances for concrete procedural and structural changes; and their efforts towards outreach spread the potential for impact beyond the immediate group. We are hopeful that further work will see the integration of collaborative engagement as a part of—instead of an addition to—the expectations and workload obligations of all stakeholders (students, staff, faculty, and community). Finally, we are also hopeful that our experiences and our insights have yielded valuable lessons the reader can pursue in their own future endeavors.

Acknowledgement The successful outreach efforts of this learning community and the recommendations shared here emerged from the hard work and commitment of many people thinking and acting together. We would like to thank our learning community colleagues for their time, creative ingenuity, flexibility, tenacity, and courageous activism working towards changing our campus climate. We would also like to thank those who read and made invaluable feedback on numerous drafts of this chapter, including Dawn Rutecki, Gloria Mileva, and Ellerie Ambrose.

Appendix

Table 10.1 Prioritized action recommendations and the strategic plan

Prioritized action recommendations		*Univ obj*
Resource and recognize legitimize for *all*	Make resources available to faculty, staff, and students who intentionally align community initiatives for increased impact Possibilities include fellowships, co-teaching grants, course release time, work study for student instructors, community partner stipends	Faculty, staff, and students believe the campus is committed to community engagement
Create collaborative *virtual* spaces database platform (Facebook, wikis)	An openly accessible platform for community, faculty, students, and staff to see *who* is doing engaged work across campus, *where* they are doing this, *what* they are doing (organized by issues), and with *which* community organizations Scholarly mechanism to reflect and learn from people who have done this work	The university has a systematic approach for reporting all engagement activities and partnerships
Create collaborative *physical* spaces	Design, create, and incentivize spaces conducive to collaborative projects 1. What does the *act of being* in another space do for the learning experience? Identify and document the literature behind this concept 2. How do we bring faculty and students into other spaces? Bring them there. Require they attend and visit and move out. Document and publicize this necessity 3. Identify models from other universities 4. Connect with established community partners to identify usable collaborative, physical spaces at their site; develop and publish a list (including the contact person) 5. Connect with facilities, campus lawyers, and risk management to develop a plan to implement innovation labs in new buildings 6. Identify corporate donors from the community to support spaces 7. Identify *public* spaces outside of corporate support—public libraries, public museums 8. Connect with faculty and staff in other departments about past success 9. Connect with records to allow off-campus locations to be formally used as classroom spaces	80% believe the university is committed to community engagement

(*continued*)

Table 10.1 (continued)

Prioritized action recommendations		*Univ obj*
Create collaborative curriculum (IDS 1 and 2 credit) (facilitated by faculty, staff, student, and community partner)	Prototype interdisciplinary studies courses co-taught by faculty, staff, student, and community partners featuring high-impact practices. Possibilities include 1 credit "community-based learning 101" co-designed and co-taught by faculty member, student ambassador, longtime community partner, and/or staff from one of the five Social Justice Centers	At least 10% of courses incorporate CBL
Create inclusive opportunities and trainings incentivize for *all*	Design trainings for collaborative engagement that give credit to faculty, students, staff, and community for attending. Possibilities include student travel funds, staff professional development, inclusive grant funding and research opportunities, collaborative conference presentations and publications; teaching awards	25% + of faculty complete training in high-impact student learning
Create collaborative positions	Create, fund, and fill positions designed to/ responsible for fostering and sustaining collaborative engagement. Possibilities include community liaisons, project managers, work study	80% believe the institution is committed to community engagement

Notes

1. See Robert Frodeman, *Sustainable Knowledge: A Theory of Interdisciplinarity* (New York: Palgrave Macmillan, 2013) and Ketevan Mamiseishvili and Vicki J. Rosser, "Examining the Relationship between Faculty Productivity and Job Satisfaction," *Journal of the Professoriate* 5, no. 2 (2011): 101–132.
2. Paul Williams, "The Competent Boundary Spanner," *Public Administration* 80, no 1 (2002): 103–124.
3. Public engagement efforts harness transdisciplinary tools to engage all stakeholders (instructors, staff, students, and community partners) in the co-creation and enactment of knowledge. Nicholas V. Longo and Cynthia M. Gibson, "Collaborative Engagement: The Future of Teaching and Learning in Higher Education," in *Publicly Engaged Scholars: The Next Generation Engagement and the Future of Higher Education* (Sterling, VA: Stylus Publishing, 2016): 65.
4. Transdisciplinarity, as the movement between one's home base and the community, requires educators engage "many perspectives to frame questions,

explore options, and develop and then apply solutions to challenges." Judith A. Ramaley, "The Changing Role of Higher Education: Learning to Deal with Wicked Problems," *Journal of Higher Education Outreach and Engagement* 18, no. 3 (2014): 111.

5. KerryAnn O'Meara, "Legitimacy, Agency, and Inequality: Organizational Practices for Full Participation of Community-engaged Faculty," in *Publicly Engaged Scholars: The Next Generation Engagement and the Future of Higher Education* (Sterling, VA: Stylus Publishing, 2016): 104.
6. See Danielle Lake, "Jane Addams and Wicked Problems: Putting the Pragmatic Method to Use," *The Pluralist* 9, no. 3 (2014): 77–94; Ramaley, "The Changing Role of Higher Education;" and Horst Rittel and Melvin Webber, "Dilemmas in a General Theory of Planning," *Policy Sciences* 4, no. 2 (1973): 155–169.
7. Matthew Hartley and John Saltmarsh, "Civic Engagement and American Higher Education," in *Publicly Engaged Scholars: The Next Generation Engagement and the Future of Higher Education* (Sterling, VA: Stylus Publishing, 2016): 36.
8. Bonnie L. Keeler, Rebecca Chaplin-Kramer, Anne D. Guerry, Prue F.E. Addison, Charles Bettigole, Ingrid C. Burke, et al., "Society is Ready for a New Kind of Science—Is Academia?" *BioScience* 67, no. 7 (2017): 591.
9. American Association of University Professors, "Background Facts on Contingent Faculty," *aaup.org*, https://www.aaup.org/issues/contingency/background-facts. (accessed August 21, 2017).
10. John Saltmarsh, Dwight E. Giles, Elaine Ward, and Suzanne M. Buglione, "Rewarding Community-Engaged Scholarship," in *New Directions for Higher Education* (2009): 25–35 and John Saltmarsh, Emily M. Janke, and Patti H. Clayton, "Transforming Higher Education Through and for Democratic Civic Engagement: A Model for Change," *Michigan Journal of Community Service Learning: The SLCE Future Directions Project* (2015): 122–127.
11. The concept of collaborative engagement is not new within the academy; it is part of a movement that has been increasingly gaining support, both from the top-down and the bottom-up within the university.
12. See Marcia Baxter Magolda, *Making their Own Way: Narratives for Transforming Higher Education to Promote Self-Development* (Sterling, VA: Stylus, 2007); and Longo and Gibson, *Publicly Engaged.*
13. Ignoring the lessons derived from employing our theories on the ground is a dangerous mistake just as failing to reflect on how our theories tend to shape our reality is also often a dangerous mistake. In moving between theory and action on the world, there is more opportunity for flexible responses to changing conditions and thus more opportunity for fruitful growth and transformation.
14. Judy Whipps and Danielle Lake, "Feminist Pragmatism," *The Stanford Encyclopedia of Philosophy*, (2016).

15. Aaron Stoller, "The Theory Gap in Higher Education," *Research in Education* 96, no. 1 (2015): 39–45.
16. John Dewey, MW 1:38.
17. John Dewey, LW 12:502. Dewey's writings also illuminate why academic institutions so often fail to cope with change and adapt to current crises, let alone collaborate with one another or with the public. On this note, he also detects the role underlying habits play in stymying our efforts at effective change.
18. Celia Bardwell-Jones and Maurice Hamington, eds., *Contemporary Feminist Pragmatism* (New York: Routledge, 2013).
19. Charlene Haddock Seigfried, *Pragmatism and Feminism: Reweaving the Social Fabric* (Chicago: University of Chicago Press, 1996), 182.
20. See Roger Koppl, "The Social Construction of Expertise, *Society* 47, no. 3 (2010): 220–226.
21. David Kolb, *Experiential Learning: Experience as the Source of Learning and Development* (Upper Saddle River, NJ: Prentice Hall, 2003), 182.
22. Ibid., 162.
23. Parker Palmer, *The Courage to Teach. Exploring the Inner Landscape of a Teacher's Life* (San Francisco: Jossey-Bass, 1998), 13.
24. Ibid., 17.
25. Grace Lee Boggs and Ossie Davis, *Living for Change: An Autobiography* (Minneapolis: University of Minnesota Press, 1998), 140.
26. Ibid., 136.
27. Frank Fischer, *Citizens, Experts and the Environment: The Politics of Local Knowledge* (Durham, North Carolina: Duke University Press, 2000), 38.
28. Faculty culture generally encourages an insular focus on "'my courses,' 'my scholarly agenda,' 'my students,' and even 'my community partner(s).'" See Kevin Kecskes, "Collectivizing our Impact: Engaging Departments and Academic Change." *Partnerships: A Journal of Service-Learning and Civic Engagement* 6, no. 3 (2015): 58.
29. For example, tenure and publication processes encourage deep but often narrow knowledge construction and thus often offer only partial perspectives. They do this by narrowing the pool of other people scholars are in dialogue with (most often subspecialists) and by honoring technical and abstract language. While such an approach may be effective for understanding technical issues and resolving complex equations, it does not create spaces and opportunity to consider the larger purpose of one's work nor its possible application.
30. John Saltmarsh and Matthew Hartley, "The Inheritance of Next-generation Engagement Scholars" in *Publicly Engaged Scholars: Next-generation Engagement and the Future of Higher Education*, edited by Margaret A. Post, Elaine Ward, Nicholas V. Longo, and John Saltmarsh (Sterling, VA: Stylus, 2016) 15–33.

31. Gary Rhoads, Judy Marquez Kiyama, Rudy McCormick, and Marisol Quiroz, "Local Cosmopolitans and Cosmopolitan Locals: New Models of Professionals in the Academy," *Review of Higher Education* 31, no. 2 (2008): 215.
32. See Baxter Magolda, *Making their Own*; Vicky Gunn, "Constraints to Implementing Learning Partnership Models and Self-authorship in the Arts and Humanities" in *The University and Its Disciplines: Teaching and Learning Within and Beyond Disciplinary Boundaries*, edited by Caroline Kreber (New York: Routledge, 2009) 169–178.
33. Post and Ward, *Publicly Engaged.*
34. Robert J. Nash, *Liberating Scholarly Writing: The Power of Personal Narrative* (New York: Teacher's College Press, 2004) 57.
35. See Hartley and Saltmarsh, "Civic Engagement" and Longo and Gibson, "Collaborative Engagement."
36. Saltmarsh and Hartley, "The Inheritance of Next Generation," 25.
37. Gunn, "Constraints to Implementing," 172.
38. However, there are research fields and methodologies where these spheres have merged, such as participatory action research, sustainability science, and transdisciplinary research. See Katja Brundiers, Arnim Wiek, and Braden Kay, "The Role of Transacademic Interface Managers in Transformational Sustainability Research and Education," *Sustainability* 5 (2013): 4614–4636. doi: 10.3390/su5114614.
39. See Dan Berrett, "Tenure Across Borders: Interdisciplinary Research and Collaboration Get Formal Recognition in New USC Guidelines for Promotion," in *Inside Higher Ed,* (July 11, 2011); Julie Thompson Klein and Holly J. Falk-Krzesinski, "Interdisciplinary and Collaborative Work: Framing Promotion and Tenure Practices and Policies," in *Research Policy* 46 (2017): 1055–1061.
40. O'Meara refers to this as a practice of "legitimacy surveillance" and considers the common practice of warning or advising engaged scholars "to spend less time on engaged work and more time on traditional scholarship to move up in systems of academic legitimacy," (98) as problematic, particularly when such warnings are accompanied by concerns about rigor and complexity. This same concept and practice can be applied to collaborative research where an individual scholar's contributions may be questioned or doubted. See O'Meara, "Legitimacy, Agency, and Inequality."
41. Rosemary Rushmer, "Responsive Research—Simple, Right? The AskFuse Case Study." *Integration and Implementation Insights,* July 11, 2017, https://i2insights.org/2017/07/11/responsive-research-askfuse-case/. (accessed August 16, 2017).
42. Rosemary Rushmer, Janet Shucksmith, and The Fuse Knowledge Exchange Group KEG, "AskFuse Origins: System Barriers to Providing the Research

that Public Health Practice and Policy Partners Say they Need, *Evidence and Policy* (2016). http://www.ingentaconnect.com/content/tpp/ep/pre-prints/content-evp_108. (accessed August 16, 2017).

43. Gunn, "Constraints to Implementing."
44. Ashley Finley, "A Brief Review of the Evidence on Civic Learning in Higher Education." Association of American Colleges and Universities, 2012, https://www.aacu.org/sites/default/files/files/crucible/CivicOutcomes Brief.pdf.
45. Klein and Falk-Krzesinski, "Interdisciplinary and Collaborative."
46. King and Kenson, 2002, p. 109.
47. Allen F. Repko, Rick Szostak, and Michelle P. Buchberger, *Introduction to Interdisciplinary Studies.* (Los Angeles, California: SAGE, 2014).
48. Saltmarsh, Hartley, and Clayton define such work as "inclusive, collaborative, and problem-oriented work in which academics share knowledge generating tasks with the public and involve community partners as participants in public problem-solving" ("Transforming Higher Education," 9).
49. Valerie Brown, "Preface: Transdisciplinarity: A Way of the future?" in *Transdisciplinary Research and Practice for Sustainability Outcomes*, edited by Dena Fam, Jane Palmer, Chris Riedy, and Cynthia Mitchell, (New York: Routledge, 2017) xxii–xxiv.
50. Brian Ó Donnchadha, "Creating a Systematic Approach for the Reflective Practice of Service-learning Academics through the Development of Communities of Reflective Practice," *Doctoral Dissertation*, (National University of Ireland, 2012).
51. Robert D. Reason, Patrick T. Terenzini, and Robert J. Domingo, "Developing Social and Personal Competence in the First Year of College," *Review of Higher Education* 30, no. 3 (2007): 271–299; Emily M. Janke and Jennifer M. Domagal-Goldman. "Institutional Characteristics and Student Civic Outcomes," *Research on Student Civic Outcomes in Service Learning: Conceptual Frameworks and Methods*, edited by Julie A. Hatcher, Robert G. Bringle, and Thomas W. Hahn (Sterling, VA: Stylus, 2017), 261–281.
52. Frodeman, *Sustainable Knowledge*, 61.
53. Pew Faculty Teaching and Learning Center, "Faculty Learning Community Participation Grant," *Grand Valley State University*, Last modified July 29, 2017, http://www.gvsu.edu/ftlc/faculty-learning-community-participation-grant-168.htm. (accessed August 16, 2017).
54. Post and Ward, *Publicly Engaged*.
55. Office for Community Engagement, "Engaged Department Initiative," *Grand Valley State University*, Last modified February 14, 2017, https://www.gvsu.edu/community/engaged-department-initiative-74.htm. (accessed August 16, 2017).

56. Office for Community Engagement, "Civic Action Plan," *Grand Valley State University,* Last modified April 24, 2017. http://www.gvsu.edu/community/civic-action-plan-105.htm. (accessed August 16, 2017).
57. New England Resource Center for Higher Education, "Carnegie Community Engagement Classification," *nerche.org,* http://www.nerche.org/index.php?option=com_content&view=article&id=341&Itemid=618. (accessed August 16, 2017).
58. U.S. Census Bureau. "Quick Facts: Michigan." July 1, 2016. https://www.census.gov/quickfacts/fact/table/MI/PST045216. (accessed August 16, 2017); Institutional Analysis, "GVSU Quick Facts: 2016–17," *Gvsu.edu,* http://reports.ia.gvsu.edu/quick_2016_02JUN17.html. (accessed August 16, 2017).
59. See Brundiers, Wiek, and Kay, "The Role of Transacademic Interface Managers."
60. Alfred Montero, "Pathways" Carleton College, *Carleton.edu,* Last modified August 26, 2016 https://apps.carleton.edu/pathways/. (accessed August 16, 2017).
61. Stoller, "The Theory Gap in Higher Education."
62. Carrie Williams Howe, Kimberly Coleman, Kelly Hamshaw, and Katherine Westdijk, "Student Development and Service-learning: A Three-phased Model for Course Design," *The International Journal of Research on Service-Learning and Community Engagement* 2 (2014): 44–62.
63. We also recommended the establishment of a set of standards to qualify community partners to teach such a class through "tested experience," thereby satisfying the Higher Learning Commission's faculty guidelines; see Higher Learning Commission, "Determining Qualified Faculty through HLC's Criteria for Accreditation and Assumed Practices: Guidelines for Institutions and Peer Review," *Higher Learning Commission,* 2016, http://download.hlcommission.org/FacultyGuidelines_2016_OPB.pdf.
64. See Nicholas V. Longo, Abby Kiesa, and Richard Battistoni, "The Future of the Academy with Students as Colleagues," in *Publicly Engaged Scholars: The Next Generation Engagement and the Future of Higher Education* (Sterling, VA: Stylus Publishing, 2016): 197–213.
65. Amy Driscoll, "Carnegie's Community-Engagement Classification: Intentions and Insights," *Change* 40 (2008): 40.
66. Ibid.
67. Ibid., 41.
68. Farrah Jacquez, Elaine Ward, and Molly Goguen, "Collaborative Engagement Research and Implications for Institutional Change," in *Publicly Engaged Scholars: The Next Generation Engagement and the Future of Higher Education* (Sterling, VA: Stylus Publishing, 2016) 104.

PART V

Future Inquiry: Higher Education in the Coming Century

Check for updates

CHAPTER 11

The Coming Revolution in (Higher) Education: Process, Time, and Singularity

Randall Auxier

Introduction

The ideas of process philosophy in general, and Alfred North Whitehead in particular, will soon come into greater use and wider familiarity. This growth will be a great aid to education and to the reforming of our institutions and practices around the very different educational (and scientific) requirements of the sort of world that sits just beyond the horizon of our present vision. There are several reasons that Whitehead's ideas, as opposed to those of many others, will be of "singular" value, if I may risk a pun.

I will try to explain the present situation with special reference to education, with its rapidly changing institutions and practices, from the viewpoint of process philosophy, and in particular I will do so in a way characteristic of Whitehead's ontology and methods. I choose education since it is primarily responsible for the conservation and transmission of whatever counts as "knowledge" in our civilization, whereas the responsibility of science extends only to the creation and confirmation or disconfirmation of one particular kind of knowledge.[1] The *critique* of science (which is a philosophical task, even when scientists themselves are doing it) is limited to the domain of possible or actual disconfirmation, since the nature of critique is reflective and has no direct relation to actual and

R. Auxier (✉)
Southern Illinois University Carbondale, Carbondale, IL, USA

A. Stoller, E. Kramer (eds.), *Contemporary Philosophical Proposals for the University*, https://doi.org/10.1007/978-3-319-72128-6_11

ongoing efforts at confirming or creating hypotheses. This difference is often obscured by scientific and popular journalism, sometimes with the cooperation of unwise scientists.

When it comes to the task of making the public aware of its results, that task is not itself science; it is journalism and public relations, and scientists have handled the task badly. When it comes to the formation of public policy to instill scientific thinking, methods, and results in the educational system, that is also not science, and the scientific community has acted dogmatically and foolishly, discrediting science as practiced by lowering it to the level of polemical exchange in the press and the school board meeting. This habit works against both the interests of the scientific community and the common good. In short, scientists may be good at science, but they are very bad at public relations and at interacting with those aspects of society that do not operate on scientific principles. Of the institutions that do examine the relations of science and society, the educational ones are the most immediately relevant and important for the dissemination and conservation of scientific knowledge. We must do better.

In an effort to join scientific ideas to the world of educational policy in a way that is limited to responsible critique, I will bring some of Whitehead's most relevant ideas to the fore for more detailed explanation and examination. Scientific ideas and the world of social processes do share a common cosmos, and they can be discussed within one ontology, but that discussion is neither quite science nor educational policy, nor is it even social philosophy. It is a kind of critical synthesis of these with ideas of process, time, and the good (or at least the better). This will be only a selective examination and very much guided by my own understanding of Whitehead.[2] Much more can and should be said about the relevance of other Whiteheadian ideas, apart from those I will discuss. But the task I have set for myself here already threatens to swell beyond its banks. There won't be much direct discussion of education in part one, so I beg the reader's patience and offer assurance that the central topic will benefit from a long introductory inquiry into metaphysics and the future.

I will finish by outlining a picture of the desirable structure and functioning of the university during the coming transition from one kind of culture to another and, indeed, to a kind of culture that includes another kind of human being. There are many relevant implications for primary and secondary education as well, but I set these aside for another time.

The Whiteheadian ideas I will discuss in part two of this inquiry also bear on the question of what education is and will become, in the most fundamental sense of the word. There will be some discontinuities with our collective past in the world to come (considerable ones), but there will also be continuities, at a very broad level, and these will be more important than the breaks with the past. Whitehead's ideas about time and possibility, and their practical applications, place us in a position to do better than guess and conjecture about what is coming. We may genuinely foresee and prepare for the future.

Although we can do better than guess and conjecture, this account is still *speculative.* But, as Whitehead says, speculation "endeavors to frame a coherent, logical, necessary system of general ideas in terms of which every element of our experience can be interpreted."[3] In short, speculation must be a disciplined process and should be judged not only by its coherence, logicality, and necessity but also, in a given inquiry, by its adequacy and applicability to the problem at hand. These are Whitehead's own criteria, and along with much else in his thinking, time has not altered them as categories of evaluation, even if the specific applications of these criteria were well beyond his imagining. In short (as I have argued elsewhere), speculation of the sort that follows is consistent with an orientation of *radical empiricism*[4] and should keep its ground and assumptions in sight at every moment in the flights of disciplined imagination.

Part One: Metaphysics and the Future

Singularity?

There has been a lot of conjecture about the future, and especially intelligent machines, during the past two decades. We have seen some of what was predicted come into existence and then wide, public use. I want to make it clear that while I do not subscribe to the particulars of the much discussed "singularity" thesis, as described by Ray Kurzweil[5] and other futurists, I do believe that we are in the midst of a cultural transition that is historically unprecedented. The term "singularity" is not the best choice for the coming change(s), indicating as it does the *incomparable uniqueness* of the moment, overemphasizing the discontinuities at the expense of continuities between the present and our impending situation. Every moment in time, and every event, taken in the sole light of its mode of difference from other moments or events is singular. Apart from exaggeration, that choice of terms also tends to minimize our efforts to form responsible, general ideas about the ongoing transition, that is, our effort to get knowledge about it for ourselves, so far as that is possible, in the present. If the coming change is so singular as to forbid our generalizing about it from the present into the future, then the quest for knowledge is futile and we might as well play checkers as talk about it.

We must try, after all, to understand what our situation will be when our machines alter, in a fundamental way, the transmission of knowledge (i.e., education) through time and across distance. Otherwise we have little chance of directing it to the better and away from the worse. In fact, the very meanings of "time" and "distance" have already been affected and will change (and grow) still more. Our machines have already so greatly altered the propagation of knowledge as to deserve a fancy name of their own. Let us be unoriginal and call it the information age. The question, then, is: what is coming that is so very different from what has already come to pass as to suggest, to some, the name "singularity"?

Before I answer, consider: *every* situation is unique in some way, and yet, every situation still allows comparison; never, so far as we know (or *can know*) does contrast stand wholly alone. If our immediate and future horizons are difficult to interpret and challenging to imagine, that is hardly a reason to label our efforts to know it, in at least *some* ways, a failure from the outset, or to shrug our shoulders and say "no one knows and no one can." To some degree, such a shrug and a statement is also true also of even the most mundane changes, as well as the most secure scientific predictions. The world is messy. To a very great extent, the claim that we cannot know the future is also simply and necessarily false (logically, if we *know* that we *cannot* know something, we still *know* at least that much, and that *is* knowledge—indeed, one must know a great deal in order to know that one cannot know, as Donald Rumsfeld so notably pointed out once[6]).

But we can know a lot about the future. The known unknowns and even unknown unknowns are part of the same "real" world as the known knowns. Being continuous with its past, the future also stands in positive relation to other matters which were unknown before and have now become known. The process of change, itself, from unknown to known is also a reliable part of relating the past and present to the future. Whatever those relations may be, they are in some degree knowable, which is to say intelligible. Further, the *continuities* in our cosmos are usually dominant over the contrasts, and overwhelmingly so, when we think about the relationship between what is real and what is known. Now, the coming changes, whatever they may be, are real. They can be understood to some extent and can be "known" (in the limited sense allowed by process epistemology) if we describe them with care, seeking continuities between what has become explicit and knowable to us now that was only implicit at the beginning our of quests to know.

Thus, I believe it is possible to see further into this impending change than even most of the *careful* artificial intelligence (AI) theorists are willing to allow. And I think this can be done without being *un*careful; indeed, I think radical empiricism of the sort we find in the thought of Whitehead, Bergson, and William James allows us to foresee and also responsibly describe what to expect. Thus, we may also project some of what we *might* want to do and even some of what we most assuredly *should* do. We know a good deal about how culture advances creatively, and we know some things about how it adjusts to massive and rapid change. Some important structural characters *will* persist through the changes we are currently experiencing, and it is possible to know at least some of what will remain more stable rather than less stable through this interesting epoch in the human adventure.

Liber et Libertas

Let me approach the present situation with an analogy from the past. I am here analogizing a past situation with the present, the information age, not with the even greater change that is on the future horizon. The world is currently undergoing a revolution at least as vast as that which followed the invention of the mechanical printing press with movable type in the mid-fifteenth century. From the very moment when mechanized printing became practicable, it was *possible* (if difficult) to foresee such things as mass literacy, and even universal, tax-supported public education, and all of the changes these would bring. The control of the masses by ecclesiastical and feudal powers would inevitably end, as people gradually understood more of the world and of themselves through reading.[7] It was the vague intuition of this possibility that led many powerful persons into the fifteenth century (and beyond) to try to suppress literacy, to control the technology, to discourage education for the masses.[8] They knew, at some level, that literacy would undermine the social order that had placed them in the lap of power and privilege. A similar but more explicit prohibition of literacy was a component of the "ethos" (if it may be called such) that grew up in support of chattel slavery following the sixteenth century. It was understood that literacy among the slaves (and among even poor, indentured whites and white overseers) would destroy the power relations that enforced slavery. Unhappily, efforts to block the underclass from becoming educated have not disappeared even in the present and take a thousand systemic forms, including the cost of obtaining higher education in the present and the crisis of student debt. It doesn't take a genius to see that a person in debt is easier to control than a debt-free person.

Controlling the movement of information after the invention of the printing press became at first difficult and then almost impossible, at least by the power structures that then existed. The people learned and the political and religious domains of power entered a long transition, as power began to equalize. The Protestant Reformation was fueled by printing and the subsequent increasing literacy. A popular press was not far behind, along with its long struggle (still ongoing) to speak freely. Each reader became an individual *ecclesia*, a church, unto himself or herself, not to mention an independent judge of the day's news.

Something analogous gradually happened in politics and in commerce. It took centuries for the *possibilities* latent in the printing press to come to full fruition, but it was foreseeable as being continuous with the deepest yearnings and aspirations of people who, since I don't have a less hackneyed phrase, *wanted to be free* (even if they were unsure what it meant). They wanted lives that were characterized by what I will later call "intensity." The press and its movable type was the technology, but literacy was the reason the technology mattered. Literacy is a gateway to intense living, and all the power that is embedded in the possession of such "knowledge" would be stored in new devices, called "printed books," external to the active human mind, and could be called up, easily, by anyone who could get books and knew how to read them. It was a potentially endless repository of externalized collective memory. Is it an accident that the Latin word for "book" is *liber* and for "freedom" is *libertas*? I don't think so.

The Current Revolution

We are presently only two decades into a change equally vast in reach and implications as the revolution of 1450. It will not require four and a half centuries for this one to come to fruition. The advent of the information age, particularly the real-time global exchange of useful data, has already altered our ways of learning, and it has radicalized our understanding of *what* knowledge is (knowledge is now access, not to books, but to the net), and *where* it resides (in a commonly accessible "cloud," soon to be replaced by still more ephemeral arrangements of electromagnetic fields[9]). The technology is the form in which the "information" is held, currently in discrete bits, foreseeably in non-discrete, non-local, low-entropy patterns of electromagnetic continua. But if access is available and if literacy means grasping how to get the information into one's hands and head, then what is knowledge?

I think it is worth considering the pieces of the word "information" in ways that help us rethink it. Take *formation* as a process, in the tradition of *bilden* and *Bildung*, and then think of it a process of *expressing* what is already *in* the process, and we have a new and more adequate way of describing what "information" is to information science, that is, a process of continuous transformation that brings to actuality something possible. "Informating" is a thus verb that runs on an energy, a dynamic fuel, if you will, of information. This kind of "information," something like Ernst Cassirer's *symbolic pregnancy*,[10] was always in those books we kept in the libraries, but they appeared to be discrete chunks of knowing, on the surface, and thus mislead us into thinking that information comes in discrete chunks. The fact then, as now, is that knowing how to read the books was only a superficial kind of access. One needed an intense engagement with what the books *meant*, their significance, their use, their application. In short, the continuity of all that information with the prospects for genuine action has always been the very key to "knowing" the books.

Thinking about books as bearers of "information" is a useful analogy here to help us grasp the current revolution. Five years ago, I was walking across the campus at my university. Behind the library, which once boasted of holding 4.4 million volumes, were several gigantic dumpsters, like trailers of the sort hauled by the big 18-wheel trucks. These were in fact recycling bins. They were filled with books and journals (especially journals, but an alarming number of books). The library was being renovated and there were workers, junior librarians and graduate assistants, presumably, heaving books into these receptacles. Librarians ... throwing away tons of books. The symbolism is clear. Something huge has come to an end. What would Guttenberg think? It is a scene almost worthy of Bradbury's *Fahrenheit 451*.

We all know that *inside* this new library, at my university, as with all research libraries today, there was not *less* "information" available, but *far more* than ever before, in all of human history. But that information no longer needs to be physically present, in the old sense of being physically contained in discrete volumes, in order to be "held" by the library. The library has already gone "non-local." Neither do the digitized bits of information that your computer is processing have to remain discrete units in the future; they will never be wholly non-physical, but their physicality can be radically altered. Your own computer, or your pad or phone, when connected to the *net* (and remember that is a metaphor), provides you with access to more information, and better, than *any* single library in history, and indeed, shockingly, *better than all of them put together through history*. That is a new situation, a revolution.

Only the antiquarian type of researcher now needs the physical materials, and even such work goes better when carried out with heavy technological mediation. Thus, we all have, at our fingertips, the quasi-discrete bits that convey most of what is useful (and much that is not useful) in the Harvard libraries and the Bodleian, and the New York Public Library, and the French National Library, and a million others. Soon, that digital *device* in your pocket also won't be needed, and manipulating its digitized, discrete bits as we do now, with thumbs and touchscreens, will look as clumsy as setting type on a Guttenberg press. No matter how much you paid for the new model, your iPhone is a transitional device. We have *already* moved beyond it in the laboratories of the information scientists. Correspondingly great cultural changes are afoot when so many have access to so much information. Not all of these changes are foreseeable in detail, but a general outline is nevertheless plain.

A few of the consequences are already apparent. To take only one example from the world of education, a "professor" is no longer valued as a sort of walking encyclopedia, the master or mistress of a "body" of knowledge. We professors were never *just* that, but it was always a *part* of our value. But no one needs that sort of "knower" in our day. It has changed in the last 20 years. Everyone carries *in hand* what the professor once carried in his/her head. And we can edit what is in hand for what we *really* need far better than we can keep the professor from telling us 50 irrelevant things for every five relevant factoids. Apart from Trivia Night at the American Legion Hall (a type of gathering soon to be obsolete), the old "walking encyclopedia" is close to useless. Teachers have been thus obliged to reexamine their roles, and many have done so. Unfortunately, many more have not and are hanging on, failing to educate any present students, and waiting for a pension. They stand before students to recite what the students can more effectively learn without a teacher, if they even had a reason to do so. The curriculum hasn't kept pace. The "reason" supplied, under the *ancien régime*, as to why students ought to learn this range and sampling of our cultural memory is now a mere artificiality. Cultural literacy beyond the fondest dreams of E.D. Hirsch is at everyone's fingertips. The truth is that the student is obliged to steer clear of this professorial obstacle for a degree, a piece of paper (printed on a fancy old press that says *we* say you're "educated"). But *we* professors are the group increasingly losing our grip on the meaning of "educated." Many people are well aware of it.

Still, all sorts of teachers must (and do) nurture students into a better command of the tools and techniques of the culture. These tools are no longer reading, writing, and arithmetic, in the traditional senses of these words. It would be more accurate to say that today's students must learn "interpretation of text and image," "the creation of text and image," and "the principles upon which computing occurs (both logical and mathematical)." This is the ICC curriculum: interpret, create, compute. To teach them anything else is to fail as a teacher (unless one has advertised oneself as a specialist in *archaica* for devotees of the ancient past, e.g., the 1960s). To operate successfully in the world of the present and future means having a fair command of these three skills, under their newer descriptions, and such ability will get you any "knowledge" (in the old-fashioned sense) you may need. It will also assist you in navigating the demands of making a living. And the transition underway isn't limited to the example of education, of course. Similar observations apply to commerce, politics, art, religion, law, and social control. None of it is what it used to be.

The adjustment I describe (and advocate) in education is still only a temporary one. The transitional standing of education (described in part three of this paper) will get us from where we are now to a time when *formal* education (i.e., classroom-based) may not be *needed*, at least in any form recognizable to us now. "Transitional education" (as I am calling it), which is what we are now doing badly but must improve, will be in evidence for 20 to 50 more years, if we do not destroy ourselves. But very soon our external access devices will shrink in size until they disappear into our bodies, installed as interfaces with the cloud and all that will follow the cloud.[11] These interfaces already exist in a rudimentary form.[12] The biological and physiological technology for implanting such devices in our bodies has existed for many years. The task is getting the interfaces to operate on the basis of our conscious intentions, and that sort of interface is under development. It will be a usable product in a decade or two (at most).

The general claim of the futurists, such as Kurzweil and Sam Harris, is that the power of computing will soon outstrip the power of physically based "thinking" and will exceed thinking to such a degree that it leaves the human race in a deeply altered situation.[13] When that happens, they think, the "access" we have to "knowledge," which is to say, "information" in the sense defined above and thus, *to each other*, will surpass what was imaginable even 40 years ago. This is not mass literacy; this is mass erudition, as it pertains to facts and available interpretations of those facts, to algebraic and geometrical reasoning, numbers and their operations, and every other operation that can be coded in 1's and 0's. And that information is the simple stuff. In this situation no individual owns the *title* to that erudition. Anyone with access will be able to "know" what is "known" and to do with it what needs doing, in at least the mechanical sense. Anyone who can follow instructions will be able to act on such "knowledge," so long as there is a body that acts. And access will, of course, be the key to the kingdom and a source of social struggle.

Education in this situation becomes, *in part*, a matter of being trained to use one's powers of attention and intention to gain fluid access to what is available. The training is informating, as a verb. Think of the analogy of a Google search. Not everyone is equally good at knowing what to type in so as to produce the most perspicacious result pattern. Now imagine training your powers of attention and intention such that your search not only succeeds but is so seamless as to require no *conscious* effort of searching. As the traditional external forms of mediation (e.g., spoken and written language) fade into an earlier stage of civilizational learning, new opportunities and accompanying challenges appear. Educators must devote themselves to those new challenges. They already exist and are growing, and they gnaw at the edges of our institutions and practices. We must now learn how to teach the arts of attention and intention as acts of inclusion and exclusion, and to build into those arts the principles that enable our students to understand what they *ought* to desire, what is *worthy* of attention, and how the *act of intending* is no morally neutral matter. Education will still be *moral* formation, in the transition that is under way *and* on the far side of that transition.

We must hold it all together, as a race, and it is technologically mediated in a profound but functionally transparent way. Some, such as Ray Kurzweil and Sam Harris are examples of thinkers who have tried very hard to foresee what our (human) situation will be. I believe that both of them, and many other futurists, have had important insights. I think those who think we can only see through a glass darkly, or who throw up their hands in doubt and despair, or who fear for our shared future should read Whitehead.

Part Two

Some Whiteheadian Ideas

There are numerous ways one might approach the continuities between the current revolution and the revolution on the horizon. The latter is, as I have said, being poorly understood and commented upon. Perhaps we can do somewhat better in this part, as the continuities appear and their implications become evident. I have chosen to use Whitehead's views about entropy and time, and their relations to order and disorder more generally, to sketch some consequences for both the singularity and for the idea of education that needs to be associated with the coming changes. In no way do I want to suggest that the directions I will take with these ideas are the only ones available from a Whiteheadian perspective. Nor do I pretend to understand all the details of the current debates in both quantum physics and its relation to AI research. I believe I understand the major lines of argument and their assumptions and consequences, and most of all I believe I clearly understand the favored styles of reasoning to which physicists, and to a lesser degree computer scientists, have wedded themselves. It is mainly in this last domain that both my criticism and my alternatives reside.

To put it briefly, I think the bad habits of reasoning currently allowed by our mainstream science, ***and*** scientific journalism, are narrow and driven by uncritical and even anti-philosophical and dogmatic attachment to a certain kind of mathematical modeling. I have written about this in greater detail elsewhere.[14] The bad reasoning is largely the product of sensationalized science for the public, in which scientists become celebrities who are asked their opinions, and these opinions come to be confused with actual science. But the problems are not limited to this domain. Mathematical reasoning (and its habit of modeling) is heavy on assumptions and often, nay, usually, uncritical at the level of ontology. This unfortunate habit has led mainstream physicists to puzzles and paradoxes that are more easily studied from a broader and more critical ontology than by the methods of science. That ontology, a piece of which I offer in what follows, casts tremendous light on our current situation and provides us with better and clearer questions about our future than the scientific celebrities and model-centric mathematical dogmatists are currently imagining.

Cosmic and Immediate Epochs

Consider: The flux (whatever it is, whether a quantum vacuum[15] or a finite perspective upon a space-time continuum) will still be fluxing on *both* sides of this misnamed "singularity." Our "singularity" is of no consequence to the flux, however world-shattering it might be to our ideas about *having* a "world" or a "cosmos." The flux will indeed be fluxing both within and beyond the confines of the present "cosmic epoch," to use Whitehead's term, that is, our physical universe and all that has occurred in its temporal passage. For Whitehead the cosmic epoch is not enclosed by a single set of physical laws; he takes it for granted that such laws develop and change. He distinguishes our "immediate epoch," in which the physical laws formulated by our best science apply with great (if not complete) uniformity to all of our observations. The *immediate* epoch is included in the broader *cosmic* epoch as an instance of what *could* be (i.e., can be) but did not necessarily *have to be* actual. The "immediate epoch" is characterized by all that is "actual," relative to our efforts at scientific knowing, and, hence, within the reach of our inquiries (including other kinds of knowledge than the scientific sort, if ideally pursued), as well as including all that is *possible* but non-actual within those limitations. Hence, we can "know" (if not quite measure) at least some of what *might have been* but *is not* and some of what *will not be* but genuinely *could be.*

To illustrate, at the broadest level, that this idea about the flux is a viable ontological posit, I want to call special attention to the second law of thermodynamics or the law of entropy, as being of crucial importance to our present discussion, both of education and of the current and impending revolutions. Entropy is a stubborn feature of our immediate epoch, but not much thought has been given to its relation to the cosmic epoch as a whole. Many philosophers and scientists have noted that the arrow of time, its so-called irreversibility, is associated closely with entropy, perhaps even as an *effect* of entropy. Some will even say entropy and time's asymmetry are one and the same thing, although I don't see any empirical warrant for so strong an identification—one would need to know more than we currently know about both time and entropy to rely on such an identification. Time could be, for all we know, far broader than the entropic version of it in this epoch (whether cosmic or immediate). We lack a contrasting case. And no thorough follower of Whitehead, at least, will hypostasize entropy into an eternal and necessary principle, inviolable in the universe. We simply don't know whether it is or isn't. Still, it could be seriously debated whether entropy characterizes more than our immediate epoch and applies also throughout the entire cosmic epoch. The issue comes down to whether one thinks of *time*, since it is the first division of the "extensive continuum" (that we hypothesize as the coordinate whole of the cosmic epoch), as giving rise to entropy, or whether entropy should be treated as equiprimordial with time. It is also possible to consider non-entropic time or whether it is valuable to conceive of the dividing of the undivided coordinate whole (the extensive continuum) as temporal but not entropic. In short, we simply don't have to decide whether the physical universe, as we know it, is a space-time continuum, or a quantum vacuum, or a fabric of 11-dimensional superstrings, or any other hypothesis that is consistent with what we do know. All we need to do is treat the cosmic epoch as a coordinate whole and originally as an undivided *but divisible* continuity. Whitehead calls this latter idea, as I have said, the "extensive continuum."[16]

In this regard, we have to consider both entropic (actual divisions) of the extensive continuum—whatever "perpetually perishes"—and non-entropic divisions, such as "prehensions" (in Whitehead's terminology), which are divisions for the sake of analysis but which are introduced as relational characters of the real process of the universe because they concretely exist, even though they do not, as non-actual divisions, perish. "Prehensions" are thus not actual divisions of the universe but are rather living concrete relations that are indivisible (irreducible) themselves and do not genuinely divide anything else.[17] Due to their relational character, prehensions presuppose a physical universe but *take no entropic toll upon the terms they relate.* To be related does not necessarily and automatically presuppose an entropic burden, although *physical* prehensions will carry such a weight in view of the fact that they are physically felt. Conceptual prehensions, by contrast, have no entropic burden. We could not say with perfect honesty that *concrete* prehension (both conceptual and physical feelings) escapes entropy altogether (since the physical aspect we observe does not so escape), but we *can* say that prehensive relations are, comparatively, low-entropy systems of relations because they do not, by hypothesis at least, require any *expending* of energy to do their proper "work" of relating (that work which is theirs alone, i.e., not reducible to the expenditures of other systems and their entropic costs).

Relations Without an Entropic Burden

Physicists err when they fail to recognize that some relations (both local and non-local) imply no serious entropic burden. Whether the idea of "work" is conceivable apart from the idea of energy is a serious question, but I will set it aside for now. I have usually argued in the past that work and energy imply one another, but that view may be fairly restricted to our immediate epoch without the need for conjecture about the whole cosmic epoch or *other* cosmic epochs. Conceptual prehension, as far as we know, only occurs where there is also physical prehension, but conceptual prehension, that is, the relating of possibilities to actualities, may not have an entropic cost *intrinsic* to its work. In more ordinary terms, the entropic cost to your body of "having an idea" is negligible, even if it isn't zero. The aspect of that idea that connects the possibilities to the actualities of the cosmic epoch appears to be a zero, when we abstract from the physical feeling that apparently supports the having of that idea. It does not appear that bearing a relation to what is merely possible (what might have been but is not and what will not be but could be) takes any observable toll on actual things.

Yet, in the higher and most complex phases of our experience, we do feel the weight of the *might have been*, for example, in the form of genuine regret, or nostalgia, or even shame and so forth. And we allow ourselves to be overwhelmed with worry about the *might be*. These stressors clearly have physical consequences, and so we must not assume that possibility comes with no concrete relation at all to entropic systems. Clearly it has such relations in some difficult-to-pin-down sense. Yet, so much possibility seems to pass by and through actual things with no effect, we must allow that having a real and concrete relation to what is possible sometimes approaches zero entropy. But let us allow that zero entropy is not, presently, of any clear use to us, since we are physical systems and will remain so even after the singularity. In short, the fundamental, ontological relations of possibility to actuality and of conceptual prehension will remain unchanged by the so-called singularity. The difference contemplated by Kurzweil and the futurists is in fact a transformation from high-entropy physical systems to much, much lower-entropy systems. But again, the continuities are greater than the differences at some levels. Indeed the continuities, at the level of meaning and value, are far more important than the physical changes contemplated, as I will argue.

As far as I know, Whitehead has the only cosmology that places us in a position to have a serious—and radically empirical—discussion about low-entropy relations in the present cosmic epoch, because only his general approach even coherently distinguishes the immediate epoch from the cosmic epoch that includes it, and provides a context for speculating responsibly and non-dogmatically about the relation between time's arrow and entropy. If *you* were to become a low-entropy system, suddenly this whole question becomes relevant to *you*. The popular cosmologies being peddled by science celebrities have no resources for a serious conversation. A point about entropy that is often lost in current discussions is that the problem is *ancient*—for example, Empedocles had a powerful discussion of it[18]—and that considering the idea of entropy involves our willingness to make a fairly firm distinction between our *philosophical* reasoning about time, energy, and entropy and our *scientific* reasoning about the same.

The relation of scientific models to experimentation remains (and must remain) deliberately vague, as do their concepts of evidence and confirmation. There are a thousand theories of evidence and confirmation, from the regression equations of the social scientists to the standard model of gravitational cosmology, but there is no consensus about either evidence or confirmation. And there never will be. For quite some time, experiments have been at best confirmations of model-dependent expectations, not tests of genuinely empirical hypotheses. The physical scientists and social scientists alike correlate numbers on computer models, at their supercolliders and in their humble offices, seeking sufficient deviation from mere noise to claim the presence of effects, artifacts, variances, of energy, that can be interpreted as either confirmation of some hypothesis, however ill-formed, and thus of physical reality, or of some trend or pattern in social life. The result of this sad situation is a nearly complete unwillingness on the part of current theoretical physicists and cosmologists and psychologists and sociologists, especially those who enjoy public recognition and being interviewed for television and the like, to think philosophically about broad, cosmological problems at all.[19] These people are far better at name-calling than they are at genuine scientific research, especially where the latter requires disciplined thinking.

Causal Laws

The next Whiteheadian idea to consider, then, apart from the cosmic and the immediate epoch, is that while this so-called singularity may pose a local problem for us from the standpoint of the physical universe, it is only one among many more unlikely *but actual* developments among billions of others. From some achieved standpoint a few billion years ago, the human species itself was so unlikely as to be unforeseeable for any knower they might want to imagine. But here we *are*. Everything actual is possible. Thus, since we are actual now, we were *possible* back then … and so was the so-called singularity we now face, and that second possibility already and always depended on the first. Thus, an important Whiteheadian lesson is to remember not to exaggerate the present situation from the standpoint of transition in the cosmos, or the concrescences of value that provide the interior unfolding, "the information" of the world, in the sense described above, that massive transition that is the flux in our cosmic epoch.

Thus we are led to consider whether entropy is or is not the determining factor in temporal flux in our immediate epoch, and assuming it is, whether that determination applies seamlessly to the *whole* cosmic epoch or whether entropic determination is only one specification (or division) of the temporal flux that *might have been* otherwise, given, for example, a different distribution of energy in the origin of the epoch (e.g., greater or lesser disequilibrium, or perhaps a space-creating profile that leads to a *slightly* less flat "cosmos," or a *slightly* flatter cosmos). Such variation might have begotten a different development of physical law, one can fairly suppose, perhaps one in which much of what we find now, in the immediate epoch would have been nearly the same, but without, for example, the nested determinations of the flux that provide for biological life. Whitehead puts this entire discussion of entropy and order in his own difficult language thus:

> The causal laws which dominate a social environment [a society of actual entities] are the products of the defining characteristic of that society. But the society is only efficient through its individual members. Thus in a society, the members can only exist by reason of the laws which dominate the society, and the laws only come into being by reason of the analogous characters of the members of the society.[20]

This means that wherever real parts are together in a manner sufficient to generate a physical history, then whatever causal laws dominate them (including their expending of energy) develop from the analogous characteristic(s) of the actual parts. To put it plainly, "causal laws" exist only as general characters of the concrete actualities that give rise to them; they are not inviolable principles that subsume individual instances in the immediate epoch, let alone in the cosmic epoch. Under the coming "singularity," there will be great disanalogies between and among the real parts we call the society of "you" now, and whatever will bear that name after your consciousness, or your memory, or your modes of receptivity have been relocated to a low-entropy electromagnetic field. But you will not be subsumed under a different law or order of laws than we now experience. You will still be you, even if the causal laws that apply to you apply at a more generalized level than before. There are some things we can know about this situation, as astonishing as it is to us. Whitehead continues:

> But there is not any perfect attainment of an ideal order whereby the infinite endurance of a society is secured. A society arises from disorder, where "disorder" is defined by reference to the ideal for that society; the favourable background of a larger environment either itself decays, or ceases to favour the persistence of the society after some stage of growth: the society then ceases to reproduce its members, and finally, after a stage of decay, passes out of existence.[21]

One might immediately see this description as simply a case of the death of a biological being, but Whitehead makes it immediately clear that he is considering entropy in its broadest sense. He continues:

> Thus, a system of "laws" determining reproduction in some portion of the universe gradually rises into dominance; it has its stage of endurance, and passes out of existence with the decay of the society from which it emanates. The arbitrary, as it were "given," elements in the laws of nature warn us that we are in a special cosmic epoch. Here the phrase "cosmic epoch" is used to mean the widest society of actual entities whose immediate relevance to ourselves is traceable. This epoch is characterized by electronic and protonic actual entities, and by yet more ultimate actual entities which can be dimly discerned in the quanta of energy. Maxwell's equations of the electromagnetic field hold sway by reason of the throngs of electrons and protons.[22]

In short, deaths of biological societies are only a special case of entropic decay that characterizes everything whose "relevance to ourselves we can trace." Among the relevant but "arbitrary factors" in our "special epoch" are the emergent "electromagnetic laws" it includes. Thus, the electromagnetic fields that will support our "consciousness" or whatever "information" we transfer to the cloud (and whatever follows the cloud) are low-entropy but not zero-entropy systems. This is not immortality. It is still physical existence in a special epoch, under the sway of the same "throngs" of electronic and protonic entities and by entities "yet more ultimate."

Protonic and Electronic Life

The importance of this point lies in the fact that as a transformation of our experience, whether we describe it as "uploading" our "consciousness," or even our "person," is *not* a move from being embodied to being disembodied. Rather, we are *differently* embodied but still subject to the same arbitrary factors that characterize our special epoch. We may contribute more deeply to different causal laws in that condition, but those causal laws will be the same ones we contribute to less vivaciously right now. The continuities from our current condition far outweigh the much-vaunted discontinuities, at the all-important level of *physical order*. To give just an example or two, there will still be "death" and hence "murder," in your protonic and electronic life, and there will still be right and wrong, and power and oppression, and overcoming of the sort dreamed of by MLK and his marchers. Where it is possible to wrong you, it is also possible to *right* you. Protonic and electronic existence has value, rights, and *life* itself in the relevant sense. I will explain this in further detail.

The *physical* concerns we have about the basic character of protonic and electronic occasions (how they exist and what they are) are vast and cannot be further considered here, but my point is that entropy, understood in cosmic terms, might be nothing more than the tendency of energy to equalize itself in "the four dimensions of the spatio-temporal continuum," which, along with other "arbitrary" factors, all come down to "the more basic fact of extensiveness."[23] This "variable space" (as we may speak of such creative extensity, in our cosmic epoch) can be conceived and even axiomatized without that space being anything dissimilar to the "space" of our immediate epoch, which we describe in Euclidean formulae.[24] I make this point to open up a space in your imagination to consider entropy, in particular, apart from the narrow way it is presented in the physicotheology of today's dogmatic physicists. We have no empirically defensible reason to think that time is symmetrical for our epoch, and thus the fancy theories of physicists such as Jack Sarfatti's "post-quantum mechanics" that rely on the possibility of actual time symmetry, while they might describe *other* universes, are inapplicable to our cosmic epoch, as far as we know.[25]

Humans have imagined a non-entropic cosmos for as long as there have been humans imagining things. They call these imaginings heaven and even hell. Neither heaven nor hell is entropic in the sense of the second law or of the stubborn association of time with entropy. Anything that is eternal exists outside of both entropy and time, but whatever is *everlasting* or *immortal* exists as temporal but still beyond the reach of entropy. My point is not that these conditions really exist. These ideas of heaven and hell may be incoherent. But people have made these distinctions since the dawn of consciousness, in thinking of the stars, for example, as unchanging watchers or personalities, and the planets as wanderers, or dynamic (even demonic) immortal beings, changing but beyond the reach of death. My point is that fantasies of low-entropy forms of existence are not new, and I don't think them absurd, but one needs an ontology that accommodates the ideas, and that ontology is very different from the anti-philosophical and dogmatic assumptions that dominate current "scientific" cosmologies (in truth they are deeply *un*scientific). The moment of the approaching singularity would be better discussed under a classical religious morality (since it has conceptual tools for discussing good and evil on a cosmic scale) than under a crypto-materialistic reductive "humanism" (which is in truth anti-humanistic). But we can do better than either of those paradoxical options: unscientific science and anti-humanistic humanism.

These observations I have made do not give anyone license to assert the empirical legitimacy of imagining such things in a scientific context today, but it is not insignificant that humankind has always been fascinated with the suggestion of what is beyond the reach of time and what is temporal but still beyond the reach of death. Protonic and electronic life may reach beyond biological death, and that could be a good thing. We need not hypothesize that any of the physical processes of our immediate epoch is wholly beyond the reach of entropy, but we must recognize an important difference between high- and low-entropy systems in the immediate epoch, and we should do our theorizing in a way that remains open regarding the currently dominant forms entropy in the immediate epoch, treating these forms as particular, even if maximally general in our observations. Entropy may be differently manifest in various immediate epochs.[26]

Electromagnetic Occasions and Consciousness

This brings us to another of Whitehead's key ideas, which takes in his views about electromagnetism. Electromagnetic occasions in the flux of our immediate epoch have astonishing characteristics, many of which are known to our current physical science, with more yet to be discovered and understood, and perhaps measured (although the last of these may prove soon to be an archaic aid to understanding, unneeded in the time to come—e.g., the quantum vacuum is unmeasurable, by hypothesis). There is a difference, of course between electromagnetic realities, whatever they are, and our current best theory about them, but there is reason to think we have *some* things more right than wrong about *some* of what electromagnetic occasions do. Among the things they permit, and apparently always accompany, are all the diverse phenomena (and their patterns) that have gone under the rudimentary names "mind" and "consciousness" and perhaps also "soul" and "spirit," although we can leave that latter discussion aside for now.

Whatever consciousness is, at bottom, our studies of it up to this point indicate that it rides a wave of physical, temporal process, even if its content defies time's arrow—consisting in "reversions" in Whitehead's terms. We study consciousness through those processes, although we are not entitled to conclude that mind or consciousness is *reducible* to those processes, or that mind and consciousness cannot *exist* without the physical flux through which we gain access to these curious (reversional) phenomena. Perhaps they are nothing apart from these processes, and perhaps they aren't. Any philosopher or computer scientist or physicist who claims to know that there is *nothing more* to these phenomena than their physical medium is a dogmatist. The claim is not knowable by any scientific, logical, or philosophical standard. It may be true, but it cannot be known to be unless we know *everything* about the universe, which manifestly we do not.

Mind and consciousness, in the sense defined, will also continue after the so-called singularity. The main change has to do with our access to them, their employment, and their perpetuation as an organized part of the flux. You may surmise: "Thus, we indirectly search for spaces, novel, *created* spaces in flux wherein phenomena appear, but we cannot know what the flux is really like."[27] I would say, in a qualified way, yes, we search for spaces, directly (with our bodies enacting the affordances of these spaces) and indirectly (by patterned inquiry, guided by reflection when required), and therefore seek especially those spaces congenial to thinking and reflecting. These are the spaces or regions in which "phenomena appear" (which is redundant, since phenomena *are* appearances), and these phenomena are that portion of the flux we can know about, by ordinary means. By "ordinary" I mean without serious technological mediation. These are the vibrations to which our bodies and, more specifically, our senses are suited.[28]

What we may succeed in "knowing" beyond these ordinary means is a serious question. Deep technological mediation requires multiple layers of "modeling" that use both mathematical and logical tools (not to mention instruments of measure), not all of which operate seamlessly at the same levels of generality. This affects the meaning of the word "knowledge," since its history is built on analogies to perception; indeed, this analogy to perception is operative even in the most mediated instances, since someone must interpret the mathematics or read the data. To "know" what the flux is as a whole (if indeed it is a "whole") evades us, but I have no basis for asserting as an iron law that it cannot be known in principle. There might be aspects of the flux unknowable to us in principle—I expect so, in our current form—and Whitehead was always pessimistic about the prospects of our moving far beyond our imaginations as they were configured in the early twentieth century. But our current form is, after all, evolutionarily transient and contingent.

Uploading Your Memory

In light of our increasing understanding of electromagnetic occasions, we may (and almost surely will) become something more rarified than we now are. What we will "know" is closer to "information" as discussed in part one of this chapter. You, the reader, will probably live to have the choice of whether to transfer your "memory" (in some form analogous to your experience of your memory) into an electromagnetic field that will permit indefinite perpetuation of that past, perhaps in a form that will permit the accumulation of new experiences and their integration with your past experiences. The computer scientists tell us that this event will follow shortly upon the advent of the singularity, although it seems likely to me that they are not taking into account the many layers of improvement that are sure to follow the initial "transfer." Caution, then, is prudent, as we think about the prospects. Early versions of Humanity 2.0 may be difficult to upgrade. If you *can* wait to get yourself transferred, I suggest you do so; oh, and you might want to make just a backup for safety's sake. Do hold out until the last possible moment for a real migration.

Soon afterward, to "exist" in the humanly meaningful sense, the futurists claim, will not require bodily perception and processing. And here we do find a reason to wonder about discontinuities, even ultimate limits. I do not know what a more rarified, low-entropy, electromagnetic version of "me" might be able to "experience" and "know" when my access to the flux is no longer mediated by the very slow processing capacity of the human body, but I am very confident that the constraints on information, at every level, from the religious to the practical, will still exist, in altered *function* but not in altered dynamic *form*. My conjecture is that access to the flux *as a whole* will be closer (if perhaps not very close in the grand scheme) and that our experience will be far less mediated than at present. The upside, then, is that "knowledge," as we currently understand that word, will be available to any and all will be vast and only thinly mediated.

If that is right, then in 200 years, no one will understand what it was like to be so completely dependent on physiological perception for the process of learning as we now are. Physiological perception will be valued, aesthetically and morally, but bypassed in learning certain kinds of facts. The power of *interpretation*, however, might still depend on physiological development. I think it likely. In the future, there will even be debates about what it was like for us to "learn" facts so slowly. Thus, I would never say we can't ever get at the flux, only that our present access is limited by our perceptual processes and processing. But the downside is that we cannot foresee presently whether the accretion of value in this coming low-entropy form of humanity will be sufficiently congruent with our present understanding of value to retain some of what we value now. Whether, for example, video games or pornography or party politics (which are not so very different in our current milieu) will entertain the low-entropy humans is doubtful. They fail to entertain many high-entropy humans, after all, and yet command, I hear, billions of dollars in the present. Granted, one might be better off dead than to have that future existence, given what we will lose in our low-entropy condition, but as I contemplate it, I see no compelling reason to think so. It might be closer, as Cephalus says in Plato's *Republic*, more like being released from bondage to a cruel master.

Still, for low entropy humans, there won't be any delicious tomatoes in season, or sunrises, or indeed, much of anything that currently takes its meaning and value from embodied aesthetic experience. There is no guarantee that such an existence might not be a nightmare on the order of Adrian Lyne's film *Jacob's Ladder*, from which oblivion would be a blessed release. These imagined scenarios are the fuel for the speculations of the futurists, and it is deeply human to indulge them, but it is more responsible to handle them bemusedly. We have always handled our transformations before. We will do so now.

And, one might add, human psychological balance is currently very delicate, even in our accustomed and evolutionarily tested embodied condition. I mean that remaining sane and well-balanced while trying to process the amount of information assailing us in the present, embodied, high-entropy condition we currently possess is a task that defeats many of us and is easy for none of us. Whether we could genuinely expect to *enjoy* a rarified low-entropy existence and not to become listless, depressed, psychotic, or catatonic is just not predictable based on our current knowledge. As I noted earlier, thinking of your low-entropy post-life on the analogy of a phone service contract, you will surely want a cancellation clause, even if it means releasing the electronic and protonic occasions that we call "you" back into the quantum vacuum.

One thing that is more securely foreseeable is that what we mean by "education" (and other primary institutions, such as "family" and "law") will be profoundly altered. But as Thomas Buford has argued,[29] there will always be some sort of institution, so long as we are humans, that passes from one generation to the next what has been sufficiently valued to be regarded as important. This is what we currently call "education." Even though we may be able to access vast quantities of "information" (in the sense defined earlier), and immediately, that does not mean all of it will be equally valued or identically interpreted. Standpoint and history will still be variable. If some information is more important than other information, and assuming that our community of "persons" is constantly undergoing addition and augmentation, some sort of education will be required. The role of an educator in such an environment is to serve as a guide to the difference between what is valued more and what is valued less and to grasp the enduring standards for such valuation. Assuming that, even in a rarified condition, not every existence is equally worthwhile, we will need educators and other sorts of guides to hold and turn the keys to that kingdom.

The Last of the Book People

Whitehead framed a philosophy that anticipates and explains and intensifies and augments what has become of us. I do not say that he saw the information age coming, although he greatly contributed to creating the logic and the mathematics that made it possible. Rather, he saw what was relatively enduring in our condition and what was painfully temporary. Our philosophical problems remain the great matters of the meaning of our existence, and of our best paths in living, of our responsibilities to one another and to ourselves, of making our lives an adventure, interesting, beautiful, peaceful, and zesty. Nothing about the singularity changes this situation. We still want to know what beauty and truth and goodness are, even if we don't have physiological bodies. We still wonder about knowledge, about the one and the many and about why there is something rather than nothing.

Still, our forms of consciousness have already changed, fundamentally, and will change a great deal more very soon. *Once* we were the humans who were obliged to spend lifetimes combing books in order to be educated. The books were collected here, there, and yon, with access controlled by whoever owned them, inconveniently cloistered behind brick walls and institutional, economic, and political barriers. That was "the library." *Now* we are humans who may instantly possess any intellectual detail in the collective store of all human "knowledge," providing only that we possess the access device and can understand how to find it in the common cloud, how to grasp its meaning, and to use it. This is a different sort of being, with different challenges, especially in the domains of ethics, aesthetics, political life, and social commitment. This is a dizzyingly dynamic being whose primary reality is change, not stability.

Thus, our newer forms of consciousness, those created by becoming interpreters and creators of image and text, will very soon eclipse completely the older forms found in the "book culture" of the past. Our present "knowledge" is of a lower-entropy sort than our previous "knowledge." We don't have to remember the truths, only to recall the access route and the passwords. In the time of Christian Roman Emperors, libraries could be burned and "knowledge" forever lost, but that would be difficult to do in a lower-entropy form of preservation. Unplug me if you will, but I can be backed up and rebooted. The delete key is a local erasure, but hardly like a fire at Alexandria's library.

At the present moment, most of the decisions that guide our lives are still being made by people who were products of "book consciousness." That will change very soon. Those of us educated in the older forms have had a "rough ride" already, so to speak, as we attempted to adjust our consciousness to navigate a world we weren't educated for, and we continue to struggle with the creeping and advancing irrelevance of our recitations of facts and figures. Meanwhile younger people, bored with our high-entropy slow pace and our insensibility to our own irrelevance, teach each other how to employ the newer technologies. As difficult as it is, we book people should welcome this change—we have no choice in any event as to whether it will occur. It has already happened.

And here we find Whitehead's philosophy awaiting not only the dying book people but reaching to the "cloud people" from their own near future. The Cartesian subject, that cogitating and self-certain ego, that modern monstrosity, was the product of a book consciousness wrestling with a budding book culture. It is not an accident that Descartes *was* thinking *the way* he was thinking *when* he was thinking about his *act* of thinking. The book culture placed the thinker in his (and it *was* "his" and not "hers," at that time) own book-filled study, comfortably before a warm fire, contemplating the meaning of existence. The creative response to this situation is a fable of a mind privately digesting its world in the linear fashion of reading, of cogitating a primal syllogism in words. This ego, without being aware of it, is dogged by the illusion of "privacy" in knowing and deceives itself into believing it has control over the knowing process by means of a method of analysis. It was never true, but it surely seemed so to that isolated ego.

This narrow and flawed interpretation of our human nature depended, more than anyone realized, on the *experience* of getting knowledge *by studying books*. But books are quite static. They say the same things every time we open them. They are "intelligibilized" stable spaces of presentation and *re*presentation. This became our model for self-knowing and, by inference, *all* knowing. That, however, is *not* the character of your smart phone. Your phone says something *different* every time you consult it. It registers changes in the world, in potency and actuality, while you are *not* consulting it and then presents you with these changes in actuality when you check it. What a wondrous book *that* would be, no? Would you like to have a book that rewrites itself, seemingly *by itself*, at every moment, to chart and arrange the world for your convenient digestion whenever you choose? Can this book be anything less than miraculous to a Cartesian subject?

Nodal Existing: Actual Entity, Society, Nexus

The fact is that Cartesian subjects are disappearing rapidly, millions dying every day, and they are not being replaced by more Cartesian subjects. The species is going extinct. A new human form is taking its place, and this form is better described as a Whiteheadian node—an "actual entity," a "society," or a "nexus," and truthfully it is *all* of these at once. Indeed, *you* are all of these at once, and you always were, but if you came from the book culture (as I did), it was difficult to learn this about yourself and, once learned, still not easy to believe when surrounded by self-certain Cartesian subjects. Yet, you are and always were a *process*. You are a semi-stable but ever-changing location, a *place*, in a coordinated dynamic whole, which you contribute to and take from in trillions of ways. You are closer to being one fish in a schooling mass or one starling in a fluctuating flock than a fixed perspective with a view of all from there. Your existence is interdependent with other beings of a similar kind, some as solid and stable as you are, some more so, some less. You are more dynamic and complex than a smart phone, presently. It has a cloud. You have a world. It may have a world soon enough, but if so, we will want to know something more about "world," and, presciently, Whitehead will be there to help us see it.

These ideas framed by Whitehead: the "actual entity" situated in its actual world, the "society" of actual entities, sufficiently interdependent to form a single history, and the living "nexus" of all things that come into relation with such entities and societies, *these* ideas are our philosophical future. They are Whitehead's ideas, but they are ours as well. These ideas are dynamic, adaptable, and they conform to and also explain the experience of subjectivity (if we still wish to call it so) that humans have now, *today*. This experience is still forming, but the old ideas that apparently depended on the supposition of a stable, even eternal and unchanging, human essence will soon lose their stranglehold on our self-understanding. It will be, as Richard Rorty phrased it, "a world well lost." It is happening all around us, rapidly and every day. If we are caught in a crisis of meaning, we have all the more reason to drop outdated ideas of the self and its supposed rationality.

Surely these "modern subjects" fabled by Descartes served their purposes and their gods, as the humans transitioned from substances to genuine souls. After Kant, these modern subjects developed both as knowers and as conditions for knowing, as described by Foucault as "Man and His

Doubles," coming to a greater sense of their situation and its power, its promise.[30] But these humans also projected the limits of their fabled subjectivity over all of science, religion, and culture, over the full complement of discursive practices that characterized their age and its fundamental idea of knowing. It was a serviceable error to do that. The constructed human subject in what Foucault calls "the age of Man" is disappearing just as he predicted, although he could not see what comes next, from the standpoint of his death in 1984.

But the knowers of the future will be more like complex quanta, robust individuals, simultaneously actual standpoints on their actual worlds, complex societies of act, and nodes of the living nexus, whose perspectives are prior to their essences (if we still wish to call it so), whose essences *are* their histories and contributions to the world, and whose standpoints are valued and assessed and wrestled with, by all and by each, in a dynamic setting we *now* call "the world," if we still wish to call it so. It is not the world of old and in that sense not really "the world" at all.

But as we try to change our ideas about ourselves, our clumsy terminology must oblige us, however slowly. Whitehead complained more about the limits of language than about anything else, and he stretched and pulled language until it reformed itself around his ideas, but it makes his books difficult to read. Today, we will struggle to adapt our old language until all of the bookish minds have passed into their perpetual perishing and these newer individuals, these nodes in the living nexus, communicate more freely, each knowing that *this* world is no longer *the* earth, or *the* universe, or even *the* creation. Our world is *a* whole adjusted *to* purpose *by* purpose, manifest and expressed accordingly. It will speak a different language (if we still wish to call it that) from the book language. Indeed, it already does.

This is the future of philosophical thought. It is not the tired questions of Cartesian subjects doubting their Kantian limits. It is processes coalescing as eddies in time to create spaces of meaning and of achievement, for what they are worth and for however long they may endure. This is the philosophy Whitehead put forward, but it came a bit too early, like Nietzsche's madman. Its time is now upon us and the overman is ... well, we are she/he. We will do ourselves, and those who come later, a great service to grasp this moment and make it decisive for our future meaning.

Part Three

Intensity: Education and the New Learning

We are now in a position to ask what becomes of the *idea* of education during the transition between the early information age which we will soon leave, through the middle ages of the information revolution, which most of us will experience, and into the late stages, during which, presumably, some of us will perhaps come to exist in a "mixed condition."

But a word needs to be said about this mixed condition. Here are some facts that need to be considered. The vast majority of speculation about the "singularity" has neglected the issue of creating new human nodes and has not been realistic about *whose* consciousness and what values will be carried from bodily life to low-entropy, protonic and electronic "life." First, insofar as human beings will choose to join the cloud and post-cloud, we are looking at an end-of-life option, not a way-of-life option. The joys of being embodied are overwhelmingly to be preferred to anything else, *ceteris paribus*, and it will be the rare individual who simply forgoes them to join the low-entropy populace.

Further, we almost always speak of uploading ourselves as *already* well-formed (i.e., educated) beings, and little thought has been given by the futurists to how one would *achieve* a mature human consciousness without going through an embodied process of, well, growing up. The process of maturation in body and mind may not be *logically* necessary to create a node, such as I have described, but it will be morally and aesthetically desirable, and overwhelmingly so. People want children and they want to raise them. Even the famous imaginative example provided by *Star Trek*'s Lt. Commander Data requires a birth/creation story. Even if we could, in principle, create nodal "perspectives" artificially, we would still have to consider how to develop those perspectives into human "standpoints." (This language of "perspective" and "standpoint" is, of course, Whitehead's.[31]) The difference between a perspective and a standpoint is what Whitehead calls the "achievement" of a "satisfaction," which is an *accretion of value*. Such satisfaction in the human case is both a moral and aesthetic process. I called it "formating" earlier.

Even if there are ways to *speed up* the process of human formation, there is little reason to think we would wish to do so or we would wish to create virtual "perspectives," nodes which we would be obliged to educate, unless they could do something for us that we could not or did not wish to do for ourselves. That situation is not on the horizon, although one must grant it is a genuine possibility. It isn't worth considering seriously at this point. Thus, we are contemplating a situation in which there will still be babies born to embodied parents, who nurture and teach those children. Gradually the infant perspective deepens and becomes a standpoint, and the standpoint matures by way of embodied experience. Even if we could speed up the biological process, we probably would not choose to do so. If and when it becomes necessary to transition any given individual to the low-entropy protonic-electronic life, one assumes that it will be done for the sake of preserving the valued standpoint, at the very least. Continuing to *deepen* the standpoint is not just highly desirable but, from a human point of view, a requirement of "life" worth living. It is not enough to go on having experiences unless these experiences accumulate in such a way as to deepen the standpoint.

In addition, there must be some capacity for low-entropy persons to initiate action and some kind of choice involved in action. In short, the standpoint must be both empowered and individualized with respect to *action*—mere activity will lack the needed depth. It isn't "life." Clearly this distinction between action and activity requires rethinking for the future.[32] Nevertheless, all of the values I have expressed in the Whiteheadian ideas employed up to this point can be summarized in a single term: "intensity." This is a technical term for Whitehead, depending on a fundamental contrast in the meaning of existence between a great "width" of existing that is "thin" and has undifferentiated relations to most everything else that exists, as opposed to a great depth of existing which has narrow relations to other existences, but is highly selective of those relations that accumulate and deepen the standpoint of the individual.[33] A "perspective" is wide but shallow, very thin; a "standpoint" is narrow but deep. Again, to be clear, *thin perspective* has more or less the same relation to all other existences, regardless of the contrasts among those existences. *Deep standpoint* has highly differential and amazingly selective, individualized relations to other existences, discriminating among them according to their value for use, for pleasure, for appreciation, for contemplation, for their capacity to call forth interpretative acts from that standpoint.

This language can be used for *all* development, for the growth of everything actual, but it is especially applicable to biological and also post-biological "life." Indeed, the very idea of life is that of a narrow but deep kind of actuality, highly selective of its few modes of vital relations and embedded in many systems of order that permit its selections. The low-entropy situatedness of protonic and electronic living will not alter the aim, the purpose, to "enjoy" (Whitehead's term, again) intensive relations. Ours is a quite delicate kind of existence, exceedingly rare in the cosmos up to the present, as far as we know, but the transformation to low-entropy forms of physical support offers some genuine changes to the *experiential* aspect of this kind of existing. The variety of intensity most characteristic of our embodied existence is deep but at the cost of narrowness. We notice only those other existences that will conform to our very limited physical senses, and among these, we give almost infinitely more attention and activity to the other existences most like ourselves; even here we are so selective as to ignore all but a small handful of other existences that are like ourselves, sharing either historical proximity or a profound sympathy of standpoint that allows for such rarified relations as "love" and "friendship" and "comradery." The narrowness is extraordinary. But then, so is the depth of actuality achieved. Our selectivity may be enhanced in the transition to a low-entropy mode of existence, although that isn't clear. Perhaps equal depth (and we won't sacrifice any depth) will be compatible with a wider nexus; perhaps we won't have to sacrifice quite as much width in order to obtain the same (or greater) depth. Perhaps we could genuinely empathize with our fellow humans and with other biological beings. It seems that not having to eat would lead to different judgments about the value inherent in the lives of those existences we now slaughter in order to get some of their energy for our own systems. Still, the human beings, whether low-entropy or high-entropy, will insist upon intensity of the narrower, selective, and deep sort. We will also insist, as a value, to take in the widest experiential nexus that is consistent with the accretions of value that maintain or deepen our actuality. In simpler language, we will insist that we not only continue to accumulate experience but that we "learn." By "learning" in this context I mean that the novel aspects of our experience be such as to enable us to act upon their meaning and to form teleological trajectories: that is, purposes.

It may occur to the reader at this point that the future, both proximate and horizonal, is a good deal like the past. Fundamental institutions and practices are going to be much closer to what we do now than the futurists prognosticate. Yet, one must grant that these continuities are highly general. There will be a form of valuing that includes both low and high-entropy persons which requires education and, indeed, *higher* education, understood as that phase of our growth toward a standpoint in which we *learn* how to take possession of our own future *learning* (and to teach ourselves to grasp autonomously what we need to "know" in the future and how to get that "knowledge"). That is now, and will be in the future, the definition of "higher education." Higher education in this scenario is, therefore, the final process of achieving an autonomous standpoint and to build a history in the future that is docile to our past.[34]

Higher Education

What then does a university look like, in terms of mission, structure, and pedagogy, which serves a society like our present one, *as it is transforming* into the foreseeable human society, which includes low-entropy persons, on the horizon? The mission we have, in effect, is already seen and stated. The final stage of our maturation is from perspectival to standpoint-relative consciousness. I call the fully developed standpoint "synoptic."[35] A synoptic worldview is more than a mature, judging consciousness. It is a genuine standpoint on *all* humane values. In essence, this is what higher education does now, so the *form* of the mission of higher education need not change, either now or in the foreseeable future. It may be desirable to see our notion of full standpoint grow to include a genuine empathy with all humanity and sympathy with all living things; this enhancement of standpoint is rare among high-entropy humans but regarded as exemplary in, for example, the lives of the Buddha and Jesus and St. Francis and Gandhi. Since we revere these exemplars in our present mode of existence, there is no reason to think we wouldn't strive for their form of universal enlightenment or love where it is to become achievable for more of us. If the low-entropy mode of human existence makes the nexus of experience wider as well as perhaps deeper, then this value will become a part of higher education. Thus, teachers would educate for more than good citizenship and intellectual and moral virtues; they would become teachers of universal enlightenment and love. Institutions that educate for this end already exist and have been there for two and a half millennia. But for some 1000 years, these have been (for the most part) separated from the institutions that emphasize intellectual and scientific knowledge, along with worldly (one is tempted to say "mundane") morality. Undeniably, in any case, the proximate goals of higher education, and the means of achieving them, have changed and will change still more.

There are several important structural changes that universities will surely enact. The brick-and-mortar campus ceased being a necessity some time ago, but as we have learned, in the foregoing inquiry, *physical* systems are not eliminated in these transformations, they simply migrate from higher- to lower-entropy physical forms. What, after all, *is* "a campus"?

It means "field." Does it exclude an electromagnetic field? I think not. My hypothesis is that as "perspective" gives way to "standpoint," the student becomes increasingly adaptable to variable learning environments. I think that the nursery is the most important physical environment, requiring the greatest individualized and high-entropy care, and that the university is the most variable and least physically restrictive setting. I love a campus as much as anyone and I grant that it has an important place in our collective history. But, truthfully, the college campus is an artifact of the nineteenth and twentieth centuries, not unlike the monastery and the Middle Ages. There will always be monasteries and there will always be college campuses, but they will not be as they have been during their respective heydays.

Some will say that the campus is necessary to the social aspects of maturation, but even if I agree that something special happens among people who are 18 to 22 at these places, I must point out that such socialization can be accomplished in more constructive ways by means of mandatory social service. By all means let us gather the young people, hormones bursting and bodies seething with energy, in places where that energy (and those hormonal disequilibria) can serve the greater good. Combining the educative task with the epoch of raging hormones has never been more than an arrangement of convenience, and the sort of maturation called for by serious reflection and study is more appropriate to a slightly later physical age. Perhaps I am not the only professor who has noticed that veterans of military service and students in their mid-to-late 20s make better university students than "traditional-aged" students. With the prospect of extending meaningful life beyond physical death on the horizon, why would we wish to hurry our young people into the workforce? It seems clear that the achievement of a mature standpoint has always awaited the age of 30 (indeed, this is the age mandated in the Jewish tradition for the beginning of a man's public life). The new university might be wisely designed for that stage that *now* occurs in early working life, that is, age 25–30, with the ages of 18–25 generally reserved for service to society and humanity, as young people learn to put their efforts behind something greater than themselves. Thus, I expect the age of intellectual maturity to be pushed back as the university matures. The university of the future will be of greater value to students who have passed their most socially engaged time. There is simply no good reason to gather them on college campuses, and there never was.

Athletics such as we associate with universities today need to be disassociated from university life and to be treated as paid, semi-professional, and developmental pursuits, just as they are in baseball. There is no reason at all to preserve intercollegiate athletics in the future. The gradual shrinking importance of campuses will make this dissociation easier. Athletics as associated with human development is very important, but as associated with the final stages of developing a standpoint, it ceases to be a factor in education. What to do with high school athletics is a completely different question. But beyond high school, specialists in physical entertainment and expression follow a course of developing a standpoint that is *essentially* embodied and must confront full intellectual maturity later than those who aim directly for the attainment of a standpoint. The university of the future has no sports teams, and the transitional university eliminates them as quickly as is reasonable.

I indicated earlier that professors would not be walking encyclopedias, but now we can see that the university professor will not be a "unified role" in the future as an individual person with a social status and tenure as we now understand that institution. As a lifelong faculty activist, I am not eager to announce this conclusion, but the days when academic freedom was protected by tenure are part of our history, not our future. Freedom to teach according to conscience is as important for the future as it always has been, but with information so freely distributed and accessible, the character of that social need has morphed into an issue of access to interpretive viewpoints. The imperative is to be exposed to those experiences that enhance the depth of our actuality. Tenure as we have cherished it in the past is not going to be needed, but analogous protections may need to be devised. Free-thinking faculty will always meet with resistance, and it will always be in the interest of the greater good to protect these voices from mere mob reaction. On the other hand, one can fairly hope that mob reaction will be moderated by wide access to information, and indeed, perhaps the committees that evaluate the performance of professors might best be disinterested (i.e., low-entropy) persons who have performed these tasks during their high-entropy lives, but no longer have a profit motive or a need to earn a living. There is no reason to imagine that striving for status, influence, and power will disappear among the low-entropy populace, but there is reason to think that power and influence will be judged less upon the basis of the ability to exert physical coercion upon those who are physically weaker and may be more directly derived from what Martin Luther King, Jr., called "the content of our character."

It seems like both noble and base motives would be easier to discern in a low-entropy community. Or perhaps I am just an optimist. Narrowed selection to enhance depth in our actuality is not the same as narrow-mindedness; it is the opposite, due to the imperative of the widest nexus. Thus, embodied faculty will be specialists of a high order, but not by any measure as narrow in spirit as the siloed specialists of the present university, who serve disciplinary standards that have become irrelevant to what students now need to learn. The students have pushed ahead of their professors in many ways.

As for the classroom, it has been clear for over a hundred years that being rendered passive by the classroom lecture does not efficiently lead to intensity in our experience. Studies measuring the content retention of today's students from a lecture-style class are discouraging. Online classes and other forms of guided study do at least as well on these scales of content retention. Students learn to become active interpreters of their worlds by actively interpreting them, not by having them spoon-fed. Thus, professors in the transitional university will be the persons who set the frames of problems and processes that lead to intense experiences (in the appropriately narrow and selective way) that take students, by means of their own actions, from perspective to standpoint. The good news is that good professors have always done just this. The more challenging news is that the curriculum of the future is not "a curriculum" at all; it is a trajectory of interpretation, criticism, and calculative reasoning. And, as always, we will, ideally speaking, need to adjust it to maximize the autonomy and future action of students at the individual level.

What sort of institutional structure will facilitate this process? I do not believe that individual universities are needed, so far as public education is concerned. I say this not because I expect greater homogenization, but because I expect less, during the transition. Professors are already becoming freelance educators, as indeed they have been at many points in history, both Western and Eastern, and whether we like it or not, that framework will grow in the future. Being a guide to the last stages in intellectual and personal maturation is surely a *calling*, but at the level of final maturation, which extends for a decade or so, it makes less and less sense to warehouse students in large passive groups. Graduating students from being high school seniors in classes of 30 to being freshmen in classes of 500 is the opposite of learning, as defined above. The further students progress, the more individualized their instruction should be. In a way, we already do this, as students progress from general education to their majors to small seminars in graduate school and finally to the dissertation, which is supposed to be the consummation of an individual standpoint. But we fail at the level of "general education" to follow the trajectory of maturation. Many private universities counteract this tendency by means of mentoring programs, but these should be the norm for public education, not just for the elite.

Thus, the public should support this stage, more in the future than in the past. But if the public universities have failed in this regard, it is just the tip of the problematic iceberg; the real difficulty is the failure of the public to see and act upon the public good. The hundreds of proprietary schools, from cosmetology to Microsoft certification, have moved in, with promises of prosperity for those who pay, and that comes as debt, and gradually blossoms into a culture of debt and incarceration—whether it is widely understood or not, it is people in debt who keep other people in prison. The public has failed to recognize that an "entrepreneurial model" for final maturation is in no one's interest. Higher education, now as ever, is about the final stages of emotional and intellectual maturation, not about how one gets a living.

What makes sense is for states, counties, and municipalities, to hold and employ a list of certified teachers in all the areas of training and study needed and desired by their populace. It makes still more sense for these teachers to be paid fairly and for students to receive their services solely at the cost of the public. These professors may be "tenured" for service and achievement in teaching, in the sense that seniority and past service ought to contribute to job security. Still, I see no natural complementarity between original research and this kind of teaching. The calling into original research, into the production of new "knowledge," into the creation of humane records and artistic expressions, this is now and always has been something different from the call to teach. Their close association in higher education in the past 125 years has been unnatural and damaging to the educational mission of the institutions that mixed them. It would not be easier to say whether rewarding faculty for research or entertaining the public with unpaid athletes has done greater damage to the university during that period, but my view is that the emphasis on research has done more to kill good teaching than athletics. The public should maintain education centers, accessible to all, and strictly maintained for the purposes of small class and individual meetings with teachers. This arrangement already works in many places. States, counties, and municipalities should also maintain centers for student social development, oriented toward public service, which are a required part of reaching final maturation.

High-end research in the sciences is going to be independent of higher education in the future. It is past time we ceased misusing our institutions of higher learning as a form of corporate welfare, providing subsidized R&D for the military industrial complex and other for-profit corporations. Certainly the public interest in research into science and health must be subsidized, but it has nothing directly to do with the education of students to intense, final maturity. The pairing of the research and teaching creates tension without producing educational advantage. Research in the humanities, on the other hand, has always been an elective affinity. There is no reason to believe that one gets better history or philosophy or poetry or theater by paying professors to produce it in endless streams of journals that no one reads. This pairing was an artifact of the stride toward scientism that took over (and ruined) many public universities in the mid-twentieth century.

The arrangement, free of the entrepreneurial motive, of athletics, and of original research, allows the public and its leadership to arrange for the final maturation of student for the economic and cultural plans they may integrate into their vision of a future community. What they need are citizens, humanly mature persons, who can communicate, listen, speak, and interpret others. It also makes sense to include within these centers the further education of low-entropy citizens, as well as the continuing education and training of those who have completed their formal schooling. One assumes that low-entropy persons may make contributions to teaching as well as learning, assuming our technology reaches this point (as it surely will), and policy here will be morally tricky. I see no reason why some aspects of the educative process would require the embodied, high-entropy teacher, but some courses of study clearly would, to some extent (e.g., medicine). Yet, the maintenance of low-entropy systems, which would, as far as we can see, still require some high-entropy hardware and maintenance, is likely to be efficient to the point of tempting administrative decision-makers to rely overmuch on virtual teaching. If you could "study" with Edgar Allan Poe, would you choose Fredric Jameson over that?

The right balance will be a matter of experimentation and adjustment, but I do not believe it would be wise to reduce any society's involvement with its teachers to a predominantly virtual arrangement. The question is when will we economize our resources such that the student is active most of the time and the teacher is in the mode of thorough response? I foresee a great increase in the need for teachers so that students can be active most of the time. This will be true from preschool to graduate school. The calling to teach needs to be counted among the fundamental humanizing and personalizing agencies in the civilization to come and should be thoroughly supported. On the other hand, bureaucratically dominated regulation and certification of teachers strikes me as counterproductive. We must move away from a labor vs. management model in all education. It has been disastrous to incentivize teachers to rise to administration (which requires utterly different skills) in order to obtain status and better pay. The administration of education in the future should be highly centralized, user-friendly, and modestly compensated. It is secretarial work, in the future, and indeed, that is all it is now, in spite of the amazing waste it begets.

It seems to me that the ancient model of allowing students to choose their teachers, at the higher levels, and from among those qualified, should serve to keep matters in balance, so long as this education is free. Allowing teachers to teach what they choose to teach has always been a part of that system. Education to full maturity should be free of charge and regarded as a civil right. Teachers may be paid by the public agencies that employ them according to the demand for their services, but under no circumstances should "demand" be correlated with number of students. Rather, hours of service is the more reasonable measure, for the transitional university. Efficiency in education is not obtained by educating huge numbers of students with the least expenditure, it is attained in producing students who are actually and maximally educated, "formated," if you will, and this process must always be individualized. John Dewey foresaw and advocated a society in which something like a third of the citizens would be teachers of some kind. This, he believed, was a key to a genuinely democratic society. He was correct.

As for curriculum and evaluation of students, what they can *do* is much more important than what they "know" in the old, Cartesian, recitative sense. That kind of knowledge is already available to everyone who has a phone. Old-fashioned tests are unhelpful, as they have been used in the past. Students must be assigned tasks to carry out and to bring back the results. They must be interviewed closely as to how they carried out these tasks within the general framework provided. They must be encouraged to think about alternative paths for the completion of tasks. These tasks must encourage initiative, experimentation with resources, and creativity—as well as patience, critical reflection, and thoroughness. Students must be taught the art and techniques of good judgment. This is consistent with the new "three R's" I mentioned early in this chapter: "interpretation of text and image," "the creation of text and image," and "the principles upon which computing occurs (both logical and mathematical)." This is the curriculum.

As for evaluative criteria, there is no question that the system of grading, whether A to F, or its common substitutes, will pass away, and the sooner the better. Standardized testing is a bad idea for the future just as it was in the past. Such methods of evaluation grew from the demand to measure, on a mass scale and with minimal expenditure of blood and treasure, something that cannot really be measured quantitatively at all: intensity. Intensive relations do admit of transitions and movements, but they flow into one another and cannot be analyzed effectively by means of quantification. They may, however, be assessed in terms of effective problem-solving and good judgment. When a task has been "completed," in an educational context, it is more than an outcome or a result, it is inclusive of the process by which it was completed and holds indefinitely broad implications for future action. Thorough interpretation of the how, the wherefore, the whence, and the whither is, therefore, the same as the evaluation. Some colleges (e.g., Sarah Lawrence) did away with grades long ago and have not suffered from doing so. They have also minimized the idea of having a "major" and substituted an "individualized course of study," also with excellent results. The transitional university should do likewise.

It will be said that this process is labor-intensive, which is true. The labor is worth the outcome. And recalling that these teachers facilitate the setting of tasks and their assessment, and are not to be responsible for lecturing to classes of young adults, much of the labor now expended for minimal return (classroom education) can be curtailed or even cut. The art of the lecture will not disappear, but it will be a matter of voluntary rather than captive audiences. It will also be said that my proposal is inefficient, and here I argue that efficiency in this domain must be tied to intensive consequences for societies and wider communities of persons, both high and low entropy. Having educated citizens with broad and adaptable interpretive skills and powers of action is never inefficient and is probably worth (in its returns) far more than we have dreamed. What is inefficient is our current behavior. It is criminally wasteful in many instances.

Without the waste that comes from hierarchical administrative structures, unpaid professional athletics, huge decorous campuses, and mass repetition of the old, high-entropy model of higher education, the savings will more than provide for the needs we genuinely have in educating the citizenry. You will perhaps complain "but we love our colleges and their campuses," to which I would reply that I see no problem with privatizing the older form of education and making it available to those who want to bear its costs for themselves. Public education is another matter. It must serve the future we will face collectively, and it must be maximally inclusive. I believe that were a plan such as I have sketched adopted by a city or even a state, gradually people would choose it. Indeed, the first city to adopt such a plan will have an advantage over other cities for decades to come. The start-up cost will be no more significant than building a major sports stadium or a new airport, and cities find the means for these regularly.

Notes

1. I should note at the outset that although Whitehead wrote extensively on education, and in ways very much applicable to what I will discuss hereafter, I will not be making explicit use of these writings. My approach is rather to examine ideas from his metaphysics and show how these foreshadow practices in the coming decades. Still, readers may find it valuable to examine Whitehead's explicit writings on education in this context. See, especially, *Aims of Education and Other Essays* (New York: Free Press, 1967 [1911]). There is a generous body of secondary literature on Whitehead's philosophy of education and the relation between education and process philosophy generally. For many years there was a scholarly society dedicated explicitly to such study, The Society for the Process Philosophy of Education, which released periodic collections of studies from its members. Most important among these scholars is George Allan. See his *Modes of Learning: Whitehead's Metaphysics and the Stages of Learning* (Albany: SUNY Press, 2013) and *Higher Education in the Making: Pragmatism, Whitehead, and the Canon* (Albany: SUNY Press, 2004).
2. For a thorough account of how I understand Whitehead, see my book, *The Quantum of Explanation: Whitehead's Radical Empiricism*, coauthored with Gary L. Herstein (London: Routledge, 2017), especially Chaps. 7–9 and 11 in relation to the current inquiry.
3. Alfred North Whitehead, *Process and Reality*, corrected edition, eds. D.R. Griffin and D.W. Sherburne (New York: Free press, 1978), p. 3.
4. See Auxier and Herstein, *The Quantum of Explanation*, Chaps. 2–3.
5. See Ray Kurzweil, *The Singularity Is Near: When Machines Transcend Humans* (New York: Penguin Books, 2006) and *The Age of Spiritual Machines* (New York: Viking, 1999).
6. See the article in Wikipedia: https://en.wikipedia.org/wiki/There_are_known_knowns, accessed November 1, 2017.
7. See, for example, Johann Gottfried Herder's observations on Martin Luther's effect of the German people. Herder, "Luther: Ein Lehrer der Deutschen Nation," in *Herder's Werke in zwei Bände* (Dortmund: Hanser Verlag, 1982), vol. 2, 632–633. Due to printing, translation of the Bible

became a viable project, and due to its mass distribution, it was possible for one person to become the "teacher" of a whole nation. The effects of translation of the Bible into vernacular language and its mass availability, added to hymnals and other worship aids (all made possible by the printing press), were *foreseeable*, even before 1517.

8. This effort was well underway before Gutenberg's press, as the storied career of John Wycliffe (d. 1384) and the wide diffusion of his English translation of the Bible makes clear. Such forces are still with us, of course, from the suppression of websites by the People's Republic of China to the abandonment of net neutrality by the Trump administration. The enemies of the free exchange of ideas and information always form a predictable portion of humanity and always for the same reasons: the maintenance of power and wealth is facilitated through keeping people in the dark. That will not change in the future. Whoever has the power will try to control the flow of information.
9. In the past, digital computing worked with discrete bits of information that behaved "classically," from a physical point of view. Quantum computing is based on "qubits" which is a kind of "information" (in a sense I will describe) that is non-discrete, that is, continuous, and which is transformed and controlled by the manipulation of entangled photons. One current theory for how triple entanglement may pave the way for the creation of analog computing systems that could physically support the low-entropy fields required for these improvements, see Paul Werbos and Ludmilla Dolmatova, "Analog Quantum Computing and the Need for Time-symmetric Physics," in *Quantum Information Processing* 15:3 (March 2016), 1273–1287. This set of ideas has received some further confirmation in Yanhua Shih's lab at University of Maryland, Baltimore County, discussed here: http://drpauljohn.blogspot.com/2016/02/new-experiment-as-important-as.html, accessed May 10, 2017. The call for a "time-symmetric physics" in this model is of interest because such a model treats the second law of thermodynamics as non-universal in principle (that it may not apply in microphysics as it does in macrophysics). This is just a theory that attempts to go around the main obstacle to treating time as symmetrical (i.e., entropy). I doubt time will ever be shown to be symmetrical (i.e., invariant and reversible) in physical fact, but that doesn't mean we cannot *model* it as such. I would say that those who are trying to model the physical universe as time symmetric could do better if continuity were defined in terms of possibility rather than using ideas about "the physical" inherited from earlier models of space.
10. See Ernst Cassirer, *The Philosophy of Symbolic Forms: The Phenomenology of Knowledge* (volume 3), trans. Ralph Mannheim (New Haven: Yale University Press, 1959 [1929]), esp. Chap. 5, pp. 191–206.

11. Taking an informal poll of my own students, 18–22 years old, I found that all of them would seriously consider having a device installed in their bodies, such as the wrist, which would give them internet access any time they wanted it, so long as they could turn it off. Yet, not one was willing to have the device installed in the cranium to be controlled with, for example, eye movements that could be learned. For some reason they perceive these as being radically different, but I think it is a clear indicator that they are a transitional generation. The idea of powering the devices with their own body-electrochemistry was met with mixed reactions.
12. Much of the research centers on language and getting computers to grasp our intentions in speaking. This can be replicated by asking computers to translate one language into another language when it has never been programmed to do so, but has been taught a third language with which to compare the two it is asked to translate. This can be done. See the article in *TechCrunch*, November 22, 2016, https://techcrunch.com/2016/11/22/googles-ai-translation-tool-seems-to-have-invented-its-own-secret-internal-language/, accessed May 5, 2017. This type of advance in getting computers to understand natural language can be built upon, although it is not yet well developed. See the article on "emotibot" in *TechNode*, March 22, 2017, http://technode.com/2017/03/22/ai-chatbot-emotibot-understand-emotions/, accessed May 5, 2017.
13. The issue of how soon is hotly debated, but it seems like a pointless dispute to me. Everyone agrees the change is coming. Whether Ray Kurzweil's overworked numbers or Sam Harris' more careful numbers prove correct, the outcome is the same.
14. See Auxier and Herstein, *The Quantum of Explanation*, esp. Chaps. 3–6, 10–11; also see my "Evolutionary Time, and the Creation of the Space of Life," in *Space, Time, and the Limits of Human Understanding*, eds. Shyam Wuppuluri and Giancarlo Ghirardi (Berlin: Springer Verlag, 2016), Chap. 31, 381–400.
15. The hypothesis I favor, and which accords with Whiteheadian cosmology, in my view, is that the flux is best characterized physically as a quantum vacuum, the lowest energy possible for physical existing, below the level of particles. See Peter W. Milonni, *The Quantum Vacuum* (New York: Academic Press, 2013). Some of the work of Giancarlo Basti is, in my view, exemplary of the approach Whitehead would favor in the physics of today, although I do not think he would embrace the theological implications Basti favors. Basti defends the idea of the universe as a quantum vacuum and emphasizes continuities in AI and physics with evaluative processes we can easily recognize. See, for example, "The Quantum Field Theory (QFT) Dual Paradigm in Fundamental Physics and the Semantic Information

Content and Measure in Cognitive Sciences" (2014), accessible here: http://www.stoqatpul.org/lat/materials/basti_paper_aisb_london.pdf. Also see Basti, "From Formal Logic to Formal Ontology: The New Dual Paradigm in Natural Sciences" (2014), accessible here: http://www.stoqatpul.org/lat/materials/basti_paper_cle_def.pdf; accessed January 2, 2018.

16. See Whitehead, *Process and Reality*, corrected ed. by D.W. Sherburne and D.R. Griffin (New York: Free Press, 1978 [1929]), pp. 61–82.
17. See Whitehead, *Process and Reality*, pp. 219–221. The prehension is an analytical division of the "actual entity" (which cannot be actually divided) rather than a real division of the extensive continuum. Many, even most, interpreters of Whitehead get this point wrong, treating prehensions as actual divisions of the real, since prehensions include physical as well as conceptual feelings, and most people cannot imagine physical existences that are indivisible themselves and which exist without actually dividing other things. Whitehead explicitly says these things, but his interpreters often forget or fail to comprehend.
18. See Empedocles' Fragments, esp. 2, 36, and 60, for example, http://history.hanover.edu/texts/presoc/emp.html#book1, accessed November 4, 2017.
19. The classic case of this regrettable attitude was the conscious strategy employed by Einstein to close down genuine philosophical discussion of general relativity. This history has been well documented by Jimena Canales in *The Physicist and the Philosopher: Einstein, Bergson, and the Debate that Changed Our Understanding of Time* (Princeton: Princeton University Press, 2015). Unfortunately Einstein and his followers gave physicists a circle of irrelevant excuses to ignore philosophical objections, to remain untrained in reasoning (apart from narrow and dogmatic, almost quasi-mystical, Platonistic interpretations of number), and to be dismissive of genuine dissent that comes from philosophical concerns. These physicists continue to reason poorly enough that they make the simplest mistakes and then hide behind their academic titles and prejudices to convince or intimidate dissenters into silence. The greatest offenders have been people like Stephen Hawking, Steven Weinberg, Neil deGrasse Tyson, Jack Sarfatti, Sean Carroll, and anyone else who takes general relativity to be an indisputable scientific fact. All are reductionists and anti-philosophical, while posing as substitutes for philosophers on matters that are more appropriately described as theological than as scientific. Indeed, "physico-theology" is the name Kant gave to the sorts of stories these people force upon the public in the name of science. Gary Herstein and I have done our best to debunk this model-centrism in our *The Quantum of Explanation*, but there is little reason for optimism that this pseudoscience (and crypto-theology) will be recognized for what it is anytime soon.

20. Whitehead, *Process and Reality*, pp. 90–91.
21. Whitehead, *Process and Reality*, p. 91.
22. Whitehead, *Process and Reality*, p. 91.
23. Whitehead, *Process and Reality*, p. 91.
24. This point is the essence of Whitehead's argument contra Einstein in *The Principle of Relativity* (Cambridge: Cambridge University Press, 1922). See also Gary L. Herstein, *Whitehead and the Measurement Problem of Cosmology* (Frankfurt am Main: Ontos Verlag, 2006).
25. To the extent that I follow the current discussion (which is fairly chaotic), it appears to me that Sarfatti and his small band of ideologues is pressing for a relaxing of the de Broglie guidance constraint so that one needs no hidden variable to account for non-local quantum communication; see Sarfatti's "On R.I. Sutherland's Retro-Causal Action-Reaction Lagrangian Quasi-Gauge Model of Relativistically Invariant Many-Particle Entangled Bohm Pilot Wave Theory in 4D Space-Time without Many-Dimensional Configuration Space," which is a working paper he has made public. See https://www.academia.edu/15700723/UPDATED_091515Post-Quantum_Theory_with_Entanglement_Signaling_for_Sentient_AI, accessed May 13, 2017. Obviously, avoiding local hidden variables is required by Bell's theorem. Sarfatti's view also remains, by his understanding, within Einstein's general relativistic interpretation of space-time and allows that the wave function collapses. The view I am suggesting, and with which I think Whitehead would agree, seems closer to that of Antony Valentini. See Antony Valentini, "Pilot-wave Theory of Fields, Gravitation and Cosmology," in *Bohmian Mechanics and Quantum Theory: An Appraisal*, eds. James T. Cushing, Arthur Fine, Sheldon Goldstein (The Hague:, Kluwer Academic Publishers, 1996), pp. 45–66. In a view like this, there is no need to accept wave-particle duality at all. Continuity in the wave function is hypothesized. This is closer to Whitehead's general attitude, but Whitehead's theory is much more general, and Valentini, along with the de Broglie-Bohm thread of interpretation, would be a special case of what Whitehead is theorizing. Whitehead can avoid the prohibitions of Bell's theorem because the hidden variable would be non local, in the required sense. The hidden variable *is* the conservation of energy in a cosmic epoch, which may allow for a decay of order at this broad level which is not necessarily a loss of energy for the cosmic epoch, and although the causal laws associated with various levels of complexity and "information" may appear to violate the first law of thermodynamics locally, the broader conservation of energy is assured, but now as a conservation of *order*. Most physicists would not accept such a distinction between order in general and the order of physical systems, but some do (e.g., Gianfranco Basti and his supporters), and still more computer scientists and mind sci-

entists are willing to entertain such hypotheses. For Whitehead, this view would only be a hypothesis, not an assertion. The trouble with Sarfatti and other contemporary model-centric theorizers is that they do not believe their theories *are* hypothetical, even when it is patently obvious they are making untestable assertions.

26. For my part I think that those who try to get formulations of "gravity" to do much theoretical work in the present have shackled themselves, and unnecessarily so, to an idea (i.e., gravity) that is almost certain to be redefined into oblivion and meaninglessness as science progresses.
27. The question and surmise came from Helen Milne in an e-mail exchange, in May of 2017, about the nature of the flux. I appreciate the question and thank her for the summary.
28. Arguably, our bodies have been created within the constraints (the modes of stability) that just are the overlapping of the vibrations congenial to the forms our present bodies use and (with the senses) interpret. This is a "space" in the relevant sense. Whether we might also say that in evolutionary time, that is, the "space" of life, these same vibrations actually create our bodies is a speculation we might make, and once that is continuous with the kinds of bodies we might have after the singularity. For more on the "space of life" in the sense I use it here, see my "Evolutionary Time, and the Creation of the Space of Life," in *Space, Time, and the Limits of Human Understanding*, eds. Shyam Wuppuluri and Giancarlo Ghirardi (Berlin: Springer Verlag, 2016), Chap. 31, 381–400.
29. See Thomas O. Buford, *Trust: Our Second Nature* (Lanham, MD: Lexington Books, 2009).
30. See Michel Foucault, *The Order of Things* (New York: Vintage Books, 1990 [1966]), Chap. 9.
31. See the detailed analysis of "perspective" and "standpoint" in Auxier and Herstein, *The Quantum of Explanation*, Chap. 7.
32. I have set out a detailed account of the differences among "act," "action," and "activity" in my book *Time, Will, and Purpose* (Chicago: Open Court, 2013), pp. 130–185.
33. This idea is far richer than I can summarize here. An excellent book-length study of this idea in Whitehead's philosophy has been published by Judith A. Jones, *Intensity: An Essay in Whiteheadian Ontology* (Nashville: Vanderbilt University Press, 1998).
34. See my discussion of "docility" in my *Time, Will, and Purpose*, Chap. 5.
35. I borrow this term and its meaning from E.S. Brightman, who might be aptly described as "the Whitehead of moral philosophy." See his *Person and Reality*, eds. R.S. Brightman, P.A. Bertocci, and J. Newhall (New York: Ronald Press, 1958); see also *Moral Laws* (New York: Abingdon Press, 1933).

Index[1]

[1] Note: Page number followed by 'n' refer to notes.

A. Stoller, E. Kramer (eds.), *Contemporary Philosophical Proposals for the University*, https://doi.org/10.1007/978-3-319-72128-6

M

N

O

P

S

T

Zeitfracht Medien GmbH
Ferdinand-Jühlke-Straße 7
99095 Erfurt, Deutschland
produktsicherheit@kolibri360.de